Music City Babylon

Music City
BABYLON

by Scott Faragher

A Birch Lane Press Book
Published by Carol Publishing Group

A Birch Lane Press Book
Published by Carol Publishing Group
Birch Lane Press is a registered trademark of Carol Communications, Inc.
Editorial Offices: 600 Madison Avenue, New York, N.Y. 10022
Sales & Distribution Offices: 120 Enterprise Avenue, Secaucus, N.J. 07094
In Canada: Canadian Manda Group, P.O. Box 920, Station U, Toronto,
    Ontario M8Z 5P9
Queries regarding rights and permissions should be addressed to
Carol Publishing Group, 600 Madison Avenue, New York, N.Y. 10022

Carol Publishing Group books are available at special discounts for bulk purchases,
for sales promotions, fund-raising, or educational purposes. Special editions can be
created to specifications. For details contact: Special Sales Department, Carol
Publishing Group, 120 Enterprise Avenue, Secaucus, N.J. 07094

Manufactured in the United States of America
10 9 8 7 6 5 4 3 2 1

Library of Congress Cataloging-in-Publication Data

Faragher, Scott.
    Music City Babylon / by Scott Faragher.
        p.   cm.
    "A Birch Lane Press book."
    ISBN 1-55972-134-0
    1. Country music—History and criticism. 2. Music trade—
Tennessee—Nashville. I. Title.
ML3524.F36   1992
781.642'09768'55—dc20   92-39070
                                                           CPI
                                                           MN

This book is affectionately dedicated to my parents

Contents

Acknowledgments

I wish to express my sincere appreciation to the following friends: the late Dick Blake, for teaching me tenacity. To Robert Ryan at the Second Avenue Exchange for literally seeing to it that I did not starve on many occasions. To Hillel Black at Carol Publishing Group, who was kind enough to serve as my editor. Special thanks for his help on the Lou Rawls chapter. To Ewell McKee at Hunter Fan Company in Memphis. Thanks also to my "therpis," Dick Lewis, for his all-too-frequent wake-up calls. My appreciation to Chad, Bard, and Wendlandt Selden of Hollywood, Mississippi, for letting me unwind at their various residences after an overdose of hillbillies.

Thanks also to the Cool Ruler, Gregory Issacs, for "Talk Don't Bother Me." Special mention to the Horse, the Earl of Knuttsford, Cadillac Jett, and all the bankers at Bud's. Don't forget Tommy Kerkeles and Don Reeves, James Branch Cabell, Clarence John Laughlin, Tennessee Williams, and Carl Jung. What about my son, Scotty? Not to mention my bastard son, Coochie? Thanks to Ray Price, whose commissions kept me alive while I finished this book. Thanks to Ed Penney at Dad's Old Books in Nashville for enabling me to eat some days. Thanks to Katye for her support and encouragement throughout the final phase of this project.

Sincere appreciation to Nashville attorney John Lentz, and those gorgeous Blackmon sisters from that Lone Star State, and Peggy Stewart of Nashville and Pansy Parpart of Dallas, my two "Fortune-Tellers."

Best wishes to Fred, Brooke, Rodentia, Paul, and Ellen. Thanks also to those who did not think that I would ever finish this book or get it published. Your negativity gave me the determination to see it through. A very sincere appreciation is extended to Reverend Ike in New York. His strong message gave me courage when everything was falling down around me.

My sincere thanks also to Sherwood Cryer, and to Mickey Gilley, without whom this book would not have been written.

Thanks for reading this book, and good luck to all.

Author to Reader

To Nashvillians today, the music industry is an accepted part of the business community. The presence of the Opryland complex, The Nashville Network, the major record labels, and publishing companies has contributed substantially to an upgraded social status for those of us who make a living through music-related work. It has not always been that way. In fact, the acceptance of "those music people" to the degree we have actually been accepted in private occurred in the last fifteen years. In the past, with a few notable exceptions, we were relegated to a lower social status and called hillbillies.

I am from Nashville and grew up there, but knew very little about country music. It was remote and distant, and yet I was always aware of its presence. Having the "hillbillies" in town was somewhat like having the Addams family living in the neighborhood. They were different, and kind of interesting, but I really did not know them and kept my distance. I knew that they were there, but our worlds never met. In the area where I lived, between Green Hills and Belle Meade, country music was almost never mentioned, and when it was, it was usually talked about with sarcasm, as if to imply that it was a lower form of music, if it could be considered music at all. In downtown Nashville on Saturdays, however, our cultures blended when for the day, our two worlds met.

On Saturdays, my friends and I would ride the bus downtown. We were in our teens then, in the mid-sixties. The British invasion was in full swing, and music was everything. Downtown Nashville was very interesting, and there were many exciting things for us to do. It was all very magical. We always hit Deaderick Street first. It was without any doubt the most important street in town. We would visit Sam Jarkey's Golden Boot Store, John G. Miller's music store, the fun shop, the pool hall, and the pawnshops—Hy's, Berry's, Friedman's—where we went to see the new batch of guitars.

This was the most important part of our Saturdays, looking at the guitars. None of us had any money and the people at the music stores and the pawnshops knew it, but put up with us anyway. We would eat lunch at the Krystal and then walk over to Hewgley's music store on Eighth and Commerce. Then it was up to Church Street to Hank Snow's music store. None of us knew who Hank Snow was back then. We knew that he was a hillbilly singer with a very bad toupee, but that was about it. They sold glossy eight-by-ten pictures of him there, as well as Fat Gibson, Gretsch, and Epiphone guitars, the kind that were mostly used by country singers.

Next it was down to lower Broadway. There were a few more pawnshops there as well as the Sho-Bud store. Sho-Bud made its own amplifiers, which were supposed to be pretty good. It was, however, world-famous for its steel guitars. We were not that interested in steel guitars because they were not used in the type of music we were listening to then, but we recognized them as works of art nonetheless.

Lower Broadway was a world apart from the rest of Nashville. First of all, it was right around the corner from the Ryman Auditorium, and on Saturdays people would line up from Fifth

Avenue in front of the Ryman, all the way down to Broadway and around the corner waiting to buy tickets to the Grand Ole Opry. Tootsie's Orchid Lounge was there, as well as Ernest Tubb's record shop, Grammar Guitars, and later the Roy Acuff Exhibits. It was truly another world.

Back then, downtown was busy and there were no shopping malls in suburban areas. People came to town from the country on Saturdays to do their shopping. Many were farmers and factory workers, from nearby towns as well as from up north. On lower Broadway though, they were there for country music. There were honky-tonks and the music rang out through the doorways and drifted down the street, steel guitars and fiddles. As we walked by those dimly lit joints we saw beer signs, jukeboxes, and people sitting at the bar, and heard women laughing. It was frightening to us in a way because it seemed all so unfamiliar and forbidding, and yet here was life, beckoning us in a disturbing way.

We did not know what to think of country music. We never listened to it on the radio, and could not understand why anybody would drive all the way down to Nashville to go to the Grand Ole Uproar, as we called it. There was something to be said for country music, however, even though we did not know much about it at the time. Country singers did their own thing. They were wild, passionate, and flamboyant, and lived by their own rules. Many of them got into trouble and were in and out of prison. They often wore cowboy boots and dressed in wild costumes. They drove big Cadillacs and Lincolns in the days when owning a Cadillac really meant something. They had money and they spread it around. Some of them even had their own airplanes.

Country singers kept mostly to themselves, did as they pleased, and were not the least intimidated by Nashville's so-called polite society. They did not seek to join country clubs. They didn't have to. If they needed a pool, they had one put in. Very few of them had any social aspirations at all. They existed on their own, generally apart from the mainstream. As their fame increased, so did their wealth, and consequently their contact with other members of the Nashville community. They bought cars, boats, houses, and farms, opened bank accounts, hired lawyers, and attracted money-spending tourists. Their impact on the city could not be ignored forever, and by degrees they became accepted and today are extremely important.

Nashville, Tennessee, actually came to be known as "Music City U.S.A." as the result of several interrelated factors. First and foremost was the Grand Ole Opry. Originally called "The WSM Barn Dance," this program of hillbilly music was first broadcast live from the studios of WSM radio in downtown Nashville in 1925. As the show's popularity grew, the location of the broadcast was changed to accommodate larger crowds. In 1941 the Opry moved to Nashville's Ryman Auditorium, a converted gospel tabernacle. It remained there until 1974, at which time it was established at its present location at the Opryland park complex in Nashville. Although there were other similar programs throughout the nation during the early part of the twentieth century, the Grand Ole Opry in time became the most important.

Another aspect of Nashville's development into Music City is the recording industry. According to Bill Malone in his book *Country Music U.S.A.*, Decca first recorded artist Red Foley at WSM's Nashville studio in mid-1945. Shortly thereafter two WSM employees started Castle Studio, Nashville's first recording studio, in the old Tulane Hotel at the corner of Eighth and Church. Castle Studio was subsequently used by almost every major company recording country music, until Owen Bradley opened "Bradley's Barn" in 1953. Next, some of the major labels opened offices in Nashville and subsequently started their own studios.

The presence of these studios and the Opry itself attracted musicians and artists, who eventually became permanent residents of Nashville. Working the Opry on weekends, they were enabled by Nashville's central location to work other shows in nearby cities during the week. Soon came the businessmen, acting as agents, managers, and music publishers.

While Nashville has been long regarded as Music City, this title had no specific relevance for the average citizen until the Opryland amusement park opened in 1974. Since that time, millions of visitors have come to town every year to visit

Opryland, to hear the Grand Ole Opry in person, and to visit the part of town known as Music Row.

While it is true that people in the music business here are no longer regarded as hillbillies, the fact remains that in spite of all the publicity, the majority of Nashvillians do not personally know anyone in the upper levels of the business. They have no idea what goes on day to day behind the scenes. In fact, there are many people within the music business itself who do not know how things really work, although they might think that they do.

The purpose of this book is to provide an insider's view of the music business through my own experiences with artists and the circumstances surrounding them. The reader will get a behind-the-scenes look at many famous entertainers and will learn how they conduct themselves in real life, away from the public eye. Everything here is presented as it happened. In cases where I did not remember an incident completely, I checked with others who were present to be sure I had it right. Where letters or other documents existed, I studied them in order to confirm that the information I have provided is correct.

As president of In Concert International, Inc., during the five years of its existence, I made some mistakes in judgment and some bad calls. Nevertheless, we all did the best we knew how, and for the most part had a good time.

Music City Babylon

Chapter One

Beginnings

Barbara Mandrell, Tammy Wynette, the Statler Brothers, George Jones, Johnny Paycheck, Ronnie Milsap, and many of country music's brightest stars owe their careers in large measure to the efforts of two men who are, for the most part, unknown to the general public. Up until their deaths, Shorty Lavender and Dick Blake were Nashville's most successful and interesting talent agents. They possessed a flair and a sense of style that are gone in Nashville now and, sadly, will probably never return.

I met both of them in late July 1973. I was out of college for the summer and living at a friend's house in Belle Meade, a suburb of Nashville. My friend had graduated from Ole Miss and had taken a job with a company called Cole, Layer, and Trumble, some sort of appraisal firm from up north that had received the contract to assess all of the business property in Nashville. He was kind enough to put in a good word for me and got me hired.

We assembled over on Murfreesboro Road every morning, checked in, and then went into our assigned parts of the city to do our work. My territory was Music Row. My work consisted of listing all of the property in each office, things like chairs, desks, typewriters, etc. This was being done for the purpose of establishing a value for those items so that they could be taxed.

It was a very hotly contested issue politically and the tax itself was ultimately declared to be unconstitutional. However I met many of Nashville's music business leaders, having no idea that I would see any of them ever again.

I remember meeting Shorty Lavender because I had always heard that "those hillbillies" often changed their names. I could not imagine anyone having a name like "Lavender" unless he had made it up himself. As his name implied, Shorty Lavender was short. He was also loud, wore a big cowboy hat, and smoked a large, inexpensive cigar. Later, at the Lavender-Blake Agency, Shorty had his desk placed on a pedestal so that he would be higher than everyone else and able to look down at them.

Dick Blake was in charge of what was left of the Hubert Long Agency when I met him that summer. He was in the SESAC building, which had been built by Hubert Long and housed the agency until its dissolution after Long's death. After Hubert died all of the agency's clients left and Dick Blake ended up with nothing. At that time, according to Blake, singer Bill Anderson quit the agency, telling Dick, "You aren't big enough to handle me." Dick Blake taught me many things, but the most important was tenacity.

At the end of the summer I went back to college to finish my last year, with the intention of becoming a lawyer. One evening on the way home, I stopped at my sister's apartment for a visit. At that time she was working as a secretary at United Talent, the agency that represented Conway Twitty and Loretta Lynn. She told me the big news in her life—that she was leaving her job to start a new agency with singer Chuck Glaser, a member of the vocal group Tompall and the Glaser Brothers, and with agent Louie Dunn, an employee of United Talent. I was happy that she was so excited but personally had no interest in the matter. She said that I should stick around for a while because she was going out to hear some band with her soon-to-be new boss, Chuck Glaser, and she wanted me to meet him. He showed up later and we talked.

With the exception of the people I had encountered while working the previous summer, I had never really even met anybody in the music business. It was very interesting listening to his history, and to how he and his brothers became successful recording acts and businessmen. I spoke with him for a couple of hours and then went back to my parents' house in Franklin. At about two o'clock in the morning I received a call from my sister saying that Chuck had been impressed with me and wanted to offer me a job in his new company, if I was interested. I was thrilled but told her that I knew absolutely nothing about country music or the music business. She said that was the way Chuck Glaser preferred things so that he could train me. I was tired of being broke and wanted to go to work, and yet I had only one year of college left.

I thought that I should finish school, but this job sounded really interesting. Later the three of us went out to dinner, and our waiter was a Ph.D. in psychology. I guess that cinched it for me. I withdrew from school and started to work for the Nova Agency.

At first we had no offices so we worked out of the Glaser Studio on Eighteenth Avenue South. The Glaser Studio was a very cool place at that time, the major hangout for the "outlaws," that renegade group of music mavericks who had just hit it big nationally. Waylon Jennings had his office there; so did Tompall Glaser, and so did Chuck. Upstairs, the studio was in full swing most of the time, with Kyle Lehning as chief engineer. It was Nashville's hottest studio.

At the Nova Agency we started with a couple of unknown acts, but within six months we had Waylon Jennings, Dr. Hook, Tompall Glaser, Jerry Lee Lewis, Jessi Colter, David Allan Coe, and Johnny Bush as clients.

I was scared to death of the tasks that lay ahead of me as an agent. I did not know whom to call or what to say. I remember making my first call. I waited until everybody was out of the whole building, locked the door, and with trembling fingers dialed a club in Chicago, the Earl of Oldtown. I asked for the owner and got him on the phone. The conversation ended quickly without my having sold him anybody. Fortunately I got over my shyness and started setting dates.

Eventually I had a falling-out with Chuck Glaser, and unable to get another job in the music business, I went back to school none the worse for the experience. I thought that I was out of the music business forever, but things turned out otherwise.

The Shorty Lavender Agency merged with Dick Blake's in 1975, creating the Lavender-Blake Agency. Two of their big-time agents, John McMeen and Jack Lynch, left almost immediately to start their own company, creating a vacancy that I filled as the result of a lunch meeting between Shorty Lavender and Marty Robbins' agent, Louie Dunn, whom I had worked with at the Nova Agency. I stayed there until 1978, when the agency disbanded because of personal differences between Shorty and Dick.

At the Lavender-Blake Agency I had become perhaps the best club agent in the nation, partly because we had a great roster of artists and partly because I had the southwest territory, which has always been the best for country music sales. As an agency we represented Johnny Rodriguez, Johnny Paycheck, Johnny Duncan, Ronnie Milsap, Barbara Mandrell, Dickey Lee, Mel Street, Tammy Wynette, George Jones, the Statler Brothers, and others.

By 1979 I was again working with Dick Blake's agency. I made my mark there, particularly with Ronnie Milsap, doing several million dollars' worth of business in one year alone. During the years 1979 to 1983, we bolstered his career; began the Marlboro Country Music tours; built the careers of Barbara Mandrell, Louise Mandrell, and Ricky Skaggs; and worked with other major artists such as Brenda Lee, the Statler Brothers, Don Williams, and Merle Haggard.

But that was the up side of the business. Now I'll tell you the rest.

Chapter Two

The Night Dick Blake Died

That October night in 1983, when I drove out to the Grand Ole Opry house, I wondered what was going to happen at Dick Blake International, at the time the number one country music agency in the world. Dick Blake's death was imminent. I had gone to the hospital that morning and there was a sign on the closed door that said FAMILY ONLY. I resented that message immensely since I was closer to Dick Blake, for whom I worked and who had been my mentor, than any of his so-called family. I sadly left, knowing that the end was indeed near. I had seen him the night before and he motioned for me to come in, which I did, but he did not have the strength to speak and drifted off at once.

I had gone to the Opry House that evening to visit Charly McClain and the Whites. Both were our clients and were scheduled to perform that night in front of a talent buyers' convention.

I had first started working with Memphis native Charly McClain back in the Lavender-Blake Agency days, in the late 1970s, when her first album *Here's Charly McClain*, was released on CBS. She had always been one of my top five female country singers. Her vocal style was smooth and erotic. In addition, she was quite attractive, petite and slender with long brown hair. She was still with CBS and was really doing well.

Charly was in a particularly good mood when we visited in her dressing room, in part because her record "Paradise Tonight," a duet with Mickey Gilley, was number one with a bullet that week in the *Billboard* charts. Her boyfriend, Wayne Massey, was also with her that evening and that pleased her immensely.

Ricky Skaggs and his manager were there visiting Ricky's wife, Sharon, who was lead singer for the Whites. They had really done better in their short career than anyone had expected them to. All three of their first singles had been top ten records nationally, and their current record was at this point number thirty-five with a bullet. We were also handling CBS artist Ricky Skaggs and had represented him since the release of his second album, *Highways and Heartaches*, in 1982. Skaggs was a nasal bluegrass whiner with a hairstyle that made him look as if a skunk had landed on his head.

I found Sherwood Cryer standing by the backstage door talking to Sandy Brokaw. Sandy and David Brokaw, Mickey Gilley's PR people, are identical twins and it is difficult to tell them apart at first glance. Sherwood Cryer has been referred to as the Howard Hughes of the country music business. He owned the world-famous Gilley's nightclub in Pasadena, Texas, and also managed singers Mickey Gilley and Johnny Lee. He was very rich and very reclusive, maintaining a circle of four or five very close friends, none of whom he trusted completely. In 1983 I was not a part of his inner circle, but would soon step inside.

I first started selling dates to Sherwood Cryer in 1973 at Gilley's. I sold him Waylon Jennings, Tompall Glaser, David Allan Coe, and Dr. Hook. We established a good relationship over the phone and talked about business in general. Like many others, I unsuccessfully tried to reach him for days or weeks, frequently staying up until 2:00 A.M. to sell him a date. I used to say that he was like God in that when you wanted him you couldn't get him but when he wanted you he always found you.

As time passed we grew closer and would talk about more than just the artists I was trying to sell him. We would ask each other's opinions on different things we were doing. He had at one time suggested that I move down to Pasadena and book Mickey Gilley and Johnny Lee. I would have done that in 1979 or 1980 if I had been able to do it out of Nashville, but Pasadena, Texas, is a terrible place—flat, humid, and monotonous. Sherwood's empire was based there and that is where he wanted it done. I couldn't live there for any amount of money.

Sherwood dismissed Sandy Brokaw and started pumping me for information. He wanted to know what I would do if and when Dick Blake died. Blake was frequently sick and required lengthy hospital stays. I told him that Blake was in rough shape, but that he had been that way many times before and would most likely make it. As his friend Jack Norman, Jr., used to say, "Dick Blake has been dying for years." Despite the fact that he had severe respiratory problems and other complications, he always pulled through. Sherwood kept on, asking me about the other acts on our roster and telling me what he thought was likely to happen. I was really not in the mood to talk about it, but he persisted. In a few minutes, fellow Dick Blake agent Joann Berry approached us and asked if she could speak to me alone for a moment. Sherwood excused us and we began walking down the corridor. She put her arm around my shoulder and told me Dick Blake had died at around 6:00 P.M.

Joann had come to Nashville from Waco, Texas, and had been hired by Dick Blake because she could bring in business. She had formerly worked as an agent for the Jim Halsey Agency in Tulsa, but had left there for some reason. As we walked down the hall, I asked Joann what she wanted to do about our business future. At that time she and I were very close and both of us assumed that we would be working together after Blake's death. Ronnie Milsap had left the agency, so my bargaining strength was not as great as I would have liked. I needed Joann, for the moment at least, due to the strength of her position with Barbara and Louise Mandrell. As Dick's health got worse, Joann had taken advantage of the circumstances and successfully jockeyed for the position within the company as Barbara's responsible agent. We had been discussing our options for the past several weeks, but I felt that Joann was holding something back. What she knew at that time and had known for some time was that Barbara Mandrell would be going out on her own as soon as Blake died.

I figured that such a move was inevitable. Barbara Mandrell had paid us nearly $400,000 in commissions during the last fiscal year. She could start her own agency, pay Joann a healthy salary, and not only save money, but make money. As powerful as Barbara Mandrell had become, it seemed quite likely she would be able to attract other artists as clients. I felt that Barbara and Joann had already made this decision. Joann would be content in having a large slice of the pie, but she was a good businesswoman and thought that if she played her hand correctly she could end up with all of the artists on the Dick Blake roster. She knew that I was the key to making that happen.

In any event, Joann had not put all of her cards on the table, but her hand was easy to imagine. We decided to talk about it later.

I returned to my conversation with Sherwood Cryer, telling him that Blake had died. He expressed his sympathy but it was obvious that he could not care less. He recalled that he had wanted me to "come on down to Texas" and book Mickey Gilley and Johnny Lee a couple of years before. I reminded him that I did not want to live in Texas. He asked me what I was going to do now that Blake was gone.

I told him that I did not know but that my intention was to stay at Dick Blake's agency. I also mentioned that we would probably lose Barbara and Louise Mandrell. Sherwood clearly wanted to make a deal, but it was my intention to keep Dick Blake International in business, with the Mandrells if possible, without them if necessary. We had enough money in the bank and commissions owed to the agency to continue operations.

There were many reasons why I wanted the Dick Blake Agency to continue. For one thing, we had all been on a gravy train. I had three company cars: A Jaguar XK-E, a Cadillac Fleetwood, and a Cadillac convertible. I had a good salary, medical insurance, and opportunities for side deals. It was a great life and I did not wish to start over at some place where I would have to dress a certain way and punch a clock. I was used to two-hour lunches and an additional hour or so for running over at the Vanderbilt track. The idea of having a real nine-to-five job terrified me. In addition, I felt that it was time I went out on my own. Under the plans that I had begun to formulate for Dick Blake, I figured I would be the chief engineer on the big gravy train. I liked the other employees, more or less, and felt that we could all work together.

In addition to a good staff, we had the following artists: Ricky Skaggs, Brenda Lee, Ronnie McDowell, Charly McClain, the Whites, Steve Wariner, and Exile. These artists had various managers, producers, and attorneys that would have to be dealt with, and soon.

In order to keep Dick Blake International rolling, it would be necessary to make some kind of deal with the family members. This would have to be done very quickly so that our clients would not panic. I knew that every agency in town would try to steal all of them and were probably already attempting to do just that. We would have to act quickly and present a unified front to the public as well as to our clients. Time was of the essence.

There was one very basic question that would have to be addressed before we did anything. Was Dick Blake International worth saving as a company? It had a sterling reputation, but in the six months before Blake's death, we had lost Ronnie Milsap and the Statler Brothers. As previously noted, we would most likely lose Barbara and Louise Mandrell as well. Our top money-makers were already gone. This was a tough question. Also, Pat Blake, Dick Blake's widow, disliked all of us to a great degree. Dick Blake frequently and without provocation referred to his family members as "a bunch of greedy bastards and thieves." This is not to say that he did not care for them, but it might be more accurate to say that he disliked us less than he disliked them. He complained about them incessantly, and I have no doubt that he spoke ill of us when he was with them. His attorney and his accountant both pleaded with him to make a will, but he would not. Even near the end, a will was taken to him at the hospital and he refused to sign. He had told us several times that he intended to let "those greedy son of a bitches" fight it out after he was gone.

I have no doubt that he perceived us to be every bit as greedy as his family. The thought that all of us might soon be fighting over his money probably cheered him on during those final days. He thrived on discord and employed it as a means to maintain control. That's just the way he was.

Thursday and Friday, the two days after his death, were filled with secret meetings. Everyone tried to figure out what everyone else was going to do. It was a strange time. Joann and I had a meeting in her office. She indicated to me at that time that Barbara Mandrell and her husband, Ken Dudney, were going to open their own agency. She added she would enjoy working with me as she had in the past and that she thought we could build a great agency and make some big money. She wanted me to deliver all of the employees. She also wanted me to deliver all of the rest of our clients. I told her that her suggestion was the best of all the options we had jointly considered.

I could have put it together if I had elected to do so and brought the entire staff and all of the clients to her new agency. The general perception of Joann around the office was not good. She was viewed as a manipulative opportunist, a Johnny-come-lately without a job who, when hired by Dick Blake against everyone's wishes except agent Dave Barton's, began taking over Barbara Mandrell as Blake's health deteriorated. I knew that she would attempt to operate behind my back if she did not perceive that I was on her side 100 percent. In fact, I felt that she would attempt to garner support for her plan anyway, without me, as she subsequently did.

Even though I wanted to keep Dick Blake International operating, I was also looking out for myself and the other employees and I did consider the possibility of working with Joann Berry and Barbara Mandrell to be a very viable option for all of us. There were, however, two points that needed to be resolved in my own mind before there was any likelihood at all of doing business with them.

I wanted a meeting with Barbara Mandrell and her husband; and Linda Edwards (corporate secretary at Dick Blake International), Allen Whitcomb (a Dick Blake agent), and myself would want some ownership in the new company.

Joann responded to the first point by saying that Barbara and Ken didn't have time for a meeting and that Barbara wanted Joann to handle everything. This was the correct position for

Joann to take from a tactical standpoint, but it was the worst position she could have taken with me. I learned long ago not to deal with anyone except principals. This was especially true in this instance, I told Joann that I understood her position and that as such it would not be a problem, which it was not, since I had decided against doing business with her anyway.

Her response to the second point was predictable but equally unacceptable. She said that there would be no ownership available in the new company for any of us, not even her. I felt that she certainly intended to own part of the new company and that she was being evasive.

I replied that although this was not the way we would prefer things ideally, we wanted to stay together as a unit and if this was the best we could hope for under the circumstances, then so be it. In other words, I told her that we had a deal, pending resolution of minor details, such as salary.

Although the possibility of a deal existed when I entered Joann's office, that option left when I walked out of the door. I have always had a sixth sense in business matters, and this was no exception. I had never considered myself as an employee anywhere and had no intention of doing so in the future. With someone like Joann at the helm, she would have considered all of us to be her employees, which in fact we would have been.

Why then did I tell her we had a deal? I knew that she would be going out on the road with Barbara Mandrell for a couple of weeks as soon as Blake's funeral was held. I wanted that time to try to figure out exactly what all of us were going to do. It was also my desire, if necessary, to discredit her as much as possible with Barbara and her husband. I wanted Joann to tell the Mandrells that she had everything under control, that she would be able to deliver Dick Blake International to them in its entirety. When she proved unable to do so, I felt that her position would be weakened.

In the meantime, I could possibly make some kind of deal with Barbara's manager-father, Irby Mandrell. He and I had always had a good relationship and I suspected that he was tired of Joann always getting in the middle of Barbara's business.

Last but not least, if I was unable to make a deal with Sherwood Cryer, and nothing could be worked out with Blake's family, then as a last resort we could make a deal with Joann. There were still way too many unresolved issues. I did not know when we would be able to meet with Blake's widow, and I felt that she would most likely stall for a while, which she did.

Dick's funeral took place on Saturday afternoon, October 15, 1983.

During the actual service itself I was seated in the second or third row from the front of the chapel. At first I felt ill at ease, realizing that the front sections in such places are usually reserved for the family. I again reflected that I was part of his real family, so I did not bother to move. As it turned out, it was fortunate that I was seated in one of the front pews during the service because before it was over I almost bit my tongue in half to avoid laughing out loud. Tears literally rolled down my face. The source of the humor was the man who delivered the eulogy. He extolled the unlimited virtues of the deceased without so much as cracking a smile. I wish that I could recall his name. He was about forty years old, red-faced and jovial and a bit pudgy, an accomplished after-dinner speaker.

He was sufficiently candid at the outset, noting quietly that he "had not had the good fortune to have known Dick Blake personally. However..." He then proceeded to describe someone whose service must have been in another part of the chapel. It was the biggest crock of shit that I have ever heard in my life, notwithstanding the fact that it was exquisitely delivered. I hung eagerly on every word, even anticipating his next salvo of perjured blasphemies.

He described Dick Blake as a kind, gentle, and loving man, someone who always placed his family first. Dick Blake was an affectionate and loving husband—loyal, understanding, and a good provider. He was a friend to all who knew him, a man with a kind word for everyone. By this time I was on the verge of hysteria, fueled by the loud and frequent sobs that followed the mention of some special virtue possessed by the deceased. I hoped that my tears of laughter would be mistaken for sorrow. The funniest part occurred when this great orator began describing Dick Blake's Christian purpose in life and his high moral standards and sense of values.

As the speaker performed, his words caused me to reflect upon some of the things he said.

A devoted husband: He would fuck anything that moved if he could have. We'd cleaned out his desk after he died, removing many incriminating notes as a courtesy to his widow.

A dedicated Christian: Blake told us once that Jim Bakker had called him. At that time I had no idea who Jim Bakker was. Dick explained that he ran the PTL Club, which he said stood for "Pass the Loot." Anyway, at some point during the conversation Jim Bakker asked Blake if he had been born again. Blake told him, "Naw, it took on me the first time."

A family man: Dick Blake skipped his only daughter's college graduation and her wedding to be on the road with the Statler Brothers.

Once he told me a story that had happened at a joint he used to operate in Indianapolis. He was married at the time, or so he said, and had a sexual relationship with one of his waitresses. One evening he told her to begin setting up tables for the night. She replied that she was not going to do it and threatened to tell his wife if he did not give her preferential treatment. He picked up the phone in front of his girlfriend and pretended to call his wife. To the young woman's amazement he confessed everything and then handed the phone to her.

"Here, my wife wants to talk to you," he said. "She is getting ready to come down here and whip your ass."

The waitress left, never to return. This was the story that Blake told. It could have been a complete fabrication, as were many of his tales.

I left the building as soon as the service was over, for in truth I had loved Dick Blake very much and I felt very sad. In a few minutes, Lincoln Lakeoff, the agency's accountant, and his wife came through the door followed by Linda Edwards, Lincoln saw that I had been crying and kind of laughed about it. He disliked Blake and felt that he was totally corrupt. He could not imagine how anyone could possibly have any feelings for him, and made some remark to that effect.

The Statler Brothers were not present at his funeral. There was no excuse for their absence. If they had to work that day then they should have changed or canceled the date. I cannot say with certainty that Dick Blake had been stealing from them at the box office, although some of his employees felt that this was the real reason they quit the agency. Even if that were the case, Blake loved them more than anyone else in his life and they should have been there.

This is perhaps the saddest commentary on the music business in Nashville. Someone devotes his life to the business, and often his peers do not show him the courtesy of attending his funeral. It was the same for Shorty Lavender. Most of the acts he had done so much to help for such a long period of time never showed up either when Shorty died. George Jones, whom Shorty had helped and supported emotionally over the years, couldn't come then, although he had managed to sing at the funeral when fellow singer Mel Street killed himself.

Joann soon joined us as Lincoln and his wife left. She asked if everything was still okay with our deal and I assured her that it was.

I wanted to make a deal with Blake's widow, Pat, as soon as possible. For some reason, she kept stalling and did not want to talk about it. In retrospect I feel that she resented our haste, since Dick Blake had not even been dead a full week. I understood her feelings, but I also knew that unless we could move quickly we would start losing clients and by the time she decided to have a meeting there would be nothing to talk about. It really was that critical.

Pat informed us that her attorney, Jack Norman, Jr., would soon arrange a meeting. She had said that she did not want to talk to me. As I mentioned earlier, she detested all of us, but me in particular. I have no doubt that she formed this opinion as a result of things Blake had told her. One time she very spitefully mentioned to me all of the money that the company had spent on my 1965 Jaguar XK-E. It was an expensive car to maintain, costing over five thousand a dollars a year for that purpose.

On the other hand, I personally netted the company somewhere in the neighborhood of $400,000 a year as a result of my efforts. As far as I was concerned, if I had spent $50,000 a year for car maintenance it would have been well deserved. I told her that Blake could have fired me any time he wanted, but chose not to. The car expenses must have been all right. My Jaguar and two Cadillacs were nothing compared to the expense of keeping up our two airplanes, which we seldom used, four buses, sound equipment, a warehouse, and sound trucks.

These things did not bother Pat, since her son was employed by our sound company. I knew one thing for certain: If we were going to be involved in the future with Dick Blake International, the sound company would be dismantled immediately and the revenues from the sale of the equipment returned to the company bank account. As for her son, Mike, I would be willing to put him to work at the agency in the position of an apprentice and see how he handled himself.

I did not know whether Pat Blake wanted to keep the place going or liquidate all of the assets and call it a day. For some reason, we were under the impression that she would like to see the company continue.

Eventually we met with Pat Blake and her attorney, but we realized that there was really no possibility of doing business with her. I remember thinking at the time what idiots they both were. I really do not have any idea what they wanted or what they expected from us. Our perception was that Pat Blake thought that she and her son would run things and that we would do what we were told. It didn't work out for any of us.

I met with Irby Mandrell, Barbara's manager and father. I thought that if I could make some kind of deal with him, the situation might yet be saved. I gathered that he had nothing to do with Barbara's agency. I didn't think that I could get Joann out of the picture, although I would have if that were possible. I did think, however, that if I could make a deal with Irby while Joann was out of town, I could reduce her strength to the extent that she could possibly be controlled. Seeing that this was not feasible, I began to consider the option of working with Sherwood Cryer as perhaps the most desirable course of action.

I called Sherwood and we discussed matters. Gilley's was at its highest point and Sherwood Cryer had the money to handle the financial load required by an agency our size. I also liked him personally. I had Linda get together all of the figures for the past several years, including total operating expenses and projected income based on the clients then in our stable. We calculated that our expenses came to $35,000 a month. This amount was really a bit more than we thought we needed at the time. After the dust settled, it ended up costing us $50,000 a month to operate. Sherwood suggested that I come down to Pasadena at once so we could put the deal together and get the show on the road. I did not want to go there, but I felt that time was running out and so were our options. We could not work with Pat Blake, and we did not want to work with the Mandrells. We wanted to stay together as a group, we all liked Sherwood Cryer, and we needed money—and he wanted to do business.

I realized that if we did make a deal with him then I needed to be perceived by my coworkers as the boss. Setting up the deal and possessing the knowledge of the conversations leading up to that point would assure my power in the overall picture. As always, knowledge is power.

I flew down to Houston's Hobby Airport and was met by Sherwood Cryer. We agreed to work together. Sherwood and I understood each other. He ran Gilley's with an iron hand. He was everywhere all the time, watching the door, looking out for fights, seeing that nobody stole anything. He was tough and whipped ass personally, although his torpedoes materialized instantly if needed. His office floor was littered with big grocery sacks full of money, thousands and thousands of dollars. Sherwood liked guns, carried one constantly, and was not afraid to use it. There were pistols on the desk, rifles propped in the corners, and machine guns in lockers. A big safe stood open against the wall, full of stacked silver ingots. This was the headquarters from which Sherwood Cryer conducted the affairs of his empire.

We made the following agreement: The majority stockholder would be Charmin, Inc. This was a booking agency owned by Sherwood's woman, Minnie Elerick. Minnie would own the majority of the stock through Charmin. The remaining 49 percent of the stock would be divided equally between agents Allen Whitcomb and Dave Barton, Linda Edwards, and myself.

Our group in Nashville would open our own company and then sell 51 percent of the company to Charmin. The money we received would be our operating capital. None of us would owe anything to anyone personally and our corporate stock would not be encumbered by any debts. It was a roll of the dice for Sherwood and Minnie. They would be taking all the risks. For us, it would be business as usual.

When I returned to Nashville, I met with Linda, Allen, and Dave and explained the situation. Most of the conversations pertaining to our plans had been conducted by Linda, Allen, and myself.

An old high school acquaintance, Bruce Honick, with the *Nashville Banner,* called, wanting to know what was happening at the agency. He'd heard some rumors that we were closing. I really didn't want to deal with the press just yet, but if he had heard rumors, than so had everyone else, so I gave him some information for a story in *Amusement Business.* I told him that it would be business as usual at Dick Blake International but that the four of us would be running the show. When this article hit the street, Pat Blake hit the roof.

I felt some sympathy for Pat. Dick had told her that she was the beneficiary on all of his insurance policies. In fact, she was the beneficiary on one policy, but the others listed the beneficiary as "the estate of Dick Blake." To further complicate matters, Dick had given the insurance companies an incorrect date of birth, one that made him two years older than he actually was. Why would he have done this? It was hard to imagine someone lying to an insurance company to make himself seem older, yet it was equally hard to believe that he could not remember his own birth date.

According to Linda Edwards, Blake had over $100,000 in a personal account, but the account had been frozen because of money owed on some sound equipment.

Blake was a mysterious man, even in death. His own wife did not know his middle name. She only found out that it was "Clair" after Linda wrote away for his birth certificate. Other things were coming to light that seemed incongruent as well. Blake had told us that he had been stabbed in the chest by a bayonet in World War II and that he had lost one lung as a result. Linda subsequently found an old insurance policy in his desk that indicated the lung had been removed in 1950 due to tuberculosis.

Blake's war stories were very interesting and we all took it for granted that they were true. Among some of the things that he told me personally are the following:

He was shot down three times in the South Pacific, twice in P-40s and once in a P-51.

He was captured by the Japanese, tortured, and buried underground for three days with nothing but a tube stuck into the ground as a source of air. He told me that they had inserted bamboo under his fingernails to torture him. It was also as a result of his time in the POW camp that he could no longer tolerate rice.

He escaped and was picked up by an American submarine.

He was with General Claire Chennault's famed Flying Tigers in China. He also knew Col. Robert L. Scott, Jr., author of *Damned to Glory,* a book about the P-40 airplane. He said Scott was a jerk.

He knew Eddie Rickenbacker in Indianapolis after the war, but he was jealous of Blake's war record. They did not like each other.

He described in great detail an aerial confrontation with one of Japan's top aces. As I recollect, he was on a routine patrol in the South Pacific, came out of the clouds, and saw this Japanese Zero flying solo at some distance ahead and below him. Blake got him in his sights and began to go after him. His guns jammed, and he had to let him go and then make a fast exit. Blake recalled meeting the famous Japanese ace in a hotel lobby some years later in San Francisco. The Japanese pilot recalled the engagement after Blake refreshed his memory.

On another occasion, Blake was returning from an aerial battle. His P-51 Mustang was badly shot up and he was coming in low. He lowered his landing gear, indicating his intentions since he feared being shot down by Americans inasmuch as he was nowhere near the landing strip. A group of black anti-aircraft gunners finished him off and the plane landed in some trees, breaking his fall to some degree. He never cared for blacks after that experience.

I mention these things to show that as well as we thought we knew Dick Blake, none of us knew him at all. Was he really married five times? Had he really done all of these things in the war, and did it matter if he had or not?

Linda's boyfriend decided to secure a copy of Dick Blake's service record, which made it clear that not only were Dick Blake's stories untrue, he had never even left the United States during the war years. Despite what I now knew, Dick Blake was still my hero. He had still kicked ass in the business world. He had done things his way in Music City. I will always respect him for that.

We had several meetings with Lincoln Lakeoff, our accountant, who knew about Dick Blake's financial misdealings. He felt we ought to get out from under Dick Blake International altogether.

We met with attorney Malcolm Mimms on November 4, 1983. We told him about Blake's side deals and chicanery. Malcolm felt it would be better for us to be on our own in case someone leaked the information and the agency got sued.

Then we told him about our employment contracts with Dick Blake International. So far these agreements had not been mentioned by any of us, mainly because we did not wish to acknowledge their existence. They had been signed by all of us in September 1982, before Blake put us on commission. Although there had been some alterations in the contracts, if they had shown up in court and been declared valid, the four of us would have been bound to Dick Blake International through September 1984.

I instructed Linda to remove the originals from her files and take them home. I told her that Pat Blake was likely to be sneaking around trying to get something on us and I did not want those contracts around. We did not know whether Pat Blake's attorney knew of their existence. I found it inconceivable that Blake would not have mentioned them to him at all, but Linda had never been asked to make any copies, so we hoped we were safe. On the other hand, those contracts had been signed with the understanding that we were each to receive 10 percent ownership in Dick Blake International.

As soon as I mentioned the employment contracts I knew that we were dealing with the wrong attorney. He said something asinine like, "I wish you hadn't shown me these because if it ever comes up in court, I will have to testify that I knew about them."

Whose side was this guy on? I want a lawyer who is extremely aggressive, who is very well informed, and who will say or do whatever is necessary to get the job done. The music business is not a duel, it's a street fight. Win or die.

Although I did not feel that Malcolm Mimms was our man, I did imagine that he could set up a corporation, a task which he handled sufficiently, and we were duly incorporated on November 7, 1983, as In Concert International. After much hashing around and checking with the musicians' union in New York, we finally settled on that name, which had been suggested by Linda.

An article appeared two days later in the *Nashville Banner,* entitled BLAKE AGENCY REOPENS UNDER NEW NAME. This story was written by artist biographer Bob Millard. As soon as the *Banner* hit the streets we began moving quickly. We now had a definite sense of purpose but we needed to solidify on several fronts. We required office space at once and we thought it best to stay where we were.

However, we faced one problem. Our present offices were leased to Dick Blake International. Linda, in another stroke of genius, suggested that we contact the lessor, Curtis Rucker. We explained the situation to him, that we had started our own company and that we did not want to be in the position of being evicted if things got nasty. I think that Dick Blake's lease had expired in December 1980 and had never been renewed. In any case we secured a new lease for In Concert with Curtis Rucker.

Next we needed to get the existing phone number transferred from Dick Blake International to the new company. This phone number had been in existence as a talent agency number for over a decade and we all felt that it was a lucky one.

As usual, Linda concocted a scheme whereby we could accomplish our aim. She went down to the phone company and secured the papers necessary for changing the billing information. These documents were presented to Pat Blake for her signature, which she provided. Her signature released her from any further liability for the phone bill, which concerned her since it had been averaging around $2,500 per month. Pat Blake's signature on this paper also released this phone number to our new company. When she found out she became furious.

In spite of the fact that we had started our own company,

Blake's widow gave us no trouble, perhaps because we wanted to give her 10 percent of the new agency as a gesture of goodwill. Our accountant thought that we were crazy to make this offer. We all insisted that this was what we wanted to do. Looking back, I see that it was not an intelligent move.

However, her lawyer never responded even after several letters, and finally the offer was withdrawn. This refusal of even a response on their part was incomprehensible to us, and even though we did not like Pat Blake, we felt sorry for her. We also felt that her attorney had really done nothing to help her.

In retrospect she was probably better off taking commissions due and all of the physical property and letting us go our own way, which is how it turned out. We had asked her to give us a price on all of the furniture, phones, computers, and other office equipment. She figured that she was going to be able to sell this stuff to us for a good sum, so she was happy about that. In addition, Linda had been helping her get things cleared up financially with Dick Blake International. It seemed that there was at least a temporary cessation of hostilities between all of us.

I was pleased with the way things were going. Sherwood was happy to be in business with us, we were all satisfied with each other, most of our acts seemed to be stabilized. Everything was okay.

Joann was, no doubt, irritated when she found out that we had started our own company and were not going with her to Barbara Mandrell's new agency, World Class Talent. In any case, we were all still on fairly good terms with Irby and Mary Mandrell, Barbara's father and mother, whose offices remained downstairs, but in the same suite as ours.

There was nothing unusual about Barbara Mandrell's husband, Ken Dudney, dropping by from time to time. On one such occasion he met with the clerical workers in the office and sought to hire them for his new agency. He offered them more money than they had been making working for Dick Blake International or would be making with us.

The women turned him down. They did not particularly like Joann Berry and to some degree did not trust her to act in their best interests. They were also loyal to me and the rest of us. I remember Judy Marie asking me what she and Lisa should do.

She told me about their job offer from the Mandrells and said that they would rather stay with us but that they wanted some security. I replied that the deal had already been concluded with Sherwood Cryer and that we were going to keep rocking. I added there was nothing to worry about and that I would take care of them, and indeed that was my intention. I did, however, have to match the offer that Barbara's husband had made.

Soon thereafter, Allen Whitcomb came to me and said that Joann had been trying to hire agent Lane Cross. I had anticipated that she would attempt some mischief of this sort and yet her actions vexed me nonetheless. Allen and I met with Lane and discussed the situation. Formerly a bus driver for the public transportation system and more recently a gofer for Top Billing, from whom we had stolen him, Lane showed great promise as an agent. He talked about his strength with the band Exile and implied that if he left the agency they would also leave.

I had no doubt that this was true and yet that is not the reason we decided to keep him by matching Joann's offer. I knew that Exile would be leaving our agency soon enough anyway and that when that happened Lane would learn a very important lesson, mainly that very few acts can be trusted. Lane was feeling his oats, thinking vainly that he had some influence over this act. We kept Lane Cross because we felt that eventually he could become a good agent.

I had also resolved that In Concert International would start out at least with all of the employees and acts who had been with Dick Blake International. I could justify the fact that we had lost the Mandrells for purely financial reasons. With as much money as Barbara had been paying in commissions it would have been foolish not to start her own agency. Louise Mandrell's departure could be explained easily enough as family loyalty. I was not prepared, however, to lose anyone else.

It is interesting to note the different ways rock and pop acts as opposed to country acts view their agents and agencies. Rock and roll acts tend to perceive the booking agency as a necessary evil, and even the larger acts, those making over $50,000 a night, pay their agency 10 percent and consider it part of the cost of doing business. From my perspective there appears to be, generally speaking, a higher degree of loyalty to agencies from rock acts than is the case with country performers. This is not to say that rock acts do not change agencies.

The phenomenon of an act leaving an agency that has significantly contributed to his success and starting his own agency seems to happen much more often with country artists. In considering the reasons for this state of affairs, I cannot attribute it to any one particular thing or circumstance. It might be merely a matter of good business sense for the country artist. More likely a lower degree of loyalty among country artists could be explained by excessive greed. With the country artist, the agency is an entity to be used until the act reaches the point where he can afford to book himself.

Examples of this abound in Nashville. Ronnie Milsap was booked for several years by his own Headline International. George Strait, Randy Travis, the Statler Brothers, Barbara Mandrell, the Judds, and Reba McEntire are a few others. The general method of operation in such cases is that the act, or the act's manager, keeps his or her own office and hires an agent to book the artist. This is a good deal for everyone; that is, except for the agency that spent the previous two or three years building the act to the point that the agency could finally begin to make some real money.

It is very disappointing to work hard for an act, making that act a high priority over a long period of time, only to see that act leave and go to another agency or leave and start his own. It has, sadly, been this way as long as I can remember. In addition to losing the act, the agency almost always loses one or two agents as well. The first few times this happens, it is likely to hurt the feelings of the particular agent who has made an act his personal priority. This sadness results from the illusion that one has been betrayed by a good friend.

In fact, something very different happened. In most cases an agent exists to be used by an artist, and any overtures of friendship from an artist are calculated to make the agent and the agency more productive on the artist's behalf. As soon as an agent begins to think that this relationship with any artist is anything more than that, he positions himself for a big letdown.

Most successful agents learn this lesson early and realize that the relationship with the client is strictly about money. He will get his feelings hurt a few times at first and then wise up. At this point, the agent begins to practice the same psychology with the artist, acting like the best of friends but maintaining a safe distance. Ultimately, the agent usually has the last laugh, for whatever goes up must come down, and any agent with any degree of longevity will witness the fall of some acts who misused him on their way up.

Chapter Three

Underway

All of us at In Concert had been through quite a bit of stress in a short period of time. We had survived the dissolution of Dick Blake International and the defection of the Mandrells, and had established In Concert International as a company. It was time to focus our attention upon keeping the artists we had, and getting some new ones.

We lost artist Steve Wariner almost immediately since his manager didn't think he ought to be at a new agency.

Brenda Lee was and is one of the greatest singers of this century, having sold over a hundred million records. I, like so many other Americans, had almost literally grown up on her music. We had worked with her at Dick Blake since 1981 and I hoped that we would be able to keep her as a client. I had my doubts, though. I felt that she was overpriced and would soon be gone as a result. She was worth $6,000 a night at this time. This is not to say that an agent might not sometimes secure a $7,500 or even an occasional $10,000 date, but at that price, very few people were interested. When Jack Johnson had entered the picture to "help with her management," he arbitrarily decided that she should be getting $10,000 a night. We were having trouble getting her dates at $7,500. He reasoned she was a living legend and had sold millions of records. This was true enough, but the talent buyer is interested in selling tickets. Someone who is not at the top of the charts currently, or even recently, is not as likely to bring in customers as a signer whose record releases are at least in the top twenty.

When a talent buyer is making a decision as to which act he should purchase, there are several factors to be considered. When given a price on an artist, he looks for other options in that same price range. If he thinks that another act at that price will sell more tickets than the one he is being pitched, then he will probably buy the one that he feels to be the best overall choice. Thus, when an act is overpriced several things happen. A significant number of buyers who would have used the act at a lower price are no longer available. They either can't afford the higher price or do not feel that the price is justified in terms of the financial risk involved. Some buyers who decide to pay the higher price lose money and vow never to use the artist again. In addition, they often tell other buyers that they lost money by using the act, so other buyers decide not to use them as well.

Any act in theory can work a certain number of dates at a given price. For example, if an act is really worth $8,000, that is, making money for promoters at that price, then he can work x number of dates. If he is willing to work for $6,000 even though he is really worth $8,000, he will be able to work as many dates as he wants. If, on the other hand, he is trying to work for $12,000 when he is really only worth $8,000, he is going to work less dates.

The other consequence of being overpriced is that an act ceases to be visible in the marketplace. As the act plays less dates in fewer cities, buyers tend to think less frequently of that artist when considering their entertainment needs. This naturally has a negative effect on an artist's career.

Our feeling at the agency was that Brenda Lee's career was over, and had been over for some time. In such cases, and this was one in point, if the artist is well off financially, she can afford to set an arbitrarily high price, since it does not matter to her whether she works or not. In this case, the logic is indeed flawless. If someone absolutely must have this particular artist, then he must pay the price.

We really did not feel that we could do much better for Brenda Lee, but we told them what they wanted to hear, not wanting to lose any more acts this early in the new game. I did appreciate their loyalty, for it helped buy us time to get things going. By the time they left us and went to the Halsey Agency in 1984, we were off and running.

We were obviously wrong about Brenda Lee's career. She has a new record deal and has had several very successful years at Opryland. Brenda's husband, Ronnie Shacklett, has served as her manager for years and has done a great job.

I next turned my attention to the situation with singer Charly McClain. I first started booking her in the late 1970s as an agent at the Lavender-Blake Agency. She and Mickey Gilley were both on CBS Records at the time, and were each doing well on their own.

Gilley was born in 1936 and grew up in Ferriday, Louisiana, with cousins Jimmy Swaggart and Jerry Lee Lewis, two real wildmen of the era. Gilley moved to Houston at age seventeen and obtained work as a laborer. Observing Jerry Lee's success, he decided to try his own hand at music. His big break happened when he became partners with Texas businessman Sherwood Cryer, who changed the name of his club on Spencer Highway in Pasadena from Shelly's to Gilley's. Gilley signed with Playboy Records in the mid-1970s and had his first hit, "Room Full of Roses."

At first considered by many to be a Jerry Lee Lewis clone, Gilley later developed his own successful style. He signed with CBS Records in Nashville and during his time at the top had seventeen number-one records.

It is interesting to note that the Country Music Association never really paid much attention to either one of these artists, despite their enormous contributions to country music. The only reason I can think of for this oversight is that neither of them were perceived as "Nashville" artists, that is, they were not part of the Nashville clique and did not spend their free time hanging around there and kissing the appropriate asses. Charly lived in Memphis and stayed there when she wasn't on the road or in the studio. Gilley was considered a "Texas" act and as such to some degree a second-class citizen by the powers that be in Nashville. He had been recognized early on by the more progressive California-based Academy of Country Music. The phenomenon that resulted from the movie *Urban Cowboy* was a tremendous boost to country music, but, then, it had not been about Nashville and was downplayed there even as the Nashville-based entertainers benefited from the increased public awareness it generated.

Gilley and McClain had run into each other in California when Charly had done a guest spot on the TV show "CHIPs." Gilley was playing Harrah's in Reno and received a call from the Brokaws to do a cameo appearance on the same show, which also included Johnny Lee. Gilley told her that he liked her singing and that they should try a duet together. As a result of that conversation their duet "Paradise Tonight" was recorded, released, and easily moved to a number-one position on *Billboard*'s country charts.

This was all well and good but the implications for me were unfavorable. With a duet album in the works it naturally followed that it would not be long before somebody came up with the idea that Mickey Gilley and Charly McClain should be touring together. I knew that this was going to happen soon.

I also knew that there was no way that In Concert could work with William Morris, Gilley's agency, in a spirit of mutual trust and cooperation. The bottom line was that either I would be able to steal Mickey Gilley from them or that they would steal Charly McClain from me. Since Gilley had been with the William Morris Agency for a couple of years and was making good money, I did not feel that my chances of luring him away would be very good. I also knew that he still had over a year and a half left on his contract.

I did not have Charly McClain under contract at all, and felt that she was an opportunist and that it would be a great boost to her career to be on tour with Gilley. This being the case, I did not expect any loyalty from her. Most likely the William Morris Agency would seek a meeting with her and explain that due to the fact that they represented Mickey Gilley, it would be necessary for her to join the William Morris Agency in order to make the tour work, since Gilley would be the headline act. Her boyfriend, Wayne Massey, was an actor and had played on the soap opera "One Life to Live."

I could almost hear Dave Douds from the William Morris Agency promise both Wayne and Charly all types of TV shows and movies. In fact, I had found Douds in their dressing room at the Opry House the night Blake died, so I already knew he was after her. Despite the fact that Dave Douds was smug and arrogant, he was a man of great ability, and not someone whom I could afford to underestimate.

It is worth mentioning at this point a little something about the hillbilly fascination with seeing themselves on the screen. It is in most cases much more a question of ego gratification provided by TV than actual career enhancement. There are, of course, some noteworthy exceptions. In the case of the Mandrells, the price of both Louise and Barbara soared as a result of their prime-time television show. However, a one-time cameo appearance on an episode of a TV show by a country artist does little to further his or her career.

Nonetheless, as Dick Blake said, "Every singer wants to be an actor and every actor wants to be a singer." This observation borders on being a universal truth, and it seems particularly so in the case of country singers. The big West Coast talent agencies like William Morris, Triad, and ICM have been able to lure many country acts to their roster by dangling the carrots of television and movies in front of them. It is a fact that these agencies do control much of the major television and movie business in the United States.

It is also true that the agents in Hollywood and Beverly Hills who are involved in such things do not give a damn about some $5,000- or $10,000-a-night country act. In most cases, they do not even know who they are. In addition, when any act, country or otherwise, reaches a certain degree of renown, they can get as much television exposure as they deserve anyway.

It still happens that country acts are duped in this fashion, seeking TV and also thinking that it is more prestigious to be represented by a West Coast–based agency. As a result the artist's date sheet frequently suffers. As I noted, the big boys in California generally do not know who the hell most country acts are anyway, and few agents in the Nashville branch of the company have any West Coast TV or movie connections at all, despite their claims to the contrary.

Returning to Mickey Gilley and Charly McClain, there was one more major obstacle that would have to be faced if I were to represent Mickey Gilley or avoid losing Charly McClain. This problem was the Brokaw Company. Based in L.A., David and Sandy Brokaw are two very shrewd operators who had been doing a good job handling public relations for Mickey Gilley. They were very loyal to the William Morris Agency since their father, Norman Brokaw, is the big wheel at that company. I am sure that Daddy was pleased by the fact that they had been instrumental in bringing Mickey Gilley and Johnny Lee to the William Morris Agency and keeping them there before, during, and after the movie *Urban Cowboy*. The combined revenue generated by Johnny Lee and Mickey Gilley during that time had no doubt been very substantial.

I knew that the Brokaw twins had Gilley's ear and that it would be very difficult to get past them. They had also done some PR for Charly McClain. This made matters worse. I was really more concerned with keeping Charly McClain as a client than I was with winning Mickey Gilley, since I was convinced Gilley would remain with the William Morris Agency.

I thought that I should join Charly McClain on tour. I flew to Houston's Hobby Airport, where I was met by one of Sherwood Cryer's "assistants." He took me to Gilley's, purportedly the largest nightclub in the world. The club was a huge Texas honky-tonk, dimly lit, with several bars, a good-size souvenir shop, a restaurant, a shoeshine stand, and the world-famous mechanical bulls. Dozens of fifty-two-inch Hunter fans droned overhead. The walls were lined with every type of electric game imaginable, and pool tables were everywhere. It seemed that the place had a low ceiling, except in the area above the large dance floor. This was merely an illusion fostered by the vastness of the place.

The club extended into the semidarkness nearly as far as the eye could see. A dirt-covered rodeo arena with a capacity of around ten thousand persons stood at the back of the club. It was difficult to estimate accurately the capacity of Gilley's club itself, and I have never been able to get a straight answer from

Sherwood Cryer as to how many people the place could actually hold.

When I finally found Sherwood, he was cordial as usual, and glad to see me. I followed him around the place as he made his rounds, and eventually ended up at his office. We discussed some business and I asked if Charly McClain had arrived. He said that she had checked in, but must be over at the hotel. She had a reputation for being at times unpleasant. Many buyers considered her aloof if not downright rude. I hoped she wouldn't show her ass tonight. As it turned out, she did only one of her scheduled two performances because she was "sick."

Sherwood justifiably felt like giving her only half of her $6,000 fee. I have no doubt that if I had not been there he would have done so. I understood his position. He ran shows at 11:00 P.M. and 1:00 A.M. That is too late for me to be out, but his intention was to keep people in the place as long as possible. He wanted to extract every cent each patron had.

The place normally closed at 2:00 A.M. When an act was supposed to do two shows and only performed one, that left him with just his house band between 12:00 and 2:00, and many patrons would call it a night at 12:00, thus costing him a large sum of money. He was angry, but I explained to him that it would be better to pay her, be nice about it, and let the situation pass. Considering that she had a duet album coming out with his client Mickey Gilley, I told him that he would make a great deal more money by letting her off the hook. She seemed rather frail to me anyway, and it could be that she really was sick. Fortunately, matters were quietly resolved and nothing more was said.

Mickey Gilley was already a big star. He worked a lot of fair dates, played the casinos, and made around $15,000 a night. Charly McClain was hot and getting hotter. Since that first single, "Paradise Tonight," went to number one, a joint tour starting in the first quarter of 1984 made a great deal of sense.

Charly told manager John Lentz to set up a meeting one night during that second week of December with Charly, Mickey Gilley, and myself at the RCA studio. The purpose of the meeting would be to discuss tour plans for the forthcoming winter and spring. We had been setting quite a few dates for

Charly and were receiving nightly fees between $6,000 and $7,000.

My main concern was to keep Charly as a client, and I was worried about the threat the William Morris Agency posed to our relationship. But everyone was in a festive mood, and as we tossed around ideas, I began to sense that I really had a chance of picking up Mickey Gilley. He complained that no matter how many hit records he had, his price seemed to have peaked.

I took advantage of the opportunity to undermine gently the William Morris Agency. I did not think it prudent at that point to disparage them directly, even though I would have gladly done so. Instead I suggested that since the urban cowboy fad was on the way out, Mickey Gilley was probably no longer the agency's priority. I also cited how we had rescued Ronnie Milsap after William Morris dropped the ball back in 1981. I would never have gotten away with these statements if someone from that agency had been at that meeting. It seemed that nobody from William Morris had been invited.

That night I called Sherwood Cryer as soon as I returned to the office and told him that I felt I had a good chance at stealing Mickey Gilley and that I was going to make my move. He reminded me that Mickey Gilley had about another year and a half left on his William Morris contract. I replied that I did not intend to wait that long.

As our conversation continued, I realized that Sherwood Cryer was pissed at William Morris. I soon found out why. The agency had placed Gilley in Reno and Atlantic City. They then put Janie Fricke on as an opening act at one place and T. G. Sheppard at the other. Sherwood had called the agent who set the dates at William Morris and told him that he would prefer to have Charly McClain opening for Gilley on those dates, since they had a new duet coming out. The agent said that the dates were set and that if Gilley did not want them, then he could put somebody else on in his place.

It should be mentioned that it is standard procedure for the headliner or main attraction to select an opening act, or if there is no preference, he at least has the right of approval. It was a breach of propriety for the agent to have taken this position with Mickey Gilley's manager.

This conversation and one other bit of insolence cost the William Morris Agency $569,437. That is the amount of commissions we took in on Mickey Gilley and Johnny Lee from 1984 to 1986. If the agency had been able to keep Gilley, they wouldn't have lost Johnny Lee, since he was also managed by Sherwood Cryer.

Furthermore, if they had kept Gilley, they would have ended up with Charly McClain as well. There would have been no way I could have kept her as a client. Her revenue for those same three years was $140,529. So, by failing to consider basic courtesy, the William Morris Agency lost $709,966 through two conversations.

The second conversation and other insolence I am referring to concerned its policy of not booking outside the agency. In other words, some idiot at the William Morris Agency told Gilley that the agency was unwilling to work through In Concert to get Charly McClain on shows with Mickey Gilley. So rather than lose a 10 percent commission on Charly McClain in order to keep Mickey Gilley happy, it lost three acts and over $700,000. Typical West Coast arrogance! These figures do not include 1987. You can add another $125,000 that we had coming in on dates we set on Gilley in the first few months of 1987.

The agent who annoyed Sherwood Cryer could have appeased him by promising him the dates that he wanted in the future and apologizing for having already put the other acts on the casino shows with Gilley.

Gilley and Sherwood had both made up their minds that they were going to work dates with Charly McClain. The William Morris Agency made a needless and costly mistake. It should have given Sherwood and Gilley what they wanted and then worked behind my back to steal Charly McClain. That is the way I would have handled it.

After my meeting with Gilley and Charly McClain, I was too wired up to sleep. I knew that Gilley would be going home for the holidays the next afternoon. I had to get a commitment from him before he left for home. I knew that he would be at the studio with Charly the next morning. As soon as I arrived at the office I picked up Allen Whitcomb and we went over to

RCA. I took Allen because he knew Mickey Gilley very well and as an agent at Gilley's former agency, United Talent, had booked him for several years.

Anyway, I went into the studio and said hello to Charly McClain. She was in a great mood and told me that she had talked to Gilley and that he was moving to In Concert. I thanked her for her help and went looking for Mickey Gilley. I found him and told him that Allen and I would like to talk to him. We made our sales pitch, but it proved to have been unnecessary. He had already made up his mind that he was leaving William Morris and coming with us.

The only thing that he was concerned about was his casino dates. He did not know if we were strong enough as an agency to be able to secure those types of dates at big casinos in Las Vegas, Reno, Lake Tahoe, and Atlantic City. I started rattling off names of people that I knew who controlled those places. I was really on good terms with many of these casino buyers because of the business I had done at Dick Blake International. I looked him in the eye and asked him if we had a deal. He replied that he was coming with us if it was okay with his manager, Sherwood Cryer.

I told him that I knew Sherwood Cryer very well and so did Allen. We doubted that he would object. The three of us shook hands and the deal was concluded. What a Christmas present! I had started out with the intention of trying to keep William Morris from stealing Charly McClain and ended up stealing Mickey Gilley and most likely Johnny Lee as well. Not bad for a day's work.

When we returned to the office I called Sherwood Cryer and told him what had happened. He said, "I don't think Gilley's manager, Mr. Sherwood Cryer, will have any objection to him going over to you boys."

"What about the Brokaws?" I asked. I knew that they would do everything in their power to try to stop Gilley from leaving the William Morris Agency. This was not paranoia on my part. It was reality. They had no loyalty to me at all, not that there was any reason that they should. I hardly knew them.

In the weeks that followed, I began to lessen their power with Mickey Gilley. I did this by explaining to Gilley that I always approved dates directly through the artist and did not want to have to waste time going through any middlemen. With this arrangement having been made at the outset, our agency now directly controlled the majority of Mickey Gilley's income. I could act autonomously and let the Brokaws know about dates only after they had been set and approved by Gilley. If I had allowed them to approve dates for Mickey Gilley, I would have been at their mercy, which is not a good place to be with the Brokaws.

Next, I went to Las Vegas for the International Association of Fairs and Expositions meeting, which started the following week. This IAFE meeting is known as the "Fair Buyers' Convention." It is actually a large trade show that takes place in Las Vegas every year. I cannot say that this is a waste of time, since many fair dates are set during this convention, but to me the whole thing lasts too long. Although the trade show and meetings do not actually start until Monday, most people begin arriving the weekend before it begins, either to set up their display booths or to party.

A trade show usually consists of a large convention room in a big hotel that is filled with various display booths that present items or services for sale to those who attend. Some of these displays are very elaborate and expensive. The 1988 Miller Brewing Company convention in Nashville was the most interesting show of its type I have ever attended. Some of the displays featured actual Grand Prix cars, stock cars, and boats sponsored by the brewery. The IAFE trade show is by contrast much less sophisticated, even though the IAFE is a useful and well-established organization.

The convention room itself is filled with hucksters of every imaginable type, selling things that would be of interest to people in the fair business, such as doughnut-making machines, draft beer dispensers, teddy bears, and other novelty items. Some larger companies offer to provide entire midway services such as Ferris wheels, roller coasters, other rides, freak shows, shooting galleries, and games of chance. Still others sell such things as light bulbs, and even unrelated items like leather jackets. Needless to say, this trade show, perhaps more than any other, is pervaded with a carnival-like atmosphere.

Most of the major talent agencies have booths at this show, hoping to sell their acts to these fair buyers. In addition, there are small agencies attempting to sell acts that nobody has ever heard of. Hundreds of people mill around in the convention room going from booth to booth picking up literature about products and services. Others chat with friends or gather in groups either at a bar or in their hotel rooms. For many, it is a chance to renew old acquaintances or to establish new business contacts.

I am bored by Sunday night, even if I only arrived the day before. By then I have usually met everyone I wish to see and am ready to come home. Las Vegas is truly like no other place in the world and is something that should be seen by everyone at least once. The entertainment is the best, and there are many good restaurants, and, of course, the casinos. The displays of neon are incredible. There must be more neon per square mile than anywhere else on earth. For me, however, the place is depressing. Underneath the surface glamour is a coldness that is all the more pronounced because all of the glamour is artificial. The city is like a painted and loveless whore whose sole purpose is to extract every cent one possesses. If you are penniless, Las Vegas must be the worst place in the world.

We ended 1983 well. Having only been in business two months, we were the hottest new kids on the block. We all had a very good holiday season and were ready to hit the ground running at the start of the new year. My first concern was the forthcoming Mickey Gilley–Charly McClain package. The potential for trouble existed from the outset, but there was also the possibility of making a great deal of money. It could go either way.

Chapter Four

Mickey Gilley and Charly McClain

The relationship between Mickey Gilley and Charly McClain was a nightmare from the start. What should have been fantastic for both of them degenerated into an unnecessary battle of wills that both lost.

According to Gilley, this is how the deal was supposed to have worked when they were touring together in 1984. Mickey Gilley was to receive his normal fee of $15,000 and Charly would be given $6,000. They would then divide between them whatever percentages were left over, with Gilley getting 60 percent and McClain receiving 40 percent.

The fact that they were singing together both on record and onstage caused some gossip initially, and generated some good publicity for the project. Charly became irritated when Gilley was asked if there was anything going on between them and he did not always, absolutely, and categorically deny it. In fact, Charly was about to be married to actor Wayne Massey. Gilley never said that there was anything between them and did deny it sometimes in interviews. At other times, he would imply there could be. He even said to me that he did not care what the public thought. If the public believed that they had something going on, it would increase record sales, no harm done. An inappropriate attitude for Mickey Gilley to take, one that was bound to cause problems.

In truth, Gilley was approaching fifty and he liked to think of himself as a ladies' man. It did his ego good for the public to think he and Charly had a thing together. He had once told me, "Hey, a good-looking guy and a good-looking girl, fuck 'em, let the public think what they want."

Under other circumstances he might have been right. In this case, however, his failure to dismiss any speculation outright made Charly's boyfriend understandably angry. Wayne Massey no doubt constantly brought up the subject to Charly. He mentioned it to me often enough. He was really angry and understandably so, not wishing to be perceived as a cuckold by the public.

The problem was further magnified by the fact, which none of us knew at the time, that Wayne Massey himself aspired to be a singer. He planned to launch his own career by ultimately introducing himself to the record-buying public through a series of duets with Charly McClain. It would be difficult for him to do so as long as Mickey Gilley was in the picture. I think then that Wayne tried in a number of ways to poison the well. He could not tell Charly that doing shows with Gilley was hurting her career. He had to wreck the situation in a more subtle way, if indeed that was his intention, which I believe it to have been.

I think that Charly McClain's remarks that Gilley was old enough to be her father must have been reported to Gilley by somebody. It was true enough. Gilley is, in fact, and has been for some time, a grandfather. Gilley's ego would not permit him to refer to her remarks about his age directly, if he was aware of them. Instead, he complained that when they performed together onstage Charly was "standoffish," which was also true enough.

It was a hostile situation all the way around and I was stuck squarely in the middle. Both artists said things to me that they would not say to each other. They expected me to work it out. The sibling rivalry factor was also very evident. I was the daddy and each wanted me to love him or her the most. Each felt that it was personally important that I understood that he or she was right and that the other was wrong. Gilley believed that he was In Concert's number-one client, which he was, and not only was he right in any dispute that might arise between him and Charly, I should agree with him. He thought Charly was a jerk.

Charly, on the other hand, felt that if it had not been for her I would not have had Mickey Gilley as a client. This was certainly true, and I appreciated the fact. I did the best I could for both Charly and Mickey, but their duet experience kept me in a trick bag the whole time. I was in constant danger of losing either one or both acts at any time if I was perceived as favoring one more than the other. I did everything I could to keep the two together as long as possible, even though they were a constant pain in the ass. Doing so was in both their interests, but more so in Charly's, since, as I have noted, Gilley was already making a minimum of $15,000 a night. Their first few dates together went off without too much trouble, but the date in Oklahoma City on March 23, 1984, was a portent of things to come.

This particular date came about as the result of a phone call from someone at CBS Records who wanted me to book Gilley and McClain together in Oklahoma City. I felt that the thing to do would be to put them in the Lloyd Noble Center in Norman, Oklahoma, which had a seating capacity of over ten thousand. Norman is considered to be the Oklahoma City market. I felt that they could both make big money there. CBS Records, however, wanted to fly in disc jockeys and program directors from all over the country. The record company sought a smaller, more intimate setting.

This would be a great opportunity for everyone, and I looked forward to putting the show together. As I have noted earlier, Charly had a bad reputation out on the road. I felt that this show would give her the opportunity to correct some of those bad impressions. It would also provide these important radio people the chance to see how well Gilley and McClain could work together.

Several people at CBS had remarked to me in the past that as a result of Charly's overall bad attitude, they did little to help her career and gave other artists publicity they would have given her if she had been easier to deal with. For example, Charly refused to do the "Nashville Now" TV show as long as Ralph

Emery was hosting it. She and Wayne Massey both said that he was a jerk. I explained to Debbie Banks in the publicity department at CBS that Charly was really very nice and that things would be different now that she had someone in her life like Wayne Massey who really cared about her. I felt that this show in Oklahoma City would give everybody a chance to work together.

I called Linda Freeman at Doc Severinsen's club in Oklahoma City and worked out the following deal: Gilley was to receive a guarantee of "union scale vs. two-thirds of the net door, less 4 percent of state tax, less 3½ percent of all mail orders, less cost of spotlight and union operator—whichever is greater." Charly had the same deal, only she was to receive "one-third of the door."

What all of that mumbo jumbo really meant was that Charly was not going to receive her $6,000 and Gilley was not going to get his $15,000. It was a promotional show and CBS Records was footing the bill, so I did not want to make the artists appear too greedy to the club owner or the record label. The record company would be providing no-cost tickets to its guests. The remainder if the tickets would be sold to the public at $12.50 a ticket.

I really did not wish to attend the show, but it was one of those situations where my attendance was expected. I flew out on the same place as John Lentz, one of Charly's managers, and we talked most of the way there.

In Oklahoma City, things looked pretty good. By show time there was a big crowd. Sherwood Cryer was there too. I made my rounds, talking with Gilley on his bus and Charly and Wayne on hers, being careful to spend enough time with each of them. The way we had it worked out was that Charly would do her show. There would then be a brief intermission, after which Mickey Gilley would come onstage. Near the end of his show, Charly would come back onstage and sing the duets with Mickey Gilley. On this particular night it was especially important that no problems erupted, due to the presence of radio, record company, and press people. The sound system was not very good, and some type of buzz or hum continued throughout the evening despite attempts to correct the problem.

Charly's show started without incident. She was perhaps a bit nervous, but warmed to the audience nicely and at one point introduced Wayne Massey. After her show, there was an intermission. When Gilley's show began, I returned to Charly's bus and visited with her for a while and then with Wayne Massey while she prepared to sing her duets with Gilley.

It was then I first became aware that Wayne Massey wanted to be a singer. Up to this point he had never mentioned it. He played a tape of fairly good rock and roll that he had recorded. Not great. Just okay. He and Charly mentioned that they would like to be working together. They also told me that they intended to get married in the near future.

In any event, we talked for a while, and then I returned to the club to watch the end of Gilley's show and to wait for Charly to return and sing the duets. Gilley finished the song "You Don't Know Me" and then said, "Once again everybody, Miss Charly McClain!" But Charly was not there. The band immediately started playing the song "Candy Man," a duet version of the old Roy Orbison song. Gilley sang his part and then when it came time for Charly to come in, he pointed to his backup singer, Ann Marie, indicating that she could sing Charly's part of the song. He then said through the microphone, "I don't know where she's at." Ann Marie knew the material already since she sang Charly's part of the duets at shows where Charly was not present.

I immediately hauled ass to Charly's bus to get her, but she was already walking onstage. She finished the song. He apologized or said something to her that the audience could not hear and put his arm around her. She gracefully broke free and said into the microphone, "Mickey's mistake! And thank you very much. No no no. Normally when we do concerts together you're supposed to start some kind of Hollywood rap and you didn't do it tonight. And they're supposed to come to the bus and get me when he starts this thing he does."

"That's because nobody's listening," Gilley replied.

"Well, they're listening," Charly said.

"When we play a concert, people listen."

"They're listening," Charly said again.

"When we play a club they're drinking and talking," Gilley replied.

"Well, it don't make no difference, you should tell me when

you're not going to do that. But anyway, I wasn't ready and I'm sorry, but you did a wonderful job [pointing to Ann Marie]."

They then performed the duet "Touch Me When We're Dancing." The sound system started cracking and popping. They then sang "Paradise Tonight." They were both ill at ease, but "Paradise Tonight" is a really up song and they loosened up as they sang. By the time it was over they were again convincing as an act. They repeated the song "Candy Man" and Charly left the stage. Gilley played another five or six songs.

I went to the bus with Charly and left Gilley onstage still singing. She was furious and firmly believed that Gilley had intentionally sabotaged her part of the show in order to make her look bad. I pointed out that they had a duet album coming out shortly. Such a deliberate action would be decidedly counterproductive. It was, I explained, an honest mistake. Gilley probably thought she was waiting behind the curtain. Her anger turned to tears and she began to think that she had been made to look like a fool in front of the audience.

Wayne and I finally succeeded in convincing her that not only had she not looked like a fool, but that she had triumphed over adverse circumstances and was most likely held in higher esteem than she would have been if nothing had happened to begin with. I clearly understood how she could be embarrassed by what had happened, but it was obviously her fault as much as Gilley's. Considering the nature and importance of the show, they should have each taken the initiative to get things worked out in advance. I winced as she related that when she heard Gilley's backup singer singing her part, she decided not to go on at all. Wayne quickly persuaded her to return to the stage.

After the show, I found Gilley drinking beer on his bus. He didn't give a shit one way or the other and seemed flippant about the incident. He felt she should have been near the stage, waiting to go on.

He was, however, pissed off about a show they had done together in Detroit three weeks before. This was a free show for some major product buyers. These people decided which artists got rack space in some of the largest chain-store outlets in the country. CBS Records had set up this deal and it was very important for both of them to make a good impression, especially with their album coming out in a little over a month. After the show, Gilley hung around, talked to the people, and signed autographs as long as anyone wanted. According to Gilley, Charly left as soon as the show was over "to go shopping," thus furthering her reputation as an unpleasant and unfriendly person. Gilley and his road manager, Cliff, both thought that she was a bitch and that Wayne Massey was trying to cause trouble.

Part of the problems between them resulted from a dispute over the arrangement of their show. Charly did not wish to do her show and then have to wait on the bus while Gilley did his show, and then return and do the duets. This is what Gilley wanted, and as an outside observer, I would say that this is the way it should have gone down. As the headline act, it should have been Gilley's decision by divine right.

Charly envisioned the show as follows: She could do her show and Gilley could come out and do their duets at the end of her show, before intermission. Or, as an option, she could come on and sing with Gilley at the very beginning of his show. Either way she could get the hell out of there much faster and without waiting around. She was right from her perspective. It would have been easier for her.

I argued from the standpoint of the show that she and Gilley should finish together. She and Wayne insisted that as much as they would like to do it that way, it would be easier on her frail voice if she could do the duets while she was warmed up. If she had to return to the bus for another hour and a half it would produce vocal stress for her to start singing cold again. Wayne and Charly and I went around and around with this issue. When I called them on their logic, Wayne stated that the real reason Gilley wanted Charly to finish the show with him was that Gilley knew that everyone would leave the auditorium as soon as Charly's part of the show was over. If I had passed that remark along to Gilley, it would have been all over.

The problems continued. Charly started to demand $7,500 to do shows with Gilley and sometimes more, instead of the $6,000 that had been agreed on initially. Charly complained about not getting the percentages that Gilley had promised. Gilley complained that Charly was not taking into account that at many of the shows both of them were using his sound equipment, which he had to pay for and haul. There were other jealousies and accusations before both of them finally cried, "No more!"

Charly McClain and Wayne Massey were married on Monday, July 16, 1984, at the Schaeffer Chapel on Poplar Avenue in Memphis. As usual, I had come to Memphis a couple of days early to mess around. The weather was hot and beautiful. Sherwood Cryer came up from Texas for the wedding and David Brokaw was in from L.A. Both of them stayed at the Peabody Hotel. After the wedding, there was a reception at the hotel with plenty of good food and conversation. This was the zenith of my relationship with Charly and Wayne.

Charly McClain and Wayne Massey continued to be a problem. As her price climbed, so did her allergy to smoke. She did not want to play clubs anymore, or if she did, she only wanted to do one show. I have never met a woman who wanted to play clubs except as a last resort, and yet the bulk of Charly's work came from those places. When she started that "one show a night" demand, it became much more difficult to sell her.

Clubs want to keep patrons there drinking as long as possible. In addition, some clubs "turn the house," meaning that they sell the first show, run that crowd out during intermission, and sell tickets to a different bunch for the second show. In theory, this doubles the amount of money that they can take in at the door. In many cases, a club or other venue cannot afford the act at all unless they turn the house, which means the act has to do two shows.

Charly and Wayne began turning down $5,000 and $6,000 tie-in dates on weeknights. I explained to them that this was insane, but they would not listen. They thought she was worth more money.

Charly also had an opportunity to work with Mickey Gilley in Atlantic City on August 1 to 7, 1984, for $25,000 plus rooms. Since she had not worked any casino dates at all, I felt that this would be a good opportunity to establish her there. I did not know how long Charly would continue to get $7,500 a night, but I knew that if I could establish her in the casino circuit, she would be able to work there for years. Wayne and Charly did not think that $25,000 was enough money so they passed, feeling that they would be able to go in as the headline act themselves soon enough. I thought they were crazy.

I discussed this with her managers, John Lentz and Gene Ferguson. They agreed with me, but Charly and Wayne were no longer listening to Gene, since they frequently found that the truth was sometimes at odds with the way they viewed the world.

Gene is a mild-mannered, quiet kind of person with a successful and extensive background both as a record company executive at CBS Records and as a manager (Charly McClain, John Anderson, Larry Boone). He is not knowm, however, for taking any crap from his clients. At any rate, Charly was not listening to him.

Her other manager, John Lentz, a Nashville attorney, is also quite capable but prefers not to rock the boat.

I like Gene and John a great deal personally, but when there was something unpleasant or controversial to be said to Charly or Wayne, the responsibility invariably fell on my shoulders. I did not wish to lose Charly as a client, and I felt that Wayne Massey had a good chance of making it as an artist on his own, but their attitude was not based on reality. Nobody in the music business, not managers, record company people, attorneys, publishers, songwriters, or even artists, knows what is really happening compared to a well-informed, top-line agent.

Charly McClain and her crew had been digging a hole for themselves for years with the buyers, the record company, and the fans. We had covered for her and made excuses as long as we could. My agents were tired of the backlash and I was weary of having to fight to get her to do what she needed to do in order to keep moving forward. She made more money with In Concert than she ever made before or since.

We could not, however, compensate for Charly and Wayne's errors in judgment forever, and their revenue began to decline. We made approximately $70,000 in 1984, $46,000 in 1985, and $24,000 in 1986 from our 10 percent commission. We continued to represent Charly through October of 1987, but I do not have those figures handy. In addition to the problems I have mentioned, Charly and Wayne were always nickel-and-diming us to death, wanting us to drop commissions on certain dates for one reason or another.

The denouement came as the result of a weekend they played in Texas in August of 1985. We got them a date in Houston for $8,000, on Saturday, August 24. I called Sherwood Cryer and asked him to take a tie-in date on Charly and Wayne on Friday, August 23. By this time Charly and Wayne were singing together and had had a couple of successful duets released. Sherwood generally used Saturdays only, but I explained my problem and he bought a date, largely as a favor to me. It was a great situation for Charly and Wayne, two days in the same city for $15,000. I had even gotten her a thousand-dollar raise since the last time she had played Gilley's.

The problems started right away. Instead of being grateful for the dates, Wayne Massey wanted to cut it from two shows to one show at Gilley's. I explained to him that this was impossible. When he finally accepted reality, he decided that he did not like the show times and wanted them changed from 11:00 P.M. and 1:00 A.M. to 10:00 P.M. and 12:00 A.M. Furthermore, Wayne did not want their show broadcast "Live From Gilley's" over the local radio station. In short, they did everything they could to sabotage the date at Gilley's.

The radio show "Live From Gilley's" was broadcast live, recorded, and syndicated nationally through a company called Westwood One. Many artists complained about having to do this show for several reasons. In the first place, they had no control over the live sound mix and consequently could not be sure that the broadcast over the radio was a desirable representation of the way they really sounded. In addition, the artist, in most cases, had no right of approval over the tape that was delivered to Westwood One for national distribution. The artist had no idea how many times the show would be broadcast, or even in which cities for that matter.

The biggest problem, however, and the real crux of the matter for most artists was that they were not receiving any additional money for this radio show; Sherwood Cryer was getting it all. Many of the performers needed the exposure nationally that "Live From Gilley's" afforded. Some of these complaints were justified, others were not. Sherwood Cryer might have been able to save himself some trouble by spelling out some of the particulars in a simple agreement that could have been attached to the contract. For whatever reasons, he elected not to do so. It was fairly well understood industry-wide that if you played Gilley's you did the radio show and subsequent rebroadcast. Some of the larger artists were able to get by without having to do the radio show. Others, I am told, had discovered that the show was broadcast and sent out for syndication without their permission.

In any case, Sherwood Cryer wanted Wayne and Charly to do the radio show. After much discussion, I was able to persuade him to forget it. Wayne also wanted me to change the show times as I mentioned. I felt that I could get this worked out too, but wanted to wait until the week of the show. My reason for waiting was to give Sherwood a chance to cool down about their refusal to do the radio show and also to mention the matter close enough to the show date for him to remember the conversation. I was sure that he had other more important things on his mind. As far as I was concerned he had made enough concessions already, giving them a thousand-dollar raise over the last time they had played six months before and letting them get by without appearing on the radio. He had bent over backward for them already. He had no intention of bending over forward.

When that Friday arrived, Charly, Wayne, and the crew checked into a hotel down the street from Gilley's in Pasadena. They went to the club but did not perform because Sherwood refused to change the show times. They said it had to be their way or not at all.

Never mind that Sherwood Cryer had paid her for two shows the time before last and only received one because Charly had been "sick." Never mind that he had come all the way from Pasadena to Memphis to attend their wedding. Never mind that there were fans in the audience who had bought tickets, hired baby-sitters, driven long distances, and in other ways rearranged their schedules to see Charly McClain and Wayne Massey.

These two performers failed to understand they were not the

employers, but the employees. They did not even spend the night at the hotel in Pasadena, but checked out and drove over thirty miles to Houston and checked into another hotel there. When I found out about this incident the following Monday, I knew that they would soon be leaving In Concert. All of us at the agency had done everything we could to help them. We were all tired of covering for them and making excuses for their behavior. Wayne Massey blamed me for not getting the show times changed. I tried to calm him down, but at that point I really did not care what they did.

When they sent in their next commission check, they deducted $2,200 to cover their expenses for the night they refused to play. I had Linda call their accountant, Marilyn Davis. There was no mistake. Wayne had instructed her to withhold that amount from our commissions.

I called Charly's acting manager, John Lentz, and told him what had happened. He said that he did not know anything about it. I told him that I was not going for that shit for any reason. He replied that we had all come too far together to rock the boat now. He calmed me down a little bit and I agreed to think about it.

I did not, however, think about it too long. Instead, I immediately called all the agents in for a meeting and explained what had happened.

"Chances are," I said, "that they are going to leave us anyway. We've got them by the nuts as far as the $2,200 is concerned. We can take that amount out of deposits so they can't beat us out of that money, ultimately. If I do that, then they are gone for sure. Let's put it to a vote. For $2,200 do we lose this act or keep the money?"

It was unanimous. All of the agents without exception said, "Let them go!" We had all bent over backward for Charly McClain and Wayne Massey, but enough was enough.

They then went to the William Morris Agency, where they remained for about three months before returning again to us. It is in some ways very gratifying to have acts leave, only to return a short time later with a new appreciation of how well things had really been before they tried something else. It is no fun when they leave, but sometimes you just have to let them go, kind of like women. Either they come back or they don't. Many times they will.

The important thing is to let them know when they leave that you are sorry to see them go, whether you really are or not. There is no reason to end a relationship of any kind on a bad note if it can be helped. This is especially true in the music business. Those of us who have been around for a while are very likely to stay around and there is no telling where or when an agent is likely to be doing business with a former client under new circumstances.

When Wayne and Charly left, I was too angry to speak directly with either one of them, but I did tell John Lentz that I thought highly of both of them and that we just needed a vacation from each other for a little while. By the time Charly and Wayne returned three months later, we all had had a little break and were again ready to get back to business.

They stayed with us awhile, then returned to the William Morris Agency, and then came back to us again. When I fired agent Jesse Garon, (he had changed his name from Errol Bach to that of Elvis's dead twin brother) Charly went with him to his new company, American Concert, where she remains along with Dan Seals and Mickey Gilley, two other ghosts from In Concert.

Charly was eventually dropped by CBS and went to Mercury Records for a short while. As far as I know she has no record deal anymore, and probably works for $2,500 a night.

Chapter Five

Johnny Lee

When I made my deal with Mickey Gilley in the lobby of the RCA Studio, he had mentioned that he wanted me to take over Johnny Lee also. I told Gilley at the time that I would be glad to do so, but first I needed a couple of months to get his own dates and schedule straightened out. I never understood Gilley's excessive regard for Johnny Lee. He was always talking Johnny up and offering to do shows with him.

Johnny Lee was born in Texas City, Texas, on July 23, 1945. He was influenced mainly by rock and roll, had a band in high school, and joined the navy. He joined Mickey Gilley as a sideman in 1971, went out on his own, and then returned to Gilley a little later.

If any one thing was responsible for Johnny Lee's rapid rise to stardom it was the movie *Urban Cowboy*. Based on an August 1978 article in *Esquire* magazine, the movie featured John Travolta and Debra Winger. It portrayed John's life as an oilfield worker and the trials of his relationship with Debra Winger. The film's action takes place for the most part in and around Gilley's in Pasadena, Texas. Music, dancing, beer drinking, sex, and cheatin' are the main activities of the characters.

The movie itself was an incredible, if artificial, boost to country music in general, and Western-flavored country music in particular.

Gilley and Lee had played together in the wake of *Urban Cowboy,* but there had been problems between them on the road. It was obvious that Johnny Lee was jealous of Mickey Gilley, and I believe Johnny Lee's envy was the source of the conflict between them. Mickey Gilley had been an ascending star for quite a while. Johnny Lee, on the other hand, had been in the house band at Gilley's until the movie had been released. Prior to that, Johnny Lee had been billed as "Johnny Lee and the Bayou City Beats," not particularly impressively. When the movie came out, he had the song "Lookin' for Love" on the soundtrack album and became a star overnight.

Johnny Lee had resented playing second fiddle to Mickey Gilley for several years. He had received some bad press recently over allegations made by his wife at the time, "Dallas" TV star Charlene Tilton, and I was informed by sources close to him that he had had a drug problem. I wasn't really that interested in taking him on as a client, but I'd promised Mickey Gilley that I would do so, and Johnny's manager, Sherwood Cryer, kept telling me that it was time to add Johnny to my roster.

What decided the issue for me was an article that came out in February 1984 in one of the trade publications. It mentioned the rapid rise of In Concert, stating that we had taken Mickey Gilley away from the William Morris Agency and that it was widely speculated throughout the industry that we would most likely take Johnny Lee as well. It pleased me then to know that the William Morris people were sitting around wondering when I was going to steal Johnny Lee. It also gave me great pleasure to know that the Brokaws knew that it was just a matter of time and there was nothing they could do to prevent it.

I called Sherwood Cryer, read him the article, and told him that I was ready to take on Johnny Lee. He was still under contract to the William Morris Agency for another couple of years, but I didn't care. Their cowardice in handling the situation with Mickey Gilley showed me that their contracts meant nothing.

Despite my outward bravado, I was honestly afraid that they would sue us any day over Mickey Gilley. I had known that he was under contract and I had deliberately interfered with that contract by inducing him to leave William Morris. To this day, I still don't understand why they didn't sue us. If the circumstances had been reversed, I would have sued them instantly.

When Gilley left William Morris, the agency attempted to beat me behind the scenes, sending people to talk to Sherwood Cryer, trying to get him to change his mind and return Gilley to his "rightful place." During this period, Sherwood and Mickey were still working together as a team and they supported each other's decisions. William Morris knew that Sherwood would have to be won over, but that never happened. They were trying to accomplish their objectives by being nice.

This method sometimes works, and to some degree it did for them, since they got Gilley back for another year, from May 1987 to May 1988. The problem in this case was that they had to wait three and a half years to do so. They could have sued us and left Mickey Gilley alone. Instead they fired Sonny Neal, the head of their Nashville office.

I like competition and I like to win, but I was very sorry to hear that Sonny Neal had been dismissed. I wasn't particularly fond of him, but he had been around for a long time, and it was not his fault that Gilley and Johnny Lee left William Morris. Sonny was a bit of a snob, but nonetheless a worthy adversary, someone who kept the game interesting.

When Sonny was fired, that really pissed me off and made me even more determined to throw a wrench into the machinery of their Nashville operation. The William Morris office succeeded because of its snob appeal. Many country artists are more concerned with what they believe to be prestigious than they are with making money. The fact of the matter is that many country artists are actually ashamed of being "country," as if being so places them on a lower rung socially. Affiliation with a well-known West Coast agency can lessen the sting to some degree.

In any case, I made the decision to add Johnny Lee to the roster in early March of 1984. I do not know the details of Johnny Lee's deal with Sherwood and Mickey. I know that Gilley owned some part of Johnny Lee, but Sherwood Cryer owned the lion's share. I do know that it was very important to both of them that Johnny's career be kept in full swing.

For some reason, I thought that Johnny Lee would be difficult to book, that it would be hard to sell dates for him. This fear had a great deal to do with my reluctance to take him on. If I had taken him as a client when I took Mickey Gilley, I would have been very much under the gun to find him work in January, February, and March, the most difficult months of the year to find work for any artist. These months are difficult for several reasons: In many parts of the country promoters are afraid of the weather. Many people are also hard up financially after the holidays and not that interested in going to shows. These months have always been basically dead for most country artists.

By waiting to take him until the end of February, I really could not be held responsible for dates that should have been played during that time. It is true that I lost commissions for those months, but what difference did it make? I knew that we could start off with a strong April and keep on rocking, even if he turned out to be a hard sell. Our performance would look all that much better if I took him after the three worst months of the year. Too bad for William Morris.

Johnny Lee was still having good record action, and shortly after he joined our agency, he and female singer Lane Brody had a duet single, "Yellow Rose of Texas," which went to number one nationally. I did not know Lane Brody and had never heard of her at that point. Her public relations were being handled by the Brokaws. Sandy Brokaw chanced to be in town and scheduled a dinner for us to meet.

I remember being stunned initially by Lane Brody's incredible beauty, but as dinner progressed she began to seem somewhat egotistical. She possessed a very high regard for herself as an artist, an impression I was unable to affirm or deny since I had not seen her perform or heard her sing. She did, however, have a deal with Capitol Records and an album due to be released sometime in 1984.

I found her to be charming, and we struck up a deal over dinner. It made sense to put her on the road with Johnny Lee, using his band to back her up, and this is what we ended up doing. As we left the restaurant and walked to her car I noticed her California license plate, which read EL VOX, meaning "The Voice." I was embarrassed by the pretense even though I liked her personally.

It turned out that Johnny Lee wasn't at all difficult to book. My decision to wait out the first quarter of 1984 did indeed prove to have been the right move. Looking back at my 1984 schedule, I saw that William Morris only had him playing twelve dates in the first three months of the year. We got him two dates in April, nine in May, and eleven in June. His price fluctuated from as low as $5,000 a night to as high as $10,000.

I still had not seen him perform and didn't for almost another year, yet he was an extremely talented artist. Reports filtered back that Johnny Lee played three, four, and five hours at his shows. Many artists I represented were interested only in doing as little as possible. Charly McClain frequently tried to do even less than the minimum amount. Jerry Lee Lewis might play for fifteen minutes or two hours.

Whatever the reasons, Johnny was a great entertainer and caused very few problems. In fact, about the only trouble he ever got into occurred when he put $5,000 down on a house in Hendersonville and then backed out of the deal. The seller then attempted to sue him for more than the price of the house. I put my lawyer, Peter Curry, in touch with Sherwood Cryer and Johnny Lee. It ended up that Johnny just went ahead and bought the house. He subsequently sold it without ever having moved in, and I think actually made a slight profit.

We did all right with Johnny Lee and made $44,965 in 1984, $63,910 in 1985, and $39,136 in 1986 in commissions, not bad for an artist that I'd started out not wanting at all. In many respects, artists are like children, and they feel that the world should revolve around their wants and needs. They complain and sulk and we put up with their tantrums and humor them, but like children, when they suddenly become silent, it usually means that something is wrong. After bitching about Sherwood Cryer for quite some time, Johnny Lee quieted down and we did not hear from him for a while.

Since Johnny lived in California, our only contact with him on a day-to-day basis was through his road manager, Terry Newman. Terry was one of those "good ole boys," the kind that northerners think of immediately when the word "South" is mentioned. He became rather haughty during the summer months of 1985, complaining about anything and everything.

I had never paid much attention to him, or to Johnny Lee either for that matter. Whenever we set a date I phoned it in to Sherwood Cryer. If it was a big money date or a small money date, we booked it and passed the information along to Sherwood. If the jump between two dates was a great distance, say, six or seven hundred miles, Sherwood said to go ahead and book it anyway, as long as Johnny had enough time to get there. We consequently had Johnny Lee making jumps in distance that we would never have suggested to another artist.

I'm sure that this irritated Johnny often, but I didn't really care, since Sherwood approved all of the dates. When and if Johnny Lee called me to complain from time to time, I blamed it on Sherwood and went about my business. My perception of Johnny Lee at the time was that he had the intellectual capacity of a Neanderthal. He reminded me somewhat of an angry Jethro Bodine. I humored him when necessary, but did not much worry about him one way or the other.

By the end of 1985, however, I knew that something was up. As it turned out, Sherwood had suddenly quit paying Johnny's $1,900-a-month rent, apparently without giving him any advance notice. Johnny Lee had also been sued by the William Morris Agency and had lost due to default. The suit had been filed against him, but Sherwood failed to answer in his behalf or to notify him so that he could act in his own defense. This one incident alone cost Johnny $19,000. I asked Sherwood about both of these matters and he responded by saying that he was not making any money off of Johnny Lee and was tired of supporting his excessive lifestyle.

Johnny Lee had once spent $6,500 chartering a jet to go to a party. He also had a Mercedes sedan that Sherwood paid for as well as a new Porsche Turbo. Sherwood no longer felt like paying his rent.

As to the lawsuit, Sherwood offered no explanation. Johnny Lee felt that Sherwood had cost him $19,000 needlessly by not responding to or informing him about the suit.

Around the middle of September, Terry Newman came to the

office and wanted copies of all of the contracts for Johnny Lee's forthcoming dates. This request to the head of our contract department immediately set off an alarm in her head and she came and told me about it. I knew that Terry was up to something, so I told her to give him what he wanted. I figured I would let Terry play his hand. That way I could see what he had in mind, though I didn't feel he was intelligent enough to get away with too much.

On September 22, I received a letter from Mark Levinson, an attorney from California who had been retained by Johnny Lee. If there was one thing I didn't want, it was some West Coast lawyer trying to make a name for himself in the country music business by sticking his nose in my affairs. This guy was going to be a nuisance and yet I could not simply ignore him.

First of all I would have to reassess my position: I had to find out where I stood with Johnny Lee and where Johnny Lee stood with this so-called lawyer. Had Johnny Lee made overtures to any other agencies? How much did the Brokaws know about this? One thing was certain, I had no intention of losing Johnny Lee as an artist; I was not about to let that happen, even though I had been taking him too much for granted.

I called Sherwood Cryer and read the letter to him. He appeared casual about the matter and said, "Yeah, I figured something was wrong when they turned in the bus the other night." I asked him what he meant and he replied that Johnny Lee's bus driver had brought the bus back to Gilley's after the weekend's dates and left off the keys, saying that Johnny would not be needing it anymore. Sherwood then laughed and said, "I guess I should have paid his rent out there after all."

It was not funny to me since I did not wish to lose Johnny Lee as a client. I knew that Sherwood had Johnny under a management contract and as his manager could force him to stay at In Concert. The bottom line, however, was something else. I had to keep Johnny Lee as a client right now, and suing him later would do me no good.

It became obvious that I would have to take some immediate action to cover myself. I don't know whether it was my idea or Sherwood's, but we decided to prepare a backdated booking contract on Johnny Lee. I had Linda Edwards find an old piece of stationery like the kind we were using back in 1984 and early 1985. I then wrote out a contract and gave it to Linda to type. It was dated January 1, 1985, and covered a period of three years, ending January 1, 1988.

The contract was sent Federal Express to Sherwood Cryer, signed by him, and immediately returned to my office. Was this an unethical action on my part? A violation of my responsibility to my client as his agent? Of course it was. What I did was wrong in every sense of the word, but ethics were not a consideration for me then. It was not that I was unethical or immoral, I was amoral. I still didn't care about Johnny Lee, other than to the extent that it was necessary in order to keep him as a client.

With my contract secure, I was now prepared to take some definite action. I called Johnny Lee and got his answering machine but did not leave a message. I did not wish to talk to his lawyer until after I'd spoken with Johnny first. He did not return my call right away.

Terry Newman, the road manager, showed up and wanted the deposits on the dates for the forthcoming weekend. This presented a bit of a problem for me. The way things had been done in the past was that after Johnny Lee had played his dates, the deposits were then sent to Sherwood Cryer. Johnny kept the money that he picked up at the show.

I knew where my power lay in this situation. Johnny Lee had no bus and he would have to pay his own expenses on the road. I knew that he did not have any money personally, and the only way that he could make any would be to work the dates we had set. Furthermore, he didn't have enough money to get to the upcoming dates unless I gave Terry Newman the deposits.

I told Terry that I would give him the deposits after I had spoken with Johnny Lee myself. He said that Johnny wanted me to work through him and that he doubted that Johnny would call me. I told him that I had no problem working with him, but that I would have to talk to Johnny Lee before I released the deposits. It was not a negotiable matter. "I am sure you can work it out," I told him.

Terry did work it out and Johnny Lee called me the next day. He told me he was leaving Sherwood Cryer and seemed rather hostile at first, but calmed down soon enough. I understood what he was complaining about. Sherwood Cryer had a tendency to view people on the same level that they were on when he first met them, regardless of how they had progressed in their chosen careers.

Sherwood had always regarded Johnny Lee as a moron and felt responsible for Johnny's success. To some degree, he was correct, but Johnny Lee was no doubt tired of being treated like a second-class citizen. Sherwood disliked Johnny Lee a great deal and wanted me to let him rot.

I explained to Sherwood that all I wanted was to make some money, and that if Johnny left the agency, neither one of us would make any money. I felt that I was in a position to keep Johnny Lee under control for the time being by doling out his deposits on a weekly basis.

I finally spoke with Johnny Lee's attorney, Mark Levinson, and he informed me that Johnny Lee wanted him to meet me as soon as possible. I replied that I would be pleased to meet him at my office in Nashville at his earliest convenience. I considered this to be a good sign.

Mark Levinson appeared about three weeks later, in the middle of October. I was cordial, as always, but very specific in terms of what I wanted. I got right to the point and explained that In Concert had done a good job for Johnny Lee and that it was my desire to keep him as a client. I realized that Johnny Lee was going through a transitional period in his career and it was my intention to help him in every way possible. I was quick to point out that this desire was, of course, contingent upon Johnny Lee remaining with In Concert. I also mentioned that I had a valid contract that had been signed in his behalf by his manager, Sherwood Cryer.

Mark then asked to see a copy of the contract, and I replied that I would gladly produce it in court if it should become necessary to do so. I further added that although I wished to be pleasant, I would sue Johnny Lee as well as any agency that professed to represent him if he tried to make any kind of move before the expiration of my contract.

Mark then asked who owned In Concert International. I told him that the answer to that question was none of his business, but that in the interest of setting the record straight, I would tell him.

I said, "In Concert International is owned by myself, Linda Edwards, and Allen Whitcomb, a former employee. It is all a matter of public record down at the courthouse. This horseshit about Sherwood Cryer was started by the William Morris Agency to cover their ineptitude when they lost Gilley and Johnny Lee. Sherwood Cryer does not own any part of this company and never has. I have heard it said that Mickey Gilley owns this company, that he and Sherwood own it together. I have also heard that Lou Rawls and the Brokaws own it. Nobody ever asks who owns William Morris or ICM. I am honored that so many people in the industry are interested in us, but sometimes it is a pain in the ass."

This seemed to satisfy him. My main fear was that Mark would take over management of Johnny Lee and put him back with the William Morris Agency. He said that he had no intention of becoming Johnny Lee's manager. In fact, he was seeking to free Johnny from the situation with his former manager, Sherwood Cryer. I felt that he was being honest, but since I do not trust lawyers, I resolved to monitor the situation closely.

I thanked him for taking time away from his busy schedule and for going to the trouble of coming all the way to Nashville to meet with me. I expressed my willingness to help him in every way possible, but stressed that it was my intention to pursue whatever means were necessary to protect my interests.

He conceded that In Concert had done a good job with Johnny Lee and he saw no reason why Johnny shouldn't remain with us. He added that his client was not interested in pursuing any additional legal battles, since the one with Sherwood Cryer would certainly keep him busy enough for quite some time.

I felt that the situation with Johnny Lee was back under control and that I could once again return to other more important matters. The ideal situation would be for Johnny Lee and Sherwood Cryer to patch things up. With this in mind, I flew to Fort Smith, Arkansas, on October 26 to visit with Johnny Lee at a club called Charlee's. I had spoken with him on the phone several times, but hadn't actually seen him since all of the trouble started. Visiting him in Fort Smith would give me the opportunity to socialize with him a bit.

When we met, Johnny told me that there was no possibility of a reconciliation with Sherwood Cryer. "I hate that mother-fucker!" he said. The visit, however, strengthened my position with him.

When the showdown came in court for Sherwood Cryer and Johnny Lee, they simply parted company. Johnny Lee was suing Sherwood for several million dollars, but all of that was dropped and they went their separate ways. Knowing Sherwood Cryer, I was surprised that he let Johnny Lee off the hook that easily, but Sherwood had grown to detest Johnny Lee and said that he had actually lost money by fooling with him. Maybe he had.

This wasn't the end of matters with Johnny Lee, however. We kept booking him but he soon stopped having hit records and was dropped by his label, Warner Brothers. His popularity started to fall as a result, and it eventually became difficult to sell dates on him at any price.

There were some further conversations with Johnny Lee's attorney but these eventually ceased, and I heard no more from him. Finally, sometime in the early part of January 1986, I was told that another agency, McFadden and Associates, was soliciting dates on Johnny Lee. This irritated me a great deal and I had my lawyer send them a cease-and-desist letter. It seemed to me that my lawyer was always too courteous in handling such matters. I felt that he should state flatly at the outset that it was our intention to sue such persons if a problem persisted. His letter did the trick, however, and I received no more reports of McFadden and Associates purporting to be Johnny Lee's agency.

Sometime during the late summer or early fall of 1986, Johnny Lee secured Jack McFadden as his manager. From an agency standpoint, I wasn't threatened by this move even though Jack operated a talent agency himself. Our contract had not been challenged in the year since the trouble with Johnny had started, and we still represented him. If Johnny had thought that our booking arrangement had been a backdated forgery, he never mentioned it to me and neither did his new manager. Jack told me later that he had spent $6,000 in legal fees trying to find a way to get out of the simple one-page contract that I had written. The reason he was unable to do so was that it was extremely simple.

Lawyers prepare contracts in legal terms that are intentionally difficult to understand and require a great deal of study by the layperson. By creating something lengthy and full of legal mumbo jumbo they seek to bewilder and confuse their own clients to the degree that the client feels that he is ending up with something that will protect him from anything short of nuclear war.

There is some validity to this approach. If lawyers prepared simple, one-page contracts, their clients would most likely feel that they had not received their money's worth. It is this very ambiguity that later creates problems, since the greater the number of provisions a contract contains, the greater the chances of another lawyer finding a loophole. I always wrote my own contracts, and they almost never exceeded a few paragraphs, and always held up under fire. It was impossible for anyone to say that he or she did not understand what had been signed.

Jack should have called me. I probably would have sold him Johnny Lee at that point for $6,000. In any case, he did not call me about the contract and was not soliciting dates on Johnny Lee. I think that Johnny Lee was just glad to be free from Sherwood Cryer and did not want to tempt fate any further at right that moment. I was really surprised that Sherwood Cryer had let him go at all. In fact, I think everyone in the business familiar with the situation was surprised.

In any case, I had a couple of meetings with Jack McFadden later on. I really knew nothing about him except that he had briefly run ICM's ill-fated attempt at a Nashville branch and had resigned for some reason. I also knew that he had been in the business for a long time, even though our paths had never crossed. Now he was Johnny Lee's manager, and had his own booking agency, McFadden and Associates. Before our meetings I had seen him around town and knew him on sight, but that was it. Our agent Lane Cross once had a confrontation with him about something and I remembered standing in Lane's office and listening to them swearing at each other over the speakerphone.

When I met Jack I liked him immediately and remembered that Allen Whitcomb held him in great esteem. What Jack said he wanted was to make some kind of deal to take over Johnny Lee's booking as well as his management. I really had no objection at this point since most of my agents were burned out on Johnny Lee and he was getting harder to sell dates for at any price. What Jack proposed was to take over Johnny Lee's bookings and pay us 5 percent on anything his company set through 1987. I could have been a hardass, but why bother? As I saw it, Jack McFadden was doing us a favor. We would get 5 percent for the remainder of 1986 and all of 1987 and would not have to waste any time or money getting it. No phone calls, no contracts, no paperwork, no hassles. I told him that I would think it over and get back to him. In the meantime I instructed our agents to set every date they could on him as soon as possible, no matter how far in the future the actual dates might be. We might as well get as many dates as we could at 10 percent before we let him go. I discussed the situation with the staff and they said, "Pharaoh, let my people go!" It was an across-the-board decision.

Now all I had to do was get it past Sherwood Cryer. I called him and explained the situation. He told me not to let Johnny Lee go. I explained it again, saying that Johnny Lee's career was over as far as I could tell and that I really did not think that my agents could set any more dates for him. Sherwood was adamant. He did not want me to let Johnny Lee go. I said that if I did not let Johnny go, he would probably leave anyway. Sherwood replied, "If he leaves, sue him. You have him under contract." I was willing to fight anybody over Johnny Lee a year and a half before, in or out of court, but as I said, I felt that his career was over.

Jack kept calling and I kept stalling. Finally, I phoned him and told him to bring over the papers and I would sign them. I sold Johnny Lee like a worn-out prizefighter. I really felt that this was the best thing for In Concert International as a company. Sherwood Cryer was irritated by my decision and subsequent actions, but it was too late. Jack McFadden was true to his word and paid us 5 percent of everything Johnny Lee made for the rest of 1986 and 1987.

I saw Johnny Lee in the Dallas airport in December of 1987. He walked by me and I shouted "Hey, Johnny!" As he turned around I thought I had made a mistake. This guy was much fatter than Johnny Lee, but it was he. He came over and we shook hands and talked for a few minutes. He had his new wife with him but he was either too inconsiderate or ill-mannered to introduce her. I wished him well and watched him waddle off down the corridor, another fallen star.

Time passed, and I felt that I owed Johnny Lee an apology for backdating that contract on him. I decided that if I ever saw him again I would tell him I was sorry for what I had done. I really do not know whether or not it was Sherwood Cryer's idea or mine; I can't remember. I do remember that I was all for it at the time, so I accept full responsibility for my actions in the matter. I recall feeling then that it was not right, that Johnny Lee should be able to have whomever he wanted as his agent. At the time, however, my baser instincts for winning prevailed.

I ran into Johnny at the Country Radio Seminar cocktail party at the Opryland Hotel in March of 1990. It was the first time I had seen him in several years. He had lost some weight, looked good, and again had a record deal. I pulled him away from several fans and told him that I owed him an apology for "some things" that happened at In Concert. I did not get specific since we were standing in the hallway and people were walking around everywhere. He said that all of that was in the past and that he had no problem with me. "We're cool," he said.

I do not wish to portray Johnny Lee as an angel or myself as a devil. I made a mistake and I wanted to clear it up. Given the circumstances and who I was at the time, I acted the only way I knew how. What's done is done, and I am glad Johnny Lee is again doing well. I have always considered him to be a man of great talent and ability as a country singer. I'm sorry that I did not take the time to get to know him better when I had the opportunity.

As regards his book, *Looking for Love,* there are a few errors that need correcting. He said that he and Gilley "built" Gilley's, implying that they were responsible to a greater degree than Sherwood Cryer. This is not true. Gilley's and the *Urban Cowboy* phenomenon would never have gotten off the ground without all of the contributors. The August 1978 *Esquire* article, the movie, Mickey Gilley, Johnny Lee, the Brokaws, the mechanical bulls, and, most important, Sherwood Cryer all made it happen. While the whole situation can be viewed as one significant event with all the ingredients coming together in exactly the right way, Sherwood Cryer was the driving force without which none of it would have happened.

Whether Sherwood Cryer stole money from Johnny Lee or didn't pay him money he owed is a matter that will remain open to conjecture. In my experience, Sherwood did everything he could to help Johnny Lee. Johnny Lee and Mickey Gilley were in the right place at the right time. Without Sherwood Cryer and Mickey Gilley, I doubt that Johnny Lee would have made it at all.

Chapter Six

The Competition

If there was one thing that I didn't want, it was more competition, especially from another West Coast company. We had done well against William Morris, and yet I knew that taking Gilley and Johnny Lee was a much bigger deal to me than losing those two acts was to them. They were so big, and had so much money that they could last forever. I knew that they could operate their Nashville branch as long as necessary, even at a loss if need be. The William Morris Agency would always be a problem for me, luring acts with their seductive talk of prestige, movies, TV, commercials, and Hollywood.

ICM was another corporate giant that had turned its basilisk eye upon the Music City. They had been close to a deal with Dick Blake shortly before his death, but things did not quite fall together. As a result, attorney Bill Carter sought to get ICM established in Nashville as soon as possible. The easiest way to do this would be to purchase an already successful Nashville agency and change its name, thus gaining agents, artists, location, and a reputation from the start. This is what the William Morris Agency had done. It simply bought and took over the Bob Neal Agency, and continued to do business.

During the first part of 1981, it was rumored ICM was on the verge of buying a Nashville agency. The rumor changed almost weekly. In most cases, we generally laughed, since there didn't seem to be a local company big enough to make it interesting, although most of the companies they were supposedly considering seemed anxious enough to be bought.

A talent agency is a rather nebulous thing in Nashville, Tennessee. In the first place, very few if any Nashville agencies had any acts actually under contract during that period. It was still for the most part a handshake business. Likewise, very few if any companies had their agents under contract either. Consequently, when it came time to discuss selling an agency, what was there to buy or sell?

An agency is certainly worth something. The physical assets are easy enough to determine, and it is simple to read the financial bottom line, but any potential buyer isn't likely to lay out good money for an agency unless the acts and the agents are prepared to sign contracts with the new owners. In such situations the acts themselves generally do not cooperate with the seller. They hate the fact that they might be used to make someone else some money. If the acts and agents aren't already signed to the existing agency, then it might be easier just to lure them away at the outset.

The pickings for ICM in Nashville seemed rather slim. They would have been in great shape if they had made a deal with Dick Blake and kept all of us and the Mandrells, but this did not happen. They finally made their move in late 1983, shortly after we opened In Concert, and created the Nashville ICM office.

The deal was put together by attorney Bill Carter, Ralph Mann of ICM, and Jack McFadden, who was to head the operation. Jack had recently moved to Nashville at that time, having just sold a radio station he owned in California. He was used to working for himself and was really not that interested in being part of a rigidly defined corporate structure.

Finally they made him an offer that he could not refuse and he agreed to take over the new ICM Nashville operation on a trial basis for one year. The contracts were signed on November 28, 1983. As part of the deal, ICM took over the offices Jack already occupied at 1717 West End Avenue. The company started with George Mallard, formerly of the Jim Halsey Agency, and Reggie Mack formerly of United Talent, as the two main agents. ICM signed Steve Wariner as its first act, and also quickly signed Sonny James, Reba McEntire, and later Charlie Daniels.

When McFadden originally set up the deal, he told board chairman Ralph Mann that the Nashville branch of ICM must be totally autonomous and apart from the New York and L.A. operations. He wanted a "hands off," no-interference policy for at least three years. A financial commitment of not less than three years would also be required. But McFadden didn't fit well into the corporate structure and left after seven months.

I don't know whether he quit or was fired; he tells me that it was a "mutual thing." His mother was very ill at this time in Sacramento, California, and he had been going out there from Nashville almost every weekend.

It was all more stress than he needed. When Jack left, Reggie Mack took over and stayed at the helm until the Nashville office abruptly shut down without any notice in April of 1985.

I was initially more afraid of ICM than of anyone else. I felt that they would easily be able to entice many gullible hillbilly artists with the same approach that William Morris had so successfully used. Since I did not know any of their agents from L.A. or New York, I really did not know whom I would be up against. I didn't then know Jack McFadden, but I did know Reggie Mack, and felt him to be a worthy adversary who would certainly be capable of providing competition I did not need or want.

ICM never succeeded in taking any acts from In Concert, although they came very close twice. One day we received a call from Buck White, leader of the then Warner/Curb group the Whites. The group consisted of Buck, a couple of musicians; and Buck's two daughters Cheryl and Sharon, Ricky Skaggs' second wife. They were well known as a bluegrass act, but had become more popular since they had been signed by a record company and had gotten some radio airplay. Their music fit well with Ricky Skaggs', and since we represented both acts, we often played them together, with the Whites opening the show.

They wanted to have a meeting with us and we told them to come on over. When they arrived, we met in Allen Whitcomb's office.

I usually conducted meetings in my office but the Whites

were very religious and conservative, and I felt that they might find my office disconcerting, if not offensive. My office was rather unusual, to put it mildly. In size it was about thirty feet long by seventeen feet wide. It had a high ceiling, which like the walls was panelled in rough-cut, pecky swamp cypress. There were guns, beer lanterns and clocks, flags, airplanes, surgical instruments, and other items hanging from the ceiling. The most singular aspect of my ceiling decor was a large velvet Elvis that faced the ceiling. Whenever I wanted to invoke the "presence of the master," I merely released a small ship's wheel behind my desk and the velvet Elvis lowered slowly and silently, to the amazement and admiration of my guests.

There were other things in my office as well. My desk was made from an old rosewood square grand piano. There was another one in the corner with a TV and video equipment. I had a Hammond B-3 organ with three Leslie speaker cabinets, a set of drums, and a giant Scully eight-track machine from a Memphis recording studio, as well as a number of old Rickenbacker guitars and different keyboard instruments. In addition to the musical equipment, there were two large mahogany judge's chairs and a big black leather sofa. There were things everywhere: books, swords, daggers, an African cape buffalo shoulder mount, a leopard rug, a couple of zebra skins, and over four thousand record albums.

The buyer from Ponderosa Park, in Salem, Ohio, dropped by my office for a visit one day. Amazed, he said, "You've got everything here but a hand grenade." I instantly handed him one, much to his amusement.

The reason that I thought the Whites might be offended by my office was that there was a voodoo display on top of my Hammond organ consisting of two human skulls with dice in the eye sockets, plus various roots, bones, voodoo dolls and Catholic statues and relics. On top of this, I had two condom machines, courtesy of Midnight Auto Supply. Sherwood Cryer had sent them to me on a truck bringing supplies to Gilley's souvenir shop. They had obviously been recently ripped out of someplace with a crowbar, since they were still full of money and had plaster-encrusted screws hanging out the back. Considering my decor, we met with the Whites in Allen's office.

Buck White is genuinely one of the nicest people I have ever met. He is as country as apple pie and possesses a charming innocence and simplicity. It's always a pleasure to be around him. On this occasion, however, things weren't quite so pleasant. The Whites had come to tell us that they were leaving In Concert. Allen and I were brilliant in dealing with them. Neither of us wanted them to leave the agency, especially since we had been representing them for a long time, before they even had a record deal.

The act was fairly difficult to book, since they wouldn't play nightclubs. Like most acts, the Whites did not care for the club atmosphere, laden with smoke, alcohol, and sex. They had done well with several single record releases like "Hanging Around" and "You Put the Blue in Me," but they were not, however, a major attraction.

I remember a meeting early in their career conducted by the controversial producer and label head, Jimmy Bowen. At the meeting were the Whites, their manager at the time, Chip Peay, agent Dave Barton, and myself. The purpose of the meeting was to tell us that the Whites had a single release planned, but nothing beyond that as yet. We were informed that the record company might put out another single if the first one did well, and might put out an album if several singles did well. In any case, we were told not to expect any help at all from the record company. In effect, if the Whites made it as an act, it would be solely as a result of their own efforts. I remember feeling sorry for them, thinking that they had been belittled in front of us. These things should have been said to us in private, not in front of them.

Although the Whites were quite frequently late in paying their commissions, we made $21,105 on them in 1984 and $25,100 in 1985. Although this was not a great deal of money, it was money that we would not have had otherwise.

Buck White was incapable of duplicity and soon told us that they were planning to go over to ICM. We took everything that ICM could have possibly told them and shredded it. We said that its agents in the Nashville office were under tremendous pressure to sign acts, any acts. "Do you really think that those people care about your career?" I asked, "Can you imagine for one moment that they actually care about you at all personally?" We hit them with everything we had.

Within an hour, ICM had been transformed into foreign, un-Christian devils. The Whites asked us to excuse them for a few minutes so they could talk things over privately. Allen and I adjourned to my office. I felt that things looked promising.

When we returned to the meeting, the Whites had decided that they wanted to stay with us at In Concert. Buck White was almost angry, feeling that he had been hoodooed by some fast talkers. The only problem was that they had signed a contract with ICM that very morning. This is so typical of country music artists. They make new deals before they even notify their present agents, managers, or even wives and husbands that they are leaving. It happens every day. Under Tennessee law, they had three days to back out of the deal. We sat there watching and listening as Buck called ICM's people and told them that he had changed his mind and that they might as well tear up the contract that they had just signed. I was very pleased with the outcome, especially so since we had snatched them out of the very jaws of ICM. That should have taught ICM a lesson. Such, however, was not the case.

I received a call from Wayne Massey, Charly McClain's husband. He and Charly wanted a meeting. This was in October of 1984. Charly McClain had just earned $110,000 in September, the biggest month of her entire career. Again, we met in Allen's office. This time it was fireworks from the very beginning. I had no intention of losing Charly McClain as a client. We had all worked entirely too hard on her career to give her up at the peak of her moneymaking potential.

Part of the problem was that Wayne and Charly were still insanely jealous of Mickey Gilley. I explained to them that Charly had always been my top priority at In Concert, which was the truth, that day. I also mentioned that the reason I had pushed so hard on the Gilley/McClain tour was that Charly McClain needed the exposure that she received as a part of that package. She appeared in places with Mickey Gilley that she would have never been able to play on her own. They always felt they were second fiddle to Mickey Gilley, so I mentioned Gilley as little as possible. But I was angry that they questioned my loyalty, priorities, and motives regarding her career, when in fact it had been just the opposite.

Mickey Gilley was already making between $15,000 and $20,000 a night. I had been using him to help her out. I cleared up that issue once and for all. It was amazing to me that they were angry. Finally, the climax came when Wayne Massey accused me of gambling with Charly's career. I did not deny it. I had rolled the dice and won. As a result of my efforts I had been subjected to constant abuse from Wayne, Charly, and Mickey Gilley as well. I did what was best for her, and I knew that I had done the right thing in keeping the Gilley/McClain package on the road as long as possible.

I was prepared to fight Wayne Massey on the spot if necessary, not that I would have won. We were both shouting, but I wasn't going to back down. For some reason, my intensity and passion saved the day and turned Wayne's attitude around 180 degrees. In the months to come, Wayne frequently referred to that meeting as if it had been some turning point in our relationship, and I guess it had been. What I didn't know at the time was that meeting was to have been "farewell." They were intending to go to ICM, but changed their minds after our showdown.

The two examples cited above give some idea of what can happen to an agency on any given day. These hillbilly singers are always looking for greener pastures, and for the most part are only as happy as they are told they are by the last person whom they have spoken to. They will try anything.

ICM had certainly been busy behind the scenes, and although it had failed to attract any of our clients, it had stirred up some measure of discontent and forced us to expend valuable time and money defending our interests.

We made fun of ICM constantly, telling artists and buyers that its people were just another example of some rich California apes who thought that they could buy their way into Nashville, people who thought that country singers and their associates were stupid and backwoods. We sliced them up and undermined them wherever possible because we knew that if they ever got a foothold here, it would be extremely difficult to get rid of them. We always speculated that one day the head honcho up in New York or L.A. would wake up in a bad mood, probably after a fight with his wife or girlfriend, make a call, and close down the Nashville office without any notice.

This was more or less what happened. The Nashville staff was given no advance notice. In April 1985 they were told, "We are closing the Nashville office."

"When?"

"Today!"

"Good riddance!"

The Jim Halsey Agency did not really bother us. They had a great client list and the clients were fairly loyal. They had Tammy Wynette, Lee Greenwood, the Judds ("The Jugs," as they are called locally), Roy Clark, the Oak Ridge Boys, Don Williams, and a few more. I felt that being based in Tulsa, Oklahoma, hurt them a great deal as far as doing business in Nashville was concerned. They had been very lucky in getting new acts that later developed into big money-makers. This was more their m.o. than pirating acts from other agencies. I really do not know whether they did not actively seek to steal acts, or if they just were not very good at it.

In any case, the only acts I remember losing to the Halsey Agency were Tammy Wynette, Brenda Lee, Merle Haggard, and Don Williams. Tammy Wynette had left the Lavender-Blake Agency in 1978 or 1979 and moved to Halsey. This would have been a substantial loss if the Lavender-Blake Agency had stayed in business.

Merle Haggard left Dick Blake International and went to Halsey in the fall of 1982. He didn't really count anyway since he was such a moron. In fact, everyone associated with him was an idiot. They all reminded me of the worst service station attendants. When we got Merle Haggard, he was making around $10,000 a night. In a few months, we were asking and getting $20,000 for most Haggard dates, with a sprinkling of $25,000 and $30,000 dates here and there.

When Haggard left, he did so abruptly, canceling all of his dates in September and October. He had one of his stooges send us a telegram, telling us to cancel all appearances except for the bass tournament in Montgomery, Alabama, because he was going to be sick. I wish I had saved the telegram since it was so stupidly worded. Merle Haggard had become jealous over Barbara Mandrell, who was making over twice what he earned per night. Haggard was still a big act, but Barbara Mandrell was at that time one of the biggest in the world. Haggard had refused to open a show with Barbara Mandrell on the bill as headliner, telling Dick Blake that she used to open for him.

Blake replied, "Hell! You used to open for Buck Owens, what difference does it make?"

Merle Haggard had not appreciated that remark even though it was true. Who opens and closes shows is a matter of great importance to most artists since the closing spot is considered to be the place of honor. I have worked with many artists who refuse to play a show unless they get to close, regardless of the money. The intelligent and emotionally secure artist usually wants to open the show so that he can get out of the auditorium and on the way home three or four hours earlier than he would if he has to wait around and go on last. Haggard did not fall into this category.

Haggard was at that time married to singer Leona Williams. He sometimes brought her along with his ex-wife Bonnie Owens, who sang too. There was also a major power struggle in progress between his two managers, Tex Whitsen and Fuzzy Owens. They sought to undermine each other constantly. The whole operation was a zoo. Anyway, for these and other reasons, losing Merle Haggard to the Halsey Agency did not count, although it bothered me at first.

Dick Blake said at the time, "Neither of us has missed a meal yet, and I don't think we will as the result of anything Merle Haggard might do."

When Brenda Lee left In Concert and went to Halsey, it was again no big deal. We were not really making any money on her anyway. I did, however, appreciate the fact that she stayed with us after Dick Blake died, long enough for us to get our feet wet.

We stole Don Williams from Halsey in 1980 or 1981 but he returned to Halsey in less than a year. I don't remember how we managed to get him as a client. It was just one of those moves artists make from time to time.

Don was then getting around $10,000 a night and was difficult to book since he was very particular about the types of shows he would play. He wouldn't play clubs, had to close the show, and wouldn't work with certain artists.

I booked a show at the auditorium in Chattanooga featuring Ronnie Milsap and Don Williams. Williams insisted on closing the show. We had just taken Don as a client, so I dropped by the dressing room to say hello, but found the atmosphere to be very inhospitable. Ronnie Milsap, on the other hand, has a good sense of humor and is for the most part fun to be around. His show is very high-energy and he all but blew Don Williams off the stage that night. The package played two more days that weekend but that was it. Milsap is a hard act to follow onstage and should have been the headliner. We always considered Williams a Halsey act we'd been lucky enough to handle for a while.

In retrospect, I guess you could say that Halsey did steal one of my important acts, Dan Seals. Dan had been a pop singer as one half of the very successful duo England Dan and John Ford Coley. As an agency we had taken Dan Seals from $1,500 a night to $10,000 in just over a year and a half. He was having a stream of number-one records, starting with his big record "Bop," a crossover hit, and continuing with songs like "You Still Move Me," "Everything That Glitters," "Meet Me in Montana" (with Marie Osmond), and so on.

Dan and his manager were under heavy pressure from someone at Capitol Records, presumably Capitol's promotion man, Lynn Schults, to move to the Halsey Agency. The pressure could have just as easily come from label head Jim Fogelsong. Dan's manager, Tony Gottleib, would never tell us exactly who was bad-mouthing us over at Capitol. If he had, I would have called the source of the problem and tried to enlighten him.

I never understood this horseshit from the record label. We had done an incredible job with Dan Seals, but his manager kept telling us he was getting pressure from "the record label" to move Dan to the Halsey Agency. This interference always irritated me. I mean, who at the record company knew anything at all about booking or agency work?

It was a constant battle and Dan Seals was a difficult act to book anyway. In the first place, we frequently got feedback from buyers that Dan Seals was boring onstage. This was well known, even within his own camp. Dan's manager had stated that he did not want Dan playing L.A. because he did not want the West Coast record people to see Dan's show. I really thought this was absurd and said so. If the show wasn't good enough for his own record company to see, then why in the hell were we busting our asses to get him $10,000 a night?

Dan Seals is a great guy, I guess. He came to my office twice in the three years that we represented him. His manager, Tony, visited frequently, but he was strange and difficult to deal with. He was extremely opinionated and frequently changed his mind completely about major issues, without advance notice.

A classic example concerned Dan Seals' first major West Coast tour as a country artist, in 1986. Bruce Shelton, our West Coast agent, had already played every other artist on our roster several times. We felt that we could set a lengthy tour, starting in Texas at the end of October, taking Seals through New Mexico and Arizona, into southern California, and returning through Nevada, Utah, Colorado, Oklahoma, and finally home.

Tony Gottlieb approved this plan and Bruce started to get the tour set up. This in itself was no easy task, since Dan Seals' travel arrangements were somewhat different from the average country singer's. Dan and his troupe went from town to town in a large van with a horse trailer full of equipment in tow. They also divided the driving responsibilities among the band members. Under these circumstances, the routing of dates was a greater consideration than it would have been if they had had a tour bus and a driver and could easily make jumps of five or six hundred miles between shows.

Bruce very carefully mapped out and booked a tour with perfect routing, easy jumps between cities, and good money. The logistics were very complicated, and once set up, should have been left alone. After the tour had been confirmed, Tony decided that six weeks straight was too long for the band to be on the road and away from home. He proposed that we interrupt the tour so the boys in the band could fly home for a few days to visit their girlfriends.

The purpose of a tour as opposed to performing weekends is to remain on the road as long as possible, playing five or six dates a week and then coming home with some real money. The idea of canceling dates that were already set and routed so that band members could see their girlfriends seemed ridiculous. After a while, Tony realized the absurdity of the suggestion and in a flash of brilliance decided to solve the problem by canceling the tour altogether.

Tony was also hot-tempered. He yelled and screamed a great deal, often irritating buyers and once actually getting arrested at a show. Gottlieb knew that Dan Seals was not an easy act to book and he realized that In Concert had been doing a great job. Finally, Tony succumbed to external pressures and told us that Dan Seals would be leaving In Concert at the end of June 1987.

Tony was a pain in the ass most of the time. His greatest fault was that he would get angry without getting all of the facts. He also cared too much what other people thought, and although he generally made his own decisions, he still worried about them afterward.

When an act leaves an agency, there are generally two positions that the losing agency can take if it wishes to keep the client it has just lost. It can immediately cease all efforts at booking its former client and hope that the new agency will not be able to do the job quickly enough and that the act will return in desperation to his or her former agency. This sometimes happens. The danger is that the new agency might get lucky fast, doing the job well from the start, and the client is lost forever.

In the other approach, the agency that has lost a client simply refuses to acknowledge the loss and continues to book dates for the artist who has left. The artist is likely to take such dates, since he or she needs them. The talent buyers most likely do not yet know that the artist has left the first agency. Unless the act in question is a major superstar, it may be some while before his or her move to another agency filters down to the level of common knowledge among the buying public at large.

The old agency is still in a really good position to throw a wrench in the machinery of the new agency. The former agency should redouble its efforts in behalf of the lost client. If an agent finds a buyer who says, "But I heard so and so moved to another agency ...," the former agent would simply tell the buyer that he has been misinformed and say something like, "I have been representing this act for over two years. So and so agency has tried unsuccessfully to steal the artist from our company, but we are still the sole exclusive agents."

If the buyer protests, it is a simple matter to say, "Look, you and I have been doing business for years. Everyone I have sold you has always shown up. Such and such agency is just trying to steal my client and it won't work. Now, let's do some business."

This approach will work long enough to set some more dates on the artist and to cause some problems for the new agency. The danger with this method is that if the act has in fact moved to another agency, the dates that the old agency continues to set take some of the immediate pressure to deliver off of the new agency. Furthermore, the new agency can excuse itself from a poor showing initially by honestly claiming that the former agency is hindering its efforts to book the act.

We continued to book Dan Seals for a while, but Tony Gottlieb wanted to give the Halsey Agency a fair chance to do a really good job for Dan Seals. In the past, I would have told my agents to keep on turning in dates and to undermine the competition in every way possible, but I honored Tony's request, mainly because I was tired of fighting.

This was in July 1987. By this time I had lost Mickey Gilley and Ronnie Milsap and was sick of dealing with hillbillies altogether. I remember Tony coming by the office to pick up some contracts right about the time a truck pulled in front of our building bringing me my first Bentley. It was a nice summer day and I had just returned from a week in the English countryside. To hell with Tony Gottlieb and Dan Seals.

I knew that the Halsey Agency would not baby-sit and humor them as we had done. I was right, and in October they were back knocking on our door. They had only been at the Halsey Agency for a few months and that was enough. There was nothing wrong with the Halsey Agency at that point, it was just not used to having to coddle clients to the extent that we did. With the big acts that they had on their roster at that time, they didn't have time to baby-sit any prima donnas.

In addition to the William Morris Agency, ICM, and Jim Halsey, there were a few others we had to contend with from time to time.

United Talent had been jointly owned by Loretta Lynn and Conway Twitty when they had both been in their prime. In addition, they had represented at one time or another Bob Luman, Kenny Dale, Cal Smith, Mickey Gilley, Warner Mack, and others. By the time In Concert came into existence, United Talent was history as a major competitor. Former boss Jimmy Jay and his two sons had left, and agents Reggie Mack and Allen Whitcomb were gone. Finally, Conway Twitty left his own agency for a brief stint at the Halsey Agency before moving to Jayson Productions and from there to the Talent Agency.

Only two people remained at United Talent, Dave Schuder, who acted as Loretta Lynn's agent, and Dave's secretary. The only reason I mention United Talent at all is to show that every once in a while an artist can surprise even the most hardened associates with a display of viciousness that seems beyond belief. What happened to agent Dave Schuder is a case in point. He had been with United Talent twelve years and was operating the company at a profit. On the day after Christmas 1986, he received a registered letter sent to his home from Loretta Lynn and her husband, "saying that they loved me and that they appreciated me, but that my services were no longer needed as of December thirtieth."

And so that was how it ended after twelve years. Merry Christmas! Dave told me that he had to fight to get two weeks' severance pay. Is it any wonder that I slept with one eye open? With this kind of thing happening constantly, repeated daily in different and sometimes subtle ways, it's very difficult to trust anyone in this business after a while. Every time I see Loretta Lynn, hear her name spoken, or hear her music on the radio, I think of Dave Schuder. Fortunately, he was well liked and was able to get a job at the Buddy Lee Agency, but Loretta Lynn's actions were, unfortunately, not atypical.

At about this same period, Loretta Lynn dismissed her longtime manager, David Skepner, also on short notice. I wasn't overly upset by this news, since David Skepner always seemed to me to be a bit patronizing. Loretta had played a show on an aircraft carrier for the U.S. Navy at some point. As a result of that engagement, David Skepner received a nice leather navy-issue flight jacket adorned with all of the appropriate squadron patches and markings. Since that time he has almost always dressed as a navy officer, in a khaki shirt and pants. At least he remains amusing.

My only experience with Skepner occurred after he took over the management of MTM Records artist Judy Rodman, whom we had just started to book. I had called on Alan Bernard, the head of MTM, to talk about moving a couple of newer acts I was working with to MTM Records. I was also curious as to whether I could acquire some new clients from his label. At the time, I was very interested in MTM Records. They had come to Nashville with plenty of money and were spending it freely. The company purchased the old Monument Records building on Sixteenth Avenue South, gutted it, and had it completely refurbished. I figured that despite the fact they had not signed any artists that were likely to make it, sooner or later they might wind up with a hit act in spite of themselves. As it turned out, they did fairly well with three acts, the Girls Next Door, Holly Dunn, and Judy Rodman.

Alan Bernard and I hit it off, and I ended up with Judy Rodman. At the time I took her on she had not released an album and had yet to score big with any of her few single records. When we met initially, I explained to Judy that it would take us at least a year to get her career off the ground. I told her I was only interested in doing business with her if she would give us a minimum commitment of at least one year.

As usual, I advised her not to go out on the road until there was a reason to do so. She seemed to understand and I felt that if I could not deal with her, at least Alan Bernard could. From my preliminary conversations with him, he seemed to realize that there was no reason to attempt to put her on tour because there was no demand for her as yet. In fact, most people had never even heard of her.

Alan Bernard and David Skepner were good friends so I wasn't surprised when I received the call informing me that David Skepner was going to serve as Judy Rodman's manager. At about this same time, Judy Rodman had her first number-one record, "Till I Met You." How it got to the top is a mystery to me. Nevertheless, my agents were doing an incredible job selling dates for Judy Rodman, considering that despite her number-one record, very few people in the marketplace had any idea as to who she was. Looking back at my 1986 route sheet, I see that she was making two to three thousand dollars a night.

One day in the fall of 1986, Alan Bernard and David Skepner dropped by for a meeting. I called in the agents as well. Bernard's and Skepner's attitudes had changed radically as a result of Judy's so-called number-one record. Now they thought that she should be getting $5,000 a night. My agents knew that this was insane.

The next remark was even more absurd. David or Alan said, "If In Concert doesn't feel that Judy Rodman is the next Barbara Mandrell, you should not be representing her."

Barbara Mandrell went from $3,500 a night to $100,000 a night, but Judy Rodman was not going to be the next Barbara Mandrell, or even the one after the next, for that matter.

It amazed me that two people with as much knowledge of the music business as David Skepner and Alan Bernard would say such things to experienced agents. It was not the first or last time that managers in Nashville or elsewhere have attempted to hype agents, but as I've said, a good agent always knows what an act is really worth far more than a manager does.

My agents found these remarks decidedly absurd, and we knew that Judy Rodman would soon be moving on to another agency. Her departure did not represent a significant loss of revenue and none of us were sorry to see her leave. With as many artists as there are out there trying to make a living, it is foolish to waste time on those whose perceptions are that far removed from reality. Whatever the agent does will never be enough.

As an interesting postscript, I received a letter from David Skepner shortly after she left with card that conferred membership in the "I Hate David Skepner Club." What an ego! I couldn't have cared less about David Skepner.

There were a few other agencies around that I had some dealings with at that time. I lost Judy Rodman and John

Anderson to the Buddy Lee Agency, but we whipped their asses in a duel over Jerry Lee Lewis once, and that was about it. I liked most of the people over there, even though the place itself, the office I mean, gave me the creeps. The decor reminded me of some private detective's office circa 1960.

We had stolen agent Allen Whitcomb and artist Ronnie McDowell from the Top Billing Agency back in the old Dick Blake days. We also intercepted Charly McClain on her way to Top Billing before Dick Blake died, and took her to In Concert. Top Billing had once been a major contender run by self-proclaimed superagent Tandy Rice. Tandy Rice is a high-profile figure in Nashville and has been for some while. He even signed up Billy Carter, the president's brother. That was a brilliant publicity move at the time, but the personal publicity Tandy received over the years hurt him more than it helped in the long run.

Several major artists, including Ronnie Milsap, told me that they never considered Top Billing because they felt that Tandy was more interested in promoting himself than his artists. That seems to be the general consensus among most of the artists I have known. Tandy Rice, however, is a very intelligent, outspoken, and visible person, one who is comfortable and graceful in the upper socioeconomic levels. As such, he had gone a long way toward changing the public's perception of his field from hillbilly music to country music.

Sometimes there is a price to pay for such visibility. Tandy, as I mentioned, has always been rather outspoken and on one occasion some remarks that he casually made caused quite a stir. *Time* magazine ran a short column under "Business Notes" entitled "Country Music, a Sad Song of Sorry Sales." The brief article said that while overall record sales were up 13 percent nationwide since 1980, country music sales had dropped 6 percent in the same period of time. This drop was attributed to economic woes in the farm and energy-producing states as well as to the public's moving away from the *Urban Cowboy* image. All of this was true enough, although none of us had begun to feel the crunch yet at In Concert. We were on an upward spiral and laughed openly at the article.

What got Tandy into trouble was a short quote at the end of

the article in which he said, "A bunch of artists rushed out to buy big fancy buses during the boom, and I think Nashville may become the biggest used-bus city in the nation."

This quote coming from a former president of the Country Music Association (1981) created quite an uproar, as the truth frequently does. One of our local newspapers, the *Nashville Banner,* came out with a front-page article the following day and a big controversy ensued, lasting several weeks. Generally speaking, Tandy Rice was villified, mainly for telling family secrets to the world at large.

I spoke to Tandy about the story and he said that he had been merely asked for a statement by *Time* stringer Pat Harris and had no idea that it would be running in *Time* magazine.

I also asked Pat Harris about the article. She said that "someone from the CMA" called her and told her that Tandy had written a letter to the Country Music Association denying having made the statement that appeared in *Time.* Tandy really prefers not to be reminded of the incident at all, understandably so.

However, his observations were quite accurate, almost prophetic in fact, simply because there are more people trying to make a living in country music than there are opportunities.

There were and are some other agencies around town: World Class, Monterey, and the Bobby Roberts Agency, to name a few. The problem is that the pie has now been cut too many ways for most agencies to do really well. In country music ego prevails and any artist is likely to hire an agent and start his own company. That's Nashville.

Many artists look first and foremost to see what other major artists are clients at an agency before making a decision as to their own representation. There is some validity in this approach. An agency that handles a number of major acts would seem to be the best bet for an act seeking representation. There is a certain prestige in having one's name on the same client list with famous and often more famous contemporaries.

The artist should look beyond this view and attempt to assess realistically his position on the priority scale if he moves to such an agency. Are there other acts in his same price range that he will have to compete with for dates within the agency? Are there other, more expensive acts, who due to their earning potential for the agency will receive more attention? Is prestige more important than money? Is there someone at the agency with whom the artist enjoys an exceptional rapport? Is the artist-to-agent ratio too high? These and other considerations are important to an artist who is thinking about making a move.

From the artist's standpoint, the first priority should be a good relationship with someone at an agency, someone who is an agent and not necessarily the president of the company. The relationship between the agent and the artist should span the major part of the artist's career. The artist should cultivate this relationship and use it to his own advantage. They should share a common goal, and as the artist's career advances, so does the agent's.

Very few artists have given enough thought to this relationship. If the agent needs a raise or wants to move to another agency, he should be able to ask the artist for leverage for their mutual good. In most cases, however, an artist will simply move to another agency and leave his responsible agent behind, thinking only of himself, but not being sufficiently intelligent to understand the long-term effects of such a move on his own career.

Given an ideal situation, the artist should try to place himself in the position of being the top act at whatever agency he chooses to affiliate with. If his career continues to move forward he may in time consider other options. He should always try to or at least offer to take his responsible agent with him if he makes a move. This almost always puts him in a better position at his new agency. For one thing, he already has someone who knows how to book him as well as what types of dates and situations are acceptable. The majority of talent buyers are familiar with his responsible agent so the move requires a shorter period of transition than it would otherwise, and therefore less down time.

One other thing should be mentioned in regard to agencies in general. Some agents employ a territory system in which the country is divided among the agents, with each agent given a certain geographical area as his or her responsibility. Other agencies let their agents develop accounts at random in any part of the country.

In the territory system, an agent is responsible for what goes on in his own area. He develops lasting relationships with his buyers, learning what nights of the week they use, what cities and venues they promote, and what types of acts they use. The good agent gets to know his buyers on a personal level, finding out their interests and hobbies, visiting them at shows from time to time, or showing them around when they come to town. The agent learns what major shows are coming into his territory and routes his own acts accordingly. He finds out what annual events and city festivals happen in his territory. He comes to know the various chambers of commerce and the radio stations, and develops a network of people who know him, like him, and will help him. Any intelligent agent does this; it just produces better results in a territory system. The agents can get together and decide at which times they will be prepared to have each of their clients in their particular territory. This gives them specific responsibilities as well as an occasional and often well-deserved rest from the demands of booking a particular artist constantly.

In addition, from the standpoint of security, an agency is better off keeping any one agent from gaining too much power outside his own territory. This lessens to some degree, however slightly, the likelihood that it will be easy for him to damage the company if he leaves and goes to work for a competitor. The territory system seems to be the best way to keep agents and artists working effectively.

As an agent, I felt that the competition was anyone, anywhere engaged in the same type of work as myself. Agents are, by their nature, aggressive, and in a great many instances unprincipled. This being the case, I regarded any agent at any level, no matter how high or low on the totem pole, as a threat. I have seduced acts away from friends as well as enemies. Life is not very secure, and those of us who have spent a great deal of time at the top tend, like many of the artists, to think that it will last forever. The truth is that unless one is self-employed, anybody is ultimately only two weeks away from being without a job.

There is one more thing I would like to mention. When In Concert was suing William Morris over Mickey Gilley, my lawyer went to L.A. to take a deposition from Dave Doud, an agent for that company. After all of the questions had been asked and answered, Dave said that he wanted to clear up one point that had been mentioned earlier. On the record, he wanted to clarify that In Concert might consider the William Morris Agency as "competition," but that the William Morris Agency did not deign to view In Concert in the same way. I can almost hear him making that statement now. I am sure that it was for my reading pleasure.

While it is undeniably true that In Concert is out of business and that the William Morris Agency is "still as strong as a monkey's tail," to quote Haiti's former president, the fact is that In Concert cost the William Morris Agency well over a million dollars and kicked their asses in almost every battle we ever had.

Chapter Seven

This Will Last Forever

Most people imagine that all country singers are rich, that the once famous, whose names are no longer heard, have retired to their expensive country homes and horse farms. This dangerous illusion is strangely enough shared by many of the country singers now at the top. They take it for granted that since they are rich and famous now, this will always be the case. The truth is that the majority of former stars have been forgotten by the public, and most of those at the top now will suffer the same fate sooner than they would ever imagine.

Most country stars of the past were on major record labels at one time or another, labels like RCA, Decca, Columbia, Epic, Liberty, Dot, United Artists, Capitol, MCA, and others.

Some of them, such as Ray Price, Roger Miller, and others, are still doing well, but for most of them, at least from the standpoint of their careers as entertainers, life is no longer quite as bright. And yet at one time, all of them had something wonderful happening. There was a buzz about them around town and around the country. They had agents, managers, lawyers, accountants, bankers, bands, buses, producers, songwriters, recording sessions, renown, publicity, husbands or wives.

They were recognized in public. People wanted to be around them, to be seen in their company, to be their friends. Some of these names may not be familiar to the public now, but they once were. Many of them had distinguished careers that spanned decades.

Where are they now? What happened to their hit records and their fame? What happened to their big Cadillacs and their fine homes? What happened to their careers?

In this chapter we will examine the rise and fall of the average country music singer. While it is certainly true that there are acts like Roy Clark, Ronnie Milsap, the Oak Ridge Boys, the Statler Brothers, and others who continue to have lasting success, it should be noted that in the overall picture, the percentage of acts with long-lasting careers is very small indeed.

Let's briefly look at why this is so. Some of these artists are comfortably retired, having put aside money when times were good. Others play the Grand Ole Opry because it is the only job they can still get. Maybe that's an unpopular and unkind thing to say, but within the music business in Nashville, it is a well-known fact. Most of these artists, those who can still get jobs, perform whenever they can for whatever amount they can get. This is reality, and a terrible one it is, the once great, the once rich and famous artist playing some high school gym for $1,500 or $2,000 a night, if he or she is indeed fortunate enough to receive that much.

It must be very depressing for an act who had eight or ten years with a record company to be unable to get past some twenty-year-old receptionist at the very building that his record sales helped pay for, but that's the way it is. The public doesn't know or care. It discards its former idols in favor of someone new. The artists on the way up or already at the top know that this is happening all around them but it is not happening to them, it is someone else, and as long as that is the case, it doesn't really matter. One less competitor in a very competitive business.

All of this is incomprehensible to the artists on the way down.

They honestly do not know what happened. Suddenly their record sales start dropping for no clearly defined reason. What happened? That last album was certainly the best they ever recorded. Everybody said so. The president of the record company said it was great. Why didn't it sell?

"It must be the record company's fault! It is that lousy promotion staff they have over there! The best album I have ever recorded, wasted because the promotion staff dropped the ball! If they had not been so busy pushing those new artists this would never have happened! I am going over to the record company and chew some ass!"

And that's just what happens. The artist raises some hell, forgetting that the record company is, after all, in business to sell records. At the next record company staff meeting, the artist's record sales figures are discussed, and it is decided that this particular artist is causing more trouble than he or she is worth.

If the record company is under contract and has to put out another record, they may go through the motions but will let the record die by giving the artist almost no promotional support. This happens much more frequently than one might suspect.

If there is an option on the part of the record company, then they may elect not to pick it up, to drop the artist from the label. It's all only bottom-line stuff for the record company. They are either making or losing money on an artist. If they are losing money, they might be willing to roll the dice again because they believe in the project and would like to get back some of the money already spent. If, on the other hand, they are losing money and the artist acts like a jerk, then the artist will most likely be dropped.

The artist who has been let go by a major record company generally has a better than average chance of getting signed by another major label. Of the country artists who were once famous, nearly all of them have been on more than one major record label. A record company is frequently interested in an artist from another label; possibly the other label didn't market him in the right way or didn't cut the right type of material. The new company may feel that it can do better. If the artist who has been dropped gets signed right away to another record company, he still has a shot at the top. This happens often, but not always with good results. Recently, several acts who had more or less been forgotten have had a successful resurgence on different record labels, notably John Anderson and Marty Stuart.

If the artist doesn't get signed, then his downward spiral has begun. Since people don't for the most part want to see an artist without current hit records, dates start falling off, and consequently income drops. The world that had seemed so friendly and secure while he was at the top begins to crumble. Important people who used to invite the artist out or ask his advice suddenly cease to call. The artist finds himself stuck with a high overhead and a great many debts, and not enough money to make ends meet. The artist in this position feels strangely disoriented and angry. What went wrong? Why are these things suddenly happening to him? He still sings and looks the same.

The artist, realizing for the first time that he really is off the charts for good, begins to panic. He lashes out at the talent agency. "Why aren't you getting me more dates?" The agency knows by this time that the artist has been dropped by the record company. At the agency, they humor him, telling him not to worry, that they have a big tour coming together in the near future. Behind the scenes at the agency, however, a decision has already been made and the agents have been instructed as follows:

"As you know, he has been dropped by the record company and his career may very well be over. On the other hand, he says that he is about to sign with another record label, so we need to keep him as long as we can. In the meantime, book what you can, but don't waste too much time on him. If he stays he stays, if he goes, he goes. It does not make any difference to us one way or the other. If he starts taking too much of your time or becomes a pain in the ass, let's put a postage stamp on his ass and send him along to another agency."

If, however, the artist in question has been hard to deal with in the past and the agency has other more important clients, then someone may simply tell the secretary to send a letter informing the artist that "unfortunately the agency feels that we are no longer able to represent you in the manner which you deserve..." In other words, "Hit the road!"

So the artist has in a very short time lost his record label deal and can't get another one. He either quits or gets fired by his agency. He still has his ego, however, and that leads him to believe that he will soon be signed to another major recording contract, but time passes and hope fades. His friends, for whom he found jobs when he was on top, are for the most part unavailable to him now. Those who are around feel vaguely uncomfortable in his presence now, as if he had some contagious disease. They already know what he will find out soon enough, that his career is over, that no major label is going to sign him again, now or ever.

In addition, if the artist was a big jerk on the way up, some of the people he mistreated will be waiting to give him a kick on his way down. There's an old saying in Nashville among insiders: "While it's a long hard climb to the top, they grease the pole for you on your way down."

The artist decides to go into the recording studio at his own expense; there is always someone willing to take his money in Nashville. He hopes to cut some hit songs on his own and then shop them to the record labels himself. He visits the publishing companies to find some good material to record, but they know that he is washed up and do not give him their best songs. They don't tell him this, that's just the way it is. Their best songs are now being held for someone else, in the same way they were once held for him.

Most successful songwriters know a hit song when they have written one. It is to their advantage to see that it is recorded by the most popular singer they can find. For this reason, most writers and publishers keep their best songs and do not even play them for lesser acts who are looking for material.

The artist goes into the studio and cuts four or five songs. They sound great to him, but he really doesn't know anymore. The songs he recorded may actually be as good as anything he has ever done before. Everybody who hears them thinks that they are great and yet for some reason he can't get a record deal.

At this point, the once great artist faces real despair. He wishes that he had saved some or all of that money he got back when it seemed like it would never end. He would like to quit the business altogether, but he can't. This is all he has ever known. It becomes increasingly difficult to get dates now, and those that he obtains are for much less money than he is used to, but his expenses remain the same.

In an effort to cut back, he sells his bus and lets some of his band members go. It will be cheaper, he thinks, to lease a bus on a day-to-day basis as he needs it. Finally his remaining band members leave him. He is not playing enough dates to pay them the money they need to get by. They find jobs playing for other artists whose careers are on the way up.

Now the artist has no record deal, no band, and no bus. He certainly didn't sell the bus at a profit. In fact, he was lucky if he was able to pay off the majority of his debt to the bank. Now he has no income. He will either have to cancel the few dates he has remaining or try to put together some musicians to work the dates on a per diem basis. All is lost or seems to be for the moment, but then he sees a ray of hope, a small light at the end of the tunnel. He can probably get a deal with an independent record label. This is really his only alternative at this point, and if he has been "recently famous" he has a good chance at success in this undertaking.

An independent label is usually considered to be any record label that does not have its own distribution network. Such labels are usually understaffed, and almost always under-capitalized. As a result of these liabilities they generally have a tough time competing in the marketplace against the large, corporate giants.

So the artist negotiates a singles deal with some independent label nobody has ever heard of. The company has no national distribution network. People will not be able to buy his music at record stores. He is aware of these inherent problems, but after all, he is a star. The disc jockeys still love him, and what the hell, he's only been out of the charts for a year and a half. He is starting to feel confident again. His record will be a hit, radio stations will play it all over the nation. This record company just has not had an artist of his renown before and it will surely get a distribution deal with a major label as a result of this record of his.

What the artist does not know, or won't admit, is that this record company is undercapitalized. It doesn't have enough money or experience to promote his record properly. Neither does he realize that he has signed his own career death warrant by placing his once famous name on a label the radio stations have never heard of. When the record is received at the station, it may be played by a few disc jockeys who liked him and used to play his records.

Most program directors, however, will throw the record in the trash to start with because they are not going to be able to get any payola from an independent label, and they do not want to risk their jobs by mentioning such an arrangement to some company that can't afford it anyway. Why risk it? They can keep getting their under-the-table money from their already established accounts. Furthermore, why play a record that won't be available in the record stores even if it is a hit? That would only serve to make the listeners angry.

The independent record predictably fails to make its mark and the artist hits bottom. He has gone from nobody to somebody to nobody again. There is nothing left but to grovel for whatever dates he can find at any price, regardless of the circumstances. He now gladly accepts dates that he would have considered insulting a short while ago. Abandoned by the formerly adoring public and shunned by those whom he once considered to be his friends, and with no hope for the future, he lives a tormented existence plagued with unanswered questions: What went wrong? Why has this happened?

There really are very few answers to these questions for most of the once great. Some of them were destroyed by drugs or alcohol. Others killed their own careers with a bad attitude. For the majority, however, there is no tangible explanation. They simply woke up one day and the world was somehow different. A few may make a temporary comeback, but for most of them, this is it—life has passed them by and there is nothing they can do about it.

What answers there might be should be examined, although they are by no means definitive. For one thing, country music has changed, and as a result has gained a wider and younger audience than it ever had in the past. This alone does not explain why most country artists sooner or later fall out of favor with the public. These days, new artists seem to go higher and succeed faster than they did in the past. But the time they spend at the top seems to be less than it was for the older ones. Faster rise, shorter career, faster decline. The public has an insatiable demand for new talent and the artist of today who has a career of ten years or more is the exception.

The record companies contribute to this situation by signing more artists than they used to and giving them much less of a commitment than they did in the past. Nowadays, if an artist does not make it early on in the game, he is more likely to be dropped by the record company fairly quickly. In addition, there are more people competing as country artists than ever before in the history of country music, with the result that there is a smaller piece of the pie for everybody. Many who never quite make it do succeed for a while in taking some of the dates, money, record deals, and airtime from more legitimate artists who might otherwise have a shot at a meaningful and long-lasting career. But then, what artist would ever consider himself to be anything less than totally legitimate or authentic?

I have briefly described the stages in the life of the average successful country artist's career. All of the formerly rich and famous don't necessarily fit this scenario, but most of them do. There are also hundreds, if not thousands, of singers who never even get close to a record deal with any company at all. They start with the enthusiasm of the young but eventually descend into the hell of lounge work or finally give up altogether. For the majority of those who do make it more or less to the top, but then drop slowly out of sight and out of the public eye, life isn't very pretty after the fall.

From the agent's point of view, dealing with the once great in their career death struggles is never easy. A few artists are actually able to accept that their time at the top is over and are thankful that fortune smiled on them for a while, but these are in the minority. Most singers, especially those who have been very successful, fight reality to their last breath. Their still incredible egos live and shield them from realizing that their careers are over and all that remains is for some kind soul to administer the last rites and put them out of everyone's misery.

Still they rage on, complaining about this or that, failing to understand that they are now only a pain in the ass and that nobody cares how they feel. Most of them finally pass quietly because the public and the powers that be in Nashville have forgotten them altogether.

Make no mistake about it, the music business in Nashville has a voracious appetite. It seduces, corrupts, destroys, and devours lives, relationships, marriages, families. Everything and everyone is grist for the mill. We all exist to serve and to feed the machine, and while it's true that a few of the fortunate ones are able to leave the game with a great deal of money, most aren't that lucky. They watch in disbelief and jealous rage as they are replaced by new faces, and adding insult to injury, these new country voices may come from Los Angeles, New York, or other urban areas, from people who have no empathy at all with the tradition or background from which country music developed.

Sometimes a new act will have a hit with a remake of an older tune and for a brief while a former star will again receive some slight recognition, but this is rare and ephemeral. As I said, it is all a big machine. Those who paved the way end up as part of the highway themselves and those on top now will be rolled over by the cosmic wheel soon enough. Today, however, they laugh, thinking that their fame and prosperity will last forever.

Chapter Eight

Around Town

Nashville is filled with hustlers of all shapes and sizes. They are immediately recognizable to the trained eye. They profess to be in the music business, but really have no specific line of work. Generally masterminds of nothing, they are more or less parasitic by nature. They move from investor to investor, preying on people who, successful in other areas, should know better. Their victims are frequently duped by some outrageous scheme into which they pour thousands and perhaps hundreds of thousands of dollars.

Ultimately, the majority of these ill-conceived business deals fail and the investor ends up feeling angry and stupid. He knows that had he not compromised his good sense to begin with, none of this would have happened. Knowing that his losses are his own fault, he is most likely to take his medicine quietly. Why advertise his stupidity? He knew better at the time, but went ahead anyway.

Why do ordinarily astute businesspeople abdicate their reason when the "music business" is involved? There are quite a few answers to this question: the desire for renown among one's colleagues at home, the challenge and excitement of risk, the lure of adventure, the need to impress others, the need to impress oneself, tax purposes, greed, the call of show business and bright lights, parties, relief of boredom, lack of common sense, the possibility of success.

There are other reasons as well. Often a successful man who owns a tire business or a feed store back home has discovered a female singer that he either has or would like to have as a mistress. He tells her that he knows somebody big up in Nashville. He makes a few phone calls and finally ends up talking to one of Nashville's many wallet surgeons, waiting to pounce upon some sucker and take his money.

The Country Music Association never mentions them, preferring instead to pretend that they do not exist. But they do exist and operate freely. Many of them are no doubt members of the Country Music Association and other legitimate organizations. These persons have companies on paper with high-sounding names, and yet their so-called organizations have no visible means of support. They attend various meetings around town, join more organizations, and are elected or appointed to various committees, but nobody really knows what they actually do for a living.

And so it goes. These people by degrees gain some acceptance in the Nashville music community, even though nobody really has any idea what they actually do. These hustlers know each other, though, and they are always "looking for some investors." It is amazing, but they somehow seem to find an abundance of people waiting to throw away their money on some wild scheme.

Some of these wallet surgeons actually succeed in an undertaking from time to time. If they succeed several times, which is rare, then they might eventually enter the real Nashville mainstream at the upper end of the spectrum. Nashville does like success. Most of the time, however, they hover around the fringe of legitimacy and respectability, never quite making it, but making a living somehow.

Some of their ideas may actually be very good. Others wish to start yet another talent agency, record label, publishing company, or management company. These enterprises last a season, if that long, and then fade away. In most cases, the investor would have been much better off writing a check for $50,000 or $100,000 to the person who hooked him to begin with, thus saving himself a great deal of additional time, trouble, and money.

Let's return to the situation of a man and his would-be mistress, since this is a frequent scenario. The investor wants to impress her with his belief in her and his sincerity. It is very difficult for him to make any real time with her in their hometown because he has a wife and a family. He is willing to come all the way to Nashville at his own expense, taking time away from his busy schedule, not because he wants anything from her, but solely because he believes in her and thinks that she really has a chance at the bright lights. Her ability is so unique, he tells her, that he feels she must be presented to the world.

She, of course, wants to believe him and begins to see this man in a different light. He is probably all right. After all, he is married, and he has never really "tried anything." She unknowingly drops her defenses. He becomes her protector, confidant, champion, and, finally, lover. This happens gradually, over a period of time. They begin to share their feelings and thoughts in a way that neither has ever done before; a real bond develops between them. Love grows.

Back home, the man's wife has reason to be alarmed. Her husband has made several trips to Nashville recently with that girl singer. She knows that it is strictly business and a hobby for her husband, that it takes his mind off the pressures at work. She also knows that the singer has a boyfriend. Besides, the girl is at least twenty years younger than he is. His interest is strictly fatherly. Or is it? She ignores her intuition. She intentionally dismisses these worrisome thoughts. She knows her husband would never cheat on her.

The husband, the "money-man," is feeling emotion he has not known in quite a while. He feels wanted, needed, and loved. He feels very young. With her, life is wonderful and he is appreciated for who he is. It is nice to be loved by someone young and beautiful. At home he is taken for granted. He has been the breadwinner for years, the one who has always been there through thick and thin. For the first time in a long time, he knows real intimacy, emotional as well as physical passion.

His own intentions have changed since this whole thing started. He is in love now and really will do whatever is necessary to make this girl happy. He lives to be with her, but he can't leave his wife and children. He tells his lover that he cannot leave them for financial reasons, but it is more than that, and he knows it. He is miserable at home, but still he stays.

Behind the scenes in Nashville, a walletectomy is about to be performed. When the money-man and his girl singer arrive for that first meeting, they are sized up, their intelligence and financial status are estimated, and the facilitator listens to what they have to say. It does not take the Nashvillian long to read between the lines. He tells the money-man, in front of his mistress, that she has what it takes.

"If I really did not feel this way," the hustler says, "I would say so." Then he adds knowingly, "It is very competitive out there, and it is going to take some money to get things rolling."

He puts the money-man on the spot in front of his mistress, forcing a commitment. And so it goes. A great deal of money is spent, times passes, and nothing happens. Finally, the money-man realizes that this could go on forever and withdraws from the arena. Meanwhile, another sucker will be coming along any moment, and so it goes.

The mistress at first believes that the money-man really will leave his family and be with her. Yes, it will cost him some money, but she is worth it. Finally, she realizes that he is not going to leave his wife, so she begins to withdraw emotionally from the relationship and ultimately runs off with someone else, possibly another man she meets in Nashville. The names and some of the details change, but the story is the same. It happens in Nashville every day.

In addition to the obvious crooks, there are literally dozens of well-known and often respected people in the music business here, people who really do not do anything that anyone can pinpoint. It is incredible, but somehow they survive and prosper.

There are others, however, whose dealings are questionable, but who are tolerated nonetheless because their activities create revenue and feed the system. The most notorious crooks are the purveyors of what are known in Nashville as "custom sessions."

The very term itself is hotly controversial within the music community here. Actually, "custom session" refers to any recording endeavor that is not under the auspices of a major record company. Thus a custom session can accurately be anything from a legitimate, union-approved session to a "scab," or nonunion, session.

In a legitimate recording session, a studio is secured, a union contractor is hired, and union musicians are selected. Whoever is bankrolling the enterprise pays the union, and the union in turn pays the musicians. In Nashville, session musicians are booked in three-hour blocks at the hours of 10:00 A.M., 2:00 P.M., 6:00 P.M. and 10:00 P.M. The musicians are paid $36.82 per hour for demo sessions. There is a two-hour minimum required and the session leader receives double scale.

In a three-hour master session, the musicians each receive $220.94 per person for the three hours' work. Again, the leader receives double scale. There is a restriction of fifteen minutes of recorded music imposed by the union. In other words, a three-hour session is not going to result in three hours worth of recorded music.

The union also has a special one-and-a-half-hour master session. The cost is $145.82 per hour for the sidemen and double for the leader. A maximum of seven-and-a-half minutes of recorded music is imposed in this case.

Custom sessions have to some degree received a bad name outside of Nashville due to the duplicity of a few unscrupulous companies and individuals. The TV program "60 Minutes" did a rather scathing report on the dirty end of this otherwise legitimate business.

Let's look at the way it generally works in Nashville. Somebody from out of town wants to record an album or a single. The artist finds a producer who offers to assist the artist for a certain fee. The producer questions the artist and thereby gains some insight into the artist's goals.

Does the artist wish to do demo- or master-quality recording? Does the artist have his own songs or does he need to go around to the publishing companies and try to find some songs that he would like to try? How many songs does the artist wish to record? How many musicians and instruments does he wish to use? Would he rather use his own band?

The producer next determines how much money the artist has available for the project. The producer then estimates what he feels the recording session will cost the artist, based upon the information the artist has provided. If the producer and artist agree to terms, a contract is signed and the artist pays the producer a deposit. The producer lines up the studio and the musicians for a specific date and time and the project is completed.

The artist returns to the hometown with a record he can sell from the bandstand or play for his friends, and everybody is happy. The producer, studio, and musicians have done their best to make this artist sound as good as he can. Everyone has been paid and all is well. No promises have been made. The artist has not been misled in any way. Everything was clearly spelled out in advance in writing and the contract is there for immediate reference if any specific questions should arise. This is how it is supposed to work, and generally speaking, this is how it does work in the majority of cases.

The artist, if he possesses an intelligence at all, can call the musicians' union in Nashville and find out what the musicians will cost. He can call the studio that has been selected and find out what that will cost. It may sound strange, but some people will come to town and record, then later feel as if they had been cheated, even though they agreed to everything and nothing was misrepresented. Some of these same people are very vocal in their discontent and consequently to some degree unfairly impart to Nashville a bad reputation. The ones with the least talent are usually the most dissatisfied. Enough said.

Not let's briefly look at the same scenario from a slightly different perspective. Most aspiring artists who come to record in Nashville hope to become successful and famous. They may say that they merely wish to make a record to sell at home, but the fact is that they secretly hope or even imagine that a famous producer might wander off the street into their session, or that an artist and repertoire (A & R) person from a record company will somehow hear their music and rush out to sign them. It is the overwhelming pervasiveness of this attitude on the part of all aspiring singers that leaves them open for a subtle but effective fleecing. The custom-session producer is in business to make money. In order to do this, he must put together recording sessions, ideally as many as possible.

Operating under some degree of legal scrutiny, the producer must be more circumspect than in the past. He must choose his words very carefully, but the bottom line is that he must close a certain number of deals in order to survive. While promising nothing that is not actually covered in the contract, he can lure the artist into his financial web in other ways.

If the artist is a songwriter, for example, he might say something like, "Listen, this is really very good material. I had no idea that you were this strong as a writer. A good friend of mine runs (some publishing company). I feel certain that he could use this material. In fact, I think that several of these songs would be just right for [famous singer]. But let's see what happens. I think that...well, in my opinion, with your voice and this material, you might be able to get a record deal yourself."

He goes on. "What we need to do is get these songs recorded right, with good musicians in a good studio. At that point, after we have a really good tape, I would be willing to call [some well-known record company head]. He is a very close friend of mine. I can't promise you anything except that he will listen to something if I send it over. I know him, though, he won't even listen to anything unless it is a really good quality master [or demo, depending on how much money the producer is trying to extract]."

By such offhand remarks, ringing with little bells of hope, the producer reels in another sucker. This is all perfectly legal and well within the boundaries of the law, despite the fact that it may very well be unethical.

The next custom session follows the same procedure as the one just mentioned. In this case, the shit gets a little deeper, and more money is involved. The producer again stays just within the limits of the law. He merely offers an extended range of services. He promises to arrange the recording session, have the music mixed and mastered, and get a record pressed. He promises to mail the record to "the radio stations." He may even offer to release the record on his own company's independent label. He tells his prospective client that his label is well known among DJs throughout the nation.

He fails to mention, however, that any record bearing the

label in question is doomed to go directly from the radio station's mailroom to its trash bin in one motion. In short, depending upon the amount of money that the producer is able to extract, he is prepared to furnish a total package to the artist.

Again, all of this is within legal limits. Since more money is involved, the producer is even more anxious to close the deal. The more services he can provide, the more he can pad the bill. The producer is again performing a legitimate service, one that he knows, however, will bear absolutely no fruit whatsoever for his "client." Again, the exact responsibilities of the producer are clearly spelled out in a written contract that protects both parties.

There is nothing, however, that protects the client from the false enthusiasm displayed by the producer and his accomplices. The enthusiasm causes the client to feel hopeful about the outcome, even though there is not a snowball's chance in hell of the project producing anything worthwhile. The producer talks about how the artist can realistically hope to gain recognition in the independent charts and maybe get noticed by "scouts" at the major labels as a result.

The fact is, however, that in the country music business such things very rarely happen, and while it is not impossible, neither is winning the lottery. In country music, as with other professions, you are either in the major leagues or you are not. There is no ground between.

The next step down is the scab session. The producers of these recordings are the most unethical of all. They will say or do almost anything to ensnare an unwary client. They may use a jerry-built studio, an incompetent engineer, and bad or at least inexperienced musicians. They operate outside of the law, often charging exorbitant sums, and are willing to take their chances of being sued at a later date. They want everything they can get out of each deal now and are not concerned with the future. These producers do not work through the musicians' union, although they may actually employ some union musicians. The "system" in Nashville allows these people to operate.

There are approximately thirty-five hundred musicians signed with the Nashville branch of the American Federation of Musicians (Musicians' Local Number 257). There are, however, more musicians wanting to do session work than there are sessions for them to play. In Nashville, many studio musicians suffer the same fate as successful artists. They are in great demand for a time and then suddenly stop getting called, despite the success of their past recordings. There is a definite clique of studio musicians in Nashville who get the majority of the recording studio work. This fact is largely responsible for the frequent observation that "all of the records that come out of Nashville sound the same."

As with artists, very few studio musicians have a successful career at the top for any great length of time. But also, as with artists, there are some who do. Styles change. The country music that is popular today may be something different next year. An excellent musician retains his skill at his chosen work for a long time, but there is no guarantee that he will be able to continue to make a living as a studio musician based solely on his ability in the studio. As with artists, successful musicians last awhile and then are out of fashion. More often than not, there are no reasons. That's just the way it is.

With hundreds of new and unknown musicians in town trying to make the big time, there is a shortage of legitimate work. Many times these unknowns will agree to play for unscrupulous producers in order to survive. In most cases, these musicians are members of the AFM.

In many cases they are not. In addition to being able to survive financially, these who are unknown obtain experience in the studio that may help them later. They are paid less than union scale, but it is always in cash. Union members who get caught playing these nonunion sessions are subject to fines, suspensions, or other disciplinary measures. But most musicians, union or otherwise, would rather work in a studio for less than union scale than not work at all.

Custom sessions are not by their nature an evil. Legitimate custom sessions do provide opportunities for many artists that would not exist otherwise. It is my experience that in the long run, almost every artist who belongs at the top gets there one way or the other anyway. Most people who do get duped by dishonest record producers to a large extent bring it upon themselves.

My advice to anyone planning a custom session is to record all conversations with these producers. If they do not have anything to hide, this should not present a problem. The artist should shop around, getting sample contracts to read at home away from the hype of the producers. On no account should an artist sign anything or hand over any money until he has first returned home and thought about the deal at great length.

Many aspiring artists are led to believe that any hesitation on their part indicates that they are not really serious about their careers. It is this very seriousness that should cause them to evaluate their options. It is in the producer's interest, not the artist's, to close the deal quickly. So many people come to Nashville, and because of impatience, or the expense of hotel rooms and meals, seek to get things done while they are there. In the long run, it is more productive and cheaper to make several trips to Nashville than it is to get roped into a bad deal.

Chapter Nine

Jerry Lee Lewis

Born in Ferriday, Louisiana, in 1935, Jerry Lee Lewis came from a poor, rural, working-class, southern background. That he succeeded at all is miraculous considering the odds against him. He got his start like Elvis, Carl Perkins, Johnny Cash, Roy Orbison, and others at Sam Phillips' Sun Records studio in Memphis in 1956. He went there seeking Sam Phillips but ended up with producer Jack Clement, who recorded four songs initially. Their second recording session yielded "Whole Lot of Shakin'," which launched his career and sold over a million records.

Jerry Lee Lewis is unique in the history of American music. Unlike many of his contemporaries, he actually has had relatively few hit records, and those within a rather brief period of time. "Great Balls of Fire," "Breathless," "High School Confidential," and "Whole Lot of Shakin'" were international hits, but nothing followed that equalled these first offerings, despite lengthy associations with record labels such as Mercury, MCA, Elektra, and others. Statistically, Jerry Lee should have faded into obscurity along with many of the other artists from his era. That he has not done so is due to several factors.

For one, Jerry Lee Lewis is extremely talented. He grew up in Louisiana with cousins Jimmy Swaggart and Mickey Gilley and learned piano from the same woman who taught both of them.

In addition to being an incredible piano player, he brought the piano into the forefront of rock music as a lead instrument. Vocally, time has deepened and enriched his voice to the extent that he is now a better singer than ever before.

Talent, however, does not necessarily have anything to do with success or longevity in the music business. Jerry Lee's success is due more to his uniqueness as an individual and his absolute refusal to compromise under any circumstances than to his talent. He has been attacked, and worse, ignored by the press. He has been denied airplay by disc jockeys and radio stations, persecuted and harassed by the Internal Revenue Service, and often abandoned by the public. In spite of the abuse that he has suffered and incredible personal tragedies such as the loss of two sons, one in a car accident and the other by drowning, he has managed to hold his head up.

Personally, his life has been a constant fight. He has been married half a dozen times, and not happily in most cases. He has been taken advantage of and cheated by a number of business associates, and has suffered severe reversals of fortune. His present wife, Kerrie, told me that he has not received any record royalties on his early hits since 1962. There is no point in going after that money, she says, since the IRS would end up with all of it anyway. Still he survives, and on his own terms.

Jerry Lee Lewis reminds me of a poor but intelligent little boy who goes to sleep hungry and dreams of being a king. He awakens the next morning and finds that it was not a dream, that he really is a king. But he has no idea how to act, and there is nobody to advise him, nobody he can trust. He remembers being poor, cold, and hungry. Now all of that has changed and he does not know why. He has done nothing but be himself, and suddenly people are telling him how great he is. The only thing he can do is act the part of king. In the meantime, there are others who are jealous and would be king themselves. There are still others who are mediocre and seek to destroy him because he is great and they are nothing. And so it goes. If he is arrogant is it any wonder?

On March 1, 1984, I paid Jerry Lee Lewis' so-called manager, Al Embry, $12,000 cash in a brown paper sack for the privilege of adding Jerry Lee Lewis to our agency roster. I doubt that

Jerry Lee Lewis ever saw any of that money. I wanted Jerry Lee
Lewis as a client, so I did not mind paying $12,000. Hell, it
wasn't my money anyway, I had gotten it from Sherwood Cryer.
I most likely could have ended up with Jerry Lee sooner or later
on my own, but time is money, and I wanted Jerry Lee Lewis
that day, not six months or a year further down the road.

This was not my first experience with Jerry Lee Lewis. When
I worked as an agent at the now defunct Nova Agency in 1973,
Chuck Glaser, president of that company, made a deal with
Memphis agent Roy Dean. Jerry Lee then passed from Roy
Dean to Robert Porter to Earl Owens and finally to Al Embry,
who has held the position of manager until the present. Al
prefers the term "Tour Director" to the title of manager.

To hear Al tell the story, he repeatedly drops Jerry Lee as a
client because Jerry Lee owes him money. Then Jerry Lee begs
Al to return as manager until Al finally relents and helps Jerry
Lee straighten out his life once again. The fact of the matter is
that every time the IRS starts digging into the Jerry Lee Lewis
files, Al takes a vacation. When things cool off, Al invariably
shows up again.

I should say a few words about Al, since he is such an integral
part of the Jerry Lee Lewis story. Al Embry in some ways
reminded me of the character Kingfish on the old "Amos 'n'
Andy" show. He did not work in the traditional sense of the
word during the time that we did business together. He often
went for days without showing up at the office. When he
appeared, it was seldom before two in the afternoon. He did,
however, have an office that we provided as part of our deal. I
also gave him a receptionist. It was a prudent move on my part,
since, given his nature, I could have his calls monitored, which I
always did.

Under most circumstances Al Embry is an interesting and
likable person, but his taste in interior decor has never been less
than totally appalling to me. His ideal office consists of a
multicolored shag carpet, some type of pseudo-Spanish
crushed-velvet sofa, and a red velvet hanging lamp, preferably
equipped with a red light bulb. His preference in end tables
runs more toward K Mart than Hepplewhite. He had a round
glass table with a pole running through the center. About

halfway up the pole hung some kind of sparkly globe, encircled in a lampshade made of some type of yarn. He felt comfortable in the equivalent of a Gay Nineties whorehouse.

One thing about Al, though, he knows how to make money. As I said, I paid him $12,000 for Jerry Lee once, and another $10,000 later; in addition to $7,500 for Fats Domino. Actually, I got the idea of paying him from Eddie Rhines, a Nashville talent agent. Eddie and I used to go to lunch from time to time at a dump downtown on Church Street called Billy's Burgers. It had formerly been an old Krystal restaurant. I would never have selected the place on my own, but Eddie liked it.

Anyway, we would go there occasionally and Eddie would tell me what he was up to. I would do him a favor from time to time by booking Jerry Lee Lewis into Gilley's. I was able to do this because I could get Sherwood Cryer on the phone and Eddie could not. Eddie began to operate a talent agency called Board Brothers, with its principal clients being Johnny Paycheck and Jerry Lee Lewis.

In any event, as soon as we got In Concert rolling, I decided that I wanted to represent Jerry Lee Lewis. I called Al and he said that he had promised Eddie a certain amount of time, but that Eddie was just not able to deliver Jerry Lee Lewis the dates that he needed.

At this point, I had known Al Embry for ten years, and had even tried to have him hire me, back in 1974. I was not, however, fully aware of the degree to which he could be moved by money. When we had our initial meeting, I concentrated more on the job that our agency could do for Jerry Lee Lewis than on the fact that I was prepared to pay off Al Embry. For one thing, I knew that given our abilities collectively as agents and our enthusiasm for the artist, we could, in fact, do a much better job than any other agency in representing Jerry Lee.

I had discussed the payoff in advance with Sherwood Cryer. His feeling was that I should do what I wanted to do. For the most part that was always Sherwood Cryer's attitude toward In Concert. I appreciated his confidence in my abilities but sometimes I would have appreciated a little more direction.

I offered Al $10,000 and he countered with $12,000. At that point I figured that we were rich, so I said OK. The deal that we agreed upon was that In Concert would get Jerry Lee Lewis for at least a year. Al tried to ease the pain by telling me how easy it was to book Jerry Lee Lewis and that Jerry Lee really preferred for Al to book him exclusively, but that Al was just too busy with other things to be able to fully devote his time to Jerry Lee. I knew that was a bunch of crap but listened patiently nonetheless. Al also wanted to receive some kind of percentage in addition to the $12,000.

He was already being paid by Jerry Lee on the other end anyway, so I held the line at $12,000 with no additional percentage from us. I also agreed to provide him with an office and use of our receptionist. All deposits would be held in escrow and controlled by In Concert. With an artist like Jerry Lee Lewis, an agent had better take his commissions out of deposits or the agency does not get paid. This arrangement suited Al because, as it turned out, most of the time we withheld money that Jerry Lee owed Al as well. One thing was certain, if Jerry Lee got the money first, it was gone for good.

My decision to pay Al proved to have been a wise one. We made $45,000 in commissions on Jerry Lee that year, 1984, even though we did not start booking him until April. There was a little grumbling around the office about the fact that I had paid Al Embry $12,000 cash, had no receipt, and did not have a contract with the artist.

I might have taken a deep breath and swallowed real hard once or twice, but I did not lose any sleep over the transaction. Al had given me his word that we would be prorating the money that I had given him on a monthly basis. In other words, if for some reason Jerry Lee went off the deep end or had a falling-out with Al, Al would repay In Concert $1,000 a month for however many months less than a year remained.

I was hotheaded and I did not think that Al would mess with me. I knew beyond any doubt that Al would not cross Sherwood Cryer. While my experiences with Sherwood were always pleasant, others were not so fortunate. He had a reputation for taking care of problems personally and was said to be violent. In any case, Sherwood Cryer provided the cash, and I made certain that he and Linda Edwards were both in my office as witnesses at the time the money was handed over to Al. The cash itself was damp and moldy, as if it had been buried underground. Sherwood Cryer has a bomb or tornado shelter in his backyard in Pasadena, Texas. It has always been speculated that he has millions of dollars stashed there.

I was very pleased with the acquisition of Jerry Lee Lewis as a client. In Concert had only been in business four months, and in addition to the acts we had started with, we had managed to pick up Mickey Gilley, Johnny Lee, Jerry Lee Lewis, and Gene Watson. We were kicking ass and everybody in the business knew it. All I cared about was getting results. How I got them was of absolutely no consequence to me. So I had bought an act. So what? Agencies do that all the time. I did know from Eddie's fate, however, that regardless of what I had paid Al, I would not be able to keep Jerry Lee Lewis as a client unless In Concert did a better job representing him than anyone else had or could do.

I must say that I did feel a slight twinge of remorse about stealing one of my best friends' only major clients. I knew, however, that Eddie Rhines would not be able to hold on to him much longer. Eddie was a little pissed off about the situation, but he soon got over it. After all, that's the way business works in Nashville.

The question from some of my competitors was why I wanted to represent an act like Jerry Lee Lewis at all. He had a well-earned reputation for skipping shows on no notice. He is an egomaniac, a drug abuser, and a heavy drinker. He has constant problems with the IRS. In spite of his difficulties, however, he is an extremely interesting man. He has been married nearly as often as Henry VIII, and two of his wives had died prematurely. His fourth wife was found dead at the bottom of a Memphis swimming pool in 1982, and his next one, Shawn Stephens, died under mysterious circumstances on August 23, 1983.

He also has a fascinating financial history, having made and squandered millions. He has been bankrupt several times and yet always manages to have expensive cars and a magnificent residence. He also has an incredible ability to persuade suckers to give him large sums of money for the rather nebulous honor of being his manager for a time. He likes old cars. He considers himself to be above the law, and has shot or shot at people he regards as friends.

Starmaker Dick Blake checks out Tammy Wynette's talents backstage at a show featuring Tammy, the Statler Brothers, and Ronnie Milsap. (Author's collection)

At a softball game during Fan Fair 1979, an annual week-long celebration which brings over twenty-five thousand fans to Music City. Left to right: Louise Mandrell, Irby Mandrell, Barbara Mandrell, and agent Eddie Rhines. This was before Mandrell's highly popular TV show. I worked with Eddie Rhines during this period, but stole Jerry Lee Lewis from him a couple of years later. (Author's collection)

Charly McClain was doing well on her own before she teamed up with Mickey Gilley in 1983, and recorded a successful string of duet hits. The tour dates she played with Gilley, however, did not do so well. Her remark "He's old enough to be my father" irritated self-proclaimed ladies' man Mickey Gilley. (Courtesy of Epic Records, Nashville)

Tammy Wynette. "Stand By Your Man." She stood by George Jones as long as she could, married again, and then divorced, but finally settled down with George Richey, one of the few competent artist managers in Nashville. (Author's collection)

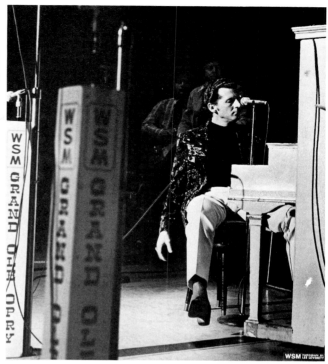

"The Killer," Jerry Lee Lewis, in a rare appearance at the Grand Ole Opry in the early 1970s. (Les Leverett, courtesy of WSM)

Left to right: Jerry Lee Lewis, Dick Blake, and Al Embry. Al prefers the term tour director over that of manager. He has outlasted all other pretenders to the management throne. I paid him $12,000 cash to bring Jerry Lee to In Concert. (Author's collection)

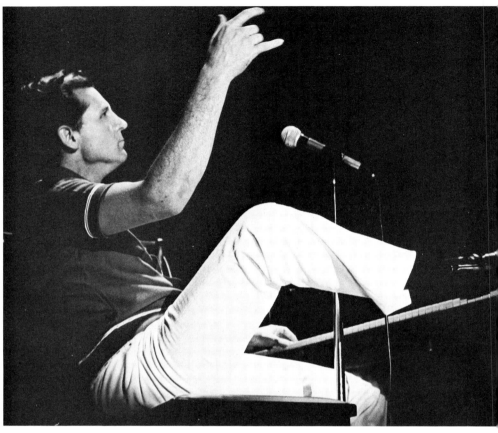

Jerry Lee Lewis. The Master at work. First draft for the Rock-and-Roll Hall of Fame. The living King of Rock and Roll. Everything that has ever been said about him is true, but that is just the beginning. (Author's collection)

Johnny Paycheck. Formerly
known as Mr. Lovemaker,
he had shed his clean-cut
image by 1977 in favor of the
"outlaw" look. This publicity
photo was a posed shot, but he
ended up in an Ohio prison
ten years later. (Courtesy of
Epic Records, Nashville)

Johnny Paycheck, 1987. He came by my office from time to time, usually for the
purpose of telling me to ignore everything his manager or road manager might
have said. Mr. Hag told his story. (Author's collection)

George "No Show" Jones. Considered by many to be the greatest country singer of all time. The license plate on his big Lexus (Toyota) reads "No Show I." He certainly earned his title. (Courtesy Epic Records, Nashville)

George and Tammy. Once they were the sweethearts of country music. After their breakup, George sang "Grand Tour," a song which many believe to be his finest offering. (Author's collection)

Randy Travis. He rescued country music from the crap that was being released at the time. Note the prominently displayed wedding ring. He married longtime manager Lib Hatcher. (Aaron Rappaport, courtesy of Warner Brothers Records, Nashville)

Ricky Skaggs, aka "Picky Ricky." For moral reasons, he refused to play where alcohol was served. He was also opposed to tobacco, but made an exception for Marlboro when they paid him twice what he usually received. (Jim McGuire, courtesy of Epic Records, Nashville)

James Brown, aka Mr. Dynamite, Mr. Please, Please, the King of Soul, the Godfather. "Mine is the only face known worldwide. . . . I am greater than Elvis. Elvis never went to Africa." (Clayton Call)

Jerry Lee Lewis, Fats Domino, and James Brown. In Concert represented all three at the time this picture was taken during the induction ceremonies of the first Rock-and-Roll Hall of Fame in New York. (Author's collection)

I took on Jerry Lee Lewis for several reasons. In the first place, I felt that it was a good gamble financially. I knew that he was likely to skip a few dates here and there, but I felt that with the size and ability of our staff, as well as our credibility with the talent buyers, we would be able to book Jerry Lee in three- and four-date blocks for good money. There was no question that he needed to reestablish his credibility with the buyers. It would take time, but I felt that we could do it, that we could turn him into a big money-maker for us.

I also liked having him for a client because he is outspoken, controversial, and eccentric. He has always had press coverage and has always been interesting. For example, Jerry Lee came by the office one day in his new Rolls-Royce convertible. It was metallic blue with factory wire wheels. This was not enough, however; he had to have a continental kit, one of those big tires stuck to the back bumper. Rolls-Royce understandably drew the line here, so Jerry Lee had some junky continental kit put on his otherwise beautiful car. He also had a red Corvette convertible with a continental kit, and told me, "As soon as people know it's my car, they'll all be putting continental kits on their cars."

I also considered representing him to be a challenge. He needed money, so I had no doubt that he would work as many dates as we could get him as long as the money was right.

There was also another reason for representing him, which to me was every bit as important as the financial considerations, and that was the fact that most of my friends, especially those out of town, held Jerry Lee Lewis in veneration. It was an ego thing for me. None of my friends ever asked me about or for that matter even mentioned acts like Charly McClain or Gene Watson. Jerry Lee Lewis is the ultimate rocker, skinny, looking like he was loaded on dope or alcohol, always in trouble with so-called authority, married half a dozen times, living life on his own terms. I would not care to emulate all of these traits in my own life, but they are fine for Jerry Lee Lewis.

I had booked Jerry Lee Lewis for the Nova Agency in the early seventies. I was amazed by him even then. He had all of these sinister-looking guys hanging around him. One of the first shows I booked him on was in Gainesville, Florida, at an old theater that had been converted to a musical showcase. Jerry

Lee rocked the joint, and during the second show he took off his shirt, jumped up on the piano, slammed the lid up and down, and tore up the stool. I was hooked.

Later on, I booked him at the Exit/In in Nashville during October of 1974. It was a small club, and the atmosphere was electric with anticipation. I could actually feel the energy. It honestly seemed to me that if someone had waved a knife through the air that it would have produced sparks.

When he finally came through the kitchen door and out into the club, the place went wild. Halfway to the piano, some woman slithered up to him and threw her arms around his neck. They started kissing and he grabbed her ass. They just stood there, writhing around. He broke away from her, went to the piano, and proceeded to rock the house down.

In a few minutes, his sister, Linda Gail, made an appearance in a long, tight, bright blue sequined dress. She was wagging it around like some kind of hula dancer.

It was all very erotic, but also very, very, decadent, like something out of a Tennessee Williams play. It was a picture from life's other side. This was a strictly southern phenomenon. The South is the birthplace of country music, jazz, black gospel, and rock and roll. The South is much more than a mere geographical area, it's a state of mind, and Jerry Lee Lewis is one of its greatest examples.

Booking Jerry Lee Lewis is not easy, even in the best of times. He is not a popular act for fair buyers. They are reluctant to take a chance on whether or not he will show up. It might be more accurate to say that for the most part, they do not use him at all. It's difficult for a responsible agent to put his reputation on the line with a fair producer, someone who represents many different fairs and selects their entertainment. To burn one of these buyers can result in the loss of hundreds of thousands of dollars.

If a producer wanted a date for Jerry Lee Lewis for one of his fairs, which was rare, we always apprised him of the risk factor, which fluctuated like the stock market from day to day. If he had been making his dates recently, there was still no guarantee whatsoever that he would make a date three months later.

At this time, Jerry Lee was earning between $10,000 and

$15,000 a night. The best assurance a buyer could have with Jerry Lee Lewis was by paying him at least $15,000 with one or more other dates for that amount of money to go along with it. I openly told buyers that I could sell them a date on Jerry Lee Lewis for $10,000, but if they wanted to be sure he would be there it would be in their best interests to pay $15,000.

In addition, Jerry Lee did not want any two-show dates, no matter how much money was involved. If he had been filling up ten-thousand-seat auditoriums, it would have been no problem. As it was, Jerry Lee Lewis generally played clubs or small theaters. In most cases, the venue was small and he needed to do two shows in order to get his price. In some cases, particularly on California tours or on weeknights that tied in with other big-money one-show dates, he could be persuaded to do two shows. At other times, under the same circumstances, he would elect to do a one-show tie-in date as opposed to doing two shows at the same place for considerably more money. In this as in other respects, he was often erratic and unpredictable.

On stage he was just as unpredictable. He still is. To the best of my knowledge he has no set show, as do most artists. He plays what he feels like playing when he feels like playing it. Often he stops in the middle of a song for no reason at all. At other times he changes songs abruptly without telling the band members, and they better change with him or he is likely to stop right onstage in the middle of the song and give them a good cursing. At still other times, he plays to himself, seemingly oblivious to the audience.

On some occasions he curses the crowd profanely if they request a particular song. He sometimes gives performances that are unenthusiastic and actually downright boring. He is just as likely to play for thirty minutes as for two hours, depending on his mood at the moment. I frequently received complaints from buyers that he only did a thirty-minute show when the contract called for fifty minutes.

After the show, he was quite likely to go down the street to some dive or even to the buyer's competitor and play two or three hours for nothing. At the same time, Jerry Lee Lewis more often than not does incredible shows.

There was also the issue of deposits. He required a 50 percent deposit on all dates, no exceptions. There were several reasons for this. In the deal that was worked out with the IRS at one point, a certain percentage was held out of the deposit money that came to our office. The Feds knew that if he got all of the money on the night of the show they would never see any of it. Also, Jerry Lee frequently needed the deposit money so that he could afford to get to the next date.

There were several problems for us as far as deposits were concerned. There are some buyers, organizations in particular, that simply do not pay deposits. Most state fairs and public functions do not. With Jerry Lee there were almost no exceptions. He did not care who the buyer was, he required a deposit of 50 percent. Sometimes we were able to get deposits from buyers who had never paid them before. More often, however, we simply lost dates that we would otherwise have secured.

There was also public backlash against Jerry Lee from time to time. We encountered some of that when we took him on in April of 1984, after the mysterious death of his wife Shawn in August 1983. Respectable buyers further distanced themselves from Jerry Lee Lewis at this point.

We tried less experienced talent buyers, explaining to them that all of the negative press made people want to see him more than they would have otherwise. This was true to some degree, but overall the bad press in that particular instance made him harder to sell.

Jerry Lee was a strange dresser. Like his tour director, Al, he is almost always attired from head to toe in polyester. When he performs, and this is still true, it is generally in some pastel polyester tuxedo with a ruffled shirt. Usually, after he gets going he takes off his jacket, vest, and bow tie, and rolls up his shirtsleeves as far as they will go. He generally wears black patent leather cowboy boots with pointed toes. The heels decline from the back of the boots in such a way that they are situated almost directly under the center of his feet.

I never could figure out how he walked with those boots on. I always told Al that he ought to get Jerry Lee to dress more appropriately onstage, but inasmuch as Al himself prefers the same kind of clothes, he did not understand what I was talking about. If someone ever dropped a match on either one of them they would melt in a flash.

Jerry Lee likes to play dumps that are patronized for the most part by the elite of the lower socioeconomic strata. There are two joints in particular in the Memphis area where he frequently performs, sometimes for the door, sometimes for the hell of it. One is located in south Memphis and is called Hernando's Hideaway. Why anyone would voluntarily go to that place is beyond my comprehension, but Jerry Lee likes it. The first and only time I went there was for his birthday party in the fall of 1985. Bruce Shelton, my West Coast agent, and I flew down to Memphis and attended the all-night affair. We stayed for about three hours and then went to my friend Bard Selden's house in Hollywood, Mississippi, and spent the night.

The Hideaway had been filled with smoke, drunks, and beehive-coiffed women, most of whom were rather fat and hard-looking. My conception of hell is to be in a place like that for eternity. Bruce and I did, however, get some good ideas as to what we should wear to Jerry Lee's next birthday party.

I had flown down to Memphis with one of my girlfriends back in the summer for a weekend getaway. At the Peabody Hotel I had seen a Jerry Lee Lewis imitator playing in the lounge. His name was Jason D. Williams. He was so much like Lewis, he could have been the son of the Killer himself. It was not hard to imagine. He looked remarkably similar to the way Jerry Lee looked in his younger days. He sounded like him vocally, and he displayed the same virtuosity on the keyboard. From what I could tell, he seemed to be as big an egomaniac as Jerry Lee Lewis, lacking, of course, the credentials to support that position. When the 1986 birthday party came around Jason D. Williams made an appearance, but I am getting ahead of myself.

The 1986 birthday party took place at the Vapors Club in Memphis. It is perhaps Memphis' most famous night spot. Long before this party rolled around Bruce and I decided that we should be the best-dressed people there. With this in mind, I purchased the trashiest 100 percent polyester suit that I had ever seen from the Goodwill store. The suit coat was a textured black with wavy raised white zigzag lines all through it.

The pants were of the same material, only black except for the belt loops, which were *x*'s of black and white, just like the coat. In addition the tops of the pants pockets, front and rear, were also highlighted with the same crap. The most distinguishing aspect of this ensemble was the lining of the coat itself, a print of bright, multicolored balloons against a white background.

Bruce, not to be outdone, dressed in a red-and-white-checked polyester sport coat, which resembled the tablecloth at an Italian restaurant. To complement this jacket, he wore some plaid pants that absolutely contrasted with his jacket. We both wore sunglasses and Bruce donned his Bing Crosby hat, which has become his trademark. We considered ourselves ambassadors from Nashville.

Thus attired, we strutted into the Nashville airport. As we expected, we immediately became the objects of many conversations, most of which we deemed to be favorable, although a few not so charming comments such as "Who are those fucking idiots?" were overheard.

Several people wanted to know where we were headed. We told them that we were Jerry Lee Lewis' agents and that we were on the way to his fiftieth birthday party in Memphis. Invariably the matter of our attire was raised, to which we responded by saying that everyone there would be similarly dressed, as indeed, for the most part, they were. Not only did we not stand out from the crowd, we were hardly noticed. In fact, the second thing Jerry Lee said was, "I like that coat, Killer!" The first thing he said was, "The last time I saw you, you were high!"

He was right. Melinda, a girlfriend at the time, had gone with me to see him perform the past summer at a short-lived joint called Andy Jack's on the wrong side of town. We had smoked a powerful reefer before we went to see him play. After that, I had wanted to get her back to her place and in bed without wasting any time, so I just stuck my head in the dressing-room door to pay my respects and left.

His memory is truly incredible. He still never fails to ask me about an old Lincoln convertible that he once saw parked outside my office several years ago.

Back to the party. I am never very comfortable around Jerry Lee Lewis. I do not see how anyone could be. He is such a volatile person. He can be laughing and cutting up one minute, having a great time, and then for some reason known only to himself, change his personality completely. The smile vanishes and he becomes hostile.

We were all sitting around the dressing room at the Vapors that evening before his first show. There were probably seven or eight people in the room, including some members of the press, who themselves were very much ill at ease. One of them asked Jerry Lee some questions. Jerry Lee was being sarcastic, laughing and throwing things.

Suddenly, for no apparent reason, he looked over at Bruce, who sat quietly by himself in the far corner of the room, minding his own business. Jerry Lee's smile faded instantly. It was as if he suddenly became oblivious to everyone else in the room. He glared at Bruce. "What's so funny, Bruce?" he asked with deadly seriousness. "You laughed! I want to know what you are laughing at!"

"Nothing," Bruce replied, forcing a smile.

But Jerry Lee was not satisfied and kept taunting Bruce. At just the moment when I was sure that Jerry Lee was going to go after Bruce, he dropped the matter as if nothing had happened, and began clowning again and showing off for all of us.

This event had rather a chilling effect on me, because I realized how very easily it could have ended differently. Al later told me that Bruce was once supposed to have made a drug connection for the Killer at a date in Kentucky and had failed to do so. After that, according to Al, Jerry Lee did not look as fondly upon Bruce as he had before. As I said, Jerry Lee has an incredible memory.

Jerry Lee did his first set at the birthday party to a packed house. After that, he returned to the dressing room, and so did I. I had had enough of that drunken, smoke-filled place and just wanted to go back to the hotel and get some sleep. I was feeling unusually lonely and just wanted to be by myself. Bard Selden and his wife came in to say good night, and as they opened the dressing-room door I heard music. The band had started playing again. I heard someone say that Jason D. Williams was onstage.

Jerry Lee went nuts and poked his finger right in Al's face and said, "Is that son of a bitch playing, Al? I want you to get his ass off that stage now! You hear!"

Bruce and I went up to the stage with Al. The crowd was loving it. Here was this imposter playing Jerry Lee Lewis songs with Jerry Lee's band at Jerry Lee's own birthday party. I could not help but respect the kid's audacity. He was good, in fact, too damn good.

When I had seen him at the Peabody Hotel he had not been playing with a band, and was still great. I did nothing to assist Al in any way. Let him deal with it. Finally they got the imposter off the stage. Bruce and I had seen enough madness for one night and returned to the hotel. We flew back to Nashville the first thing the next morning, glad to be home.

Jerry Lee constantly kept us amused, tearing up hotel rooms and skipping dates. Bruce and I were sitting around in my office one morning and Judy's voice came over the box, saying that there was some guy on the phone from Florida and that Jerry Lee had trashed the hotel room. I put him on the speakerphone, intending to have a little fun with him. This man was very courteous and pleasant, with a good sense of humor. I had expected him to be angry and therefore intended to play with his mind. Our conversation went more or less as follows.

Hotel Manager: "When the maid went to clean up Mr. Lewis' room this morning, she found quite a mess. It seems Mr. Lewis tore the place up."

Myself: "Sir, there must be some mistake. Either someone broke into his room after he left or your maid must have gotten the room numbers confused. Jerry Lee Lewis is a fine Christian man and he is, despite his reputation, constitutionally incapable of such a wanton and senseless act of destruction. It is, sir, completely against his nature."

Hotel Manager: "No, it was his room all right."

Myself: "Well, what damage actually occurred?"

Hotel Manager: "Several syringes were stuck into the macramé wall decorations. The sofa had been overturned as well, and someone had slashed it and pulled out some of the stuffing. All of the plants had been dumped on the floor. It looks like someone punched several holes in the wall with their fists. Several spoons were bent double, I really don't understand that, and it looks like somebody vomited on the wall."

Myself: "That is incredible." [*Shocked!*]

Hotel Manager: "It's not really as bad as it looked at first. The maid has pretty well cleaned the place already and maintenance is patching up the holes in the wall right now. About the only real problem is the sofa, and that was made locally."

I had intended to give this guy some bullshit, but he was so nice and calm about it all that I ended up apologizing for his inconvenience and asked him to send me some pictures and told him to let us know the damages and we would send him a check.

Situations like that happened with some frequency. When we told Al about this, he said, "Why does Jerry do that? I tell him, 'Jerry, you don't need to do that.'"

Al then related another recent story that we had not heard. Again, they were in a hotel suite and were walking down the hallway to catch the elevator in order to check out. At the last moment Jerry Lee said that he had forgotten something in the room and told Al that he would meet him at the desk in a few minutes.

Al went down and Jerry Lee returned to the room and stuffed a washcloth down the drain of the wet bar and turned the water on full blast. He then left the room, locking the door behind him, and met Al back at the registration desk downstairs, saying nothing to Al about the incident. It cost over $800 to have the carpet replaced. When Al later asked him why he had done that, Jerry Lee replied that he had ordered two syrups at breakfast and room service had only brought him one.

One of our last experiences with Jerry Lee Lewis at In Concert occurred at the Mid-South Fair in Memphis in 1987. I had been working on that date quite a while, hoping to get it set so that I would have another good excuse to party in Memphis and relax in Mississippi. The date was finally set with the fair for $15,000 and contracts were sent. By this time, Jerry Lee was again in heavy trouble with the IRS and it was causing problems at dates. I guess that it had some kind of interoffice memo that instructed all IRS agents nationwide to contact the Memphis office if they heard it advertised that Jerry Lee Lewis was scheduled to play a date anywhere in the country.

The IRS could then rush up to the place of performance and put a levy upon the promoter and the auditorium, meaning that from that moment on they could not pay, give, hold out, or in any other way deal with or handle money targeted for Jerry Lee Lewis. For a while, this had been no problem for us or for Jerry

Lee Lewis, because by the time the IRS heard the advertising, we had already been paid in full. There was nothing it could do about it. It was certainly after Jerry Lee Lewis, however. At that time he owed it around $1,700,000. It was obvious that the IRS was never going to get that money, and it was our opinion that it knew that and wanted to make an example out of him by simply putting him out of business.

A company called Killer, Inc., had been established in 1984 "for the services of" Jerry Lee Lewis. The existence of this company had made it possible for him to work from 1984 until midway through 1987. Finally, Jerry Lee quit paying the IRS altogether under that arrangement, so it pulled out all stops in its attempts to get him. I asked Al about it and he said that with all the money and interest Jerry Lee owed, the harder he worked, the more taxes were due. In other words, no matter what Jerry Lee paid on the account, it was growing faster than he could keep up with, so finally he just said, "Hell with it!"

As long as Killer, Inc., had been operative, Jerry Lee was able to work shows without interference from the IRS. Now it was going to try to stop him from working at all. Jerry Lee's wife Kerrie had told me over the phone that Jerry Lee had done exactly as agreed with Killer, Inc., and was all paid up, but that the lawyers had stolen all of the money.

In any case, there was absolutely no doubt whatsoever that as soon as the IRS heard about the Mid-South Fair date there were going to be some problems. I explained this to the people at the fair in very clear terms at the outset. My contract was mailed to them on June 5, 1987. It called for a $7,500 deposit immediately with another $7,500 due prior to performance upon demand, day of show. The contract was between the Mid-South Fair and Killer, Inc., for the services of Jerry Lee Lewis.

Between the time that the contract was sent and the date of the show, Killer, Inc., had been abandoned. Al warned me to get that other $7,500 in my hands before the IRS got wind of the show. I repeatedly warned the fair's people that they should go ahead and send in the rest of the money. I told them that if the IRS showed up at the fair and prevented Jerry Lee from getting the rest of the money that there would not be any show at all.

On Monday, September 28, 1987, the IRS placed a levy on the

Mid-South Fair. About an hour later they did the same thing to In Concert. This meant that neither one of us, the fair or In Concert, could handle any money for Jerry Lee Lewis from that point forward.

I immediately contacted Kevin Nicholas at the IRS in Memphis, who was in charge of Jerry Lee's account. I was talking to him on one phone and Kerrie Lewis on the other. The bottom line was that it could have been worked out, but Jerry Lee would end up with less than $5,000 out of the $15,000 fee.

It would seem that for a man who was almost flat broke, it would have been worth the short drive to Memphis to pick up that money.

Such, however, was not the case. In fact, I received a call from several of the directors of the fair, who held the phone to the television for an interview with Jerry Lee Lewis on the ten o'clock news. This was still two days before the date was scheduled to play.

On TV Jerry Lee said that he would be glad to play the Mid-South Fair but that he had not been asked. He acted as if he knew nothing about it at all. It was incredible. He was lying through his teeth. It was typical, though, just one more insane incident in a lifetime of insanity. I was not angry at Jerry Lee over the incident. If the fair's people had done what I had told them to do there would have been no problem. As far as the IRS was concerned, I was very surprised that it had not put a levy on us much earlier than it did.

From my position as president of In Concert, a $12,000 under-the-table deal had netted us quite a bit of money over a three-and-a-half-year period. We had done business with Jerry Lee Lewis throughout that period against overwhelming odds. It is sad to think how much money we all could have made if we had not been faced with so many unnecessary obstacles. We made money, but more important, we had a good time. There was always some new challenge, another moron to be reckoned with, or some other problem, but it was never boring. There was, is, and shall remain but one Jerry Lee Lewis, and I consider it my greatest honor as an agent to have been able to represent him. He is the living king of rock and roll.

Chapter Ten

Fats Domino

T here had been good and bad times with Jerry Lee Lewis and with Al Embry as well. In one of the up periods, Al Embry started talking about Fats Domino, saying that he'd met with him and was putting together a deal to handle all of his dates. In all probability this meant that Al was fishing for a deal with me. I sent Bruce to New Orleans with Al to visit Fats in person and to make sure that everything was on the up and up. After some further conversations I agreed to give Al $7,500 and 2 percent of the gross. I would have preferred not to have given Al that 2 percent, but I was anxious to make a deal. We set a price on Fats somewhere between $12,500 and $15,000 a night.

Antoine "Fats" Domino had turned fifty-seven when we began to represent him. He was born in New Orleans in 1928, learned to play the piano early, and developed his own unique vocal style, which brought him recognition even in the Crescent City, and area overflowing with legendary musicians and singers. He was discovered at the age of twenty-one by local bandleader David Bartholomew while playing a joint called the Hideaway. He was signed to Imperial Records in 1953 and a string of hits resulted. "Walking to New Orleans," "My Girl Josephine," "I'm Walkin'," "Ain't It a Shame," "Whole Lotta Loving," "Blueberry Hill," and others became American standards.

Fats Domino was not on the cutting edge of rock and roll. He was not a rebel. He was, however, a consistent hitmaker and eventually sold over sixty million records for labels like Imperial, ABC, and Mercury. When the first inductees for the Rock and Roll Hall of Fame were announced, Fats Domino was among that number, as were Jerry Lee Lewis and James Brown, both of whom we were representing then at In Concert.

The addition of Fats to our roster proved a big plus for the agency. On the other hand, with professional jealousies being what they are in Nashville, we were under constant attack as a result of representing black artists. Competitors frequently told our country artists that In Concert was getting out of the country music business altogether and even went so far as to say that I did not like country music. I dismissed these rumors whenever they came to my attention, but I am sure that they took their toll.

As agent for the western part of the country, Bruce Shelton quickly set a California tour for Fats Domino in August 1985. Many of these dates were played with Jerry Lee Lewis, and some of them were played with Ricky Nelson. I sent Bruce out on the road to keep an eye on things. This was the first time Fats had played California in over twenty years and was considered to be a big deal. He played the Memorial Auditorium in Sacramento, the Concord Pavilion, the Universal Amphitheater, and other dates in Escondido, Fresno, and Colton. The tour ended at the Sands in Las Vegas.

Fats didn't like to work, and after his California run the only other dates we could persuade him to accept were April 11 and 12, 1986, at Gilley's club in Texas. Booking him wasn't difficult, but getting him to play dates was another matter altogether. This problem most likely resulted from the fact that Fats, unlike so many of his contemporaries, was financially well off and could afford not to perform too often. He preferred to spend most of his time at his home in New Orleans. As with Jerry Lee Lewis during that period, we cleared the dates on Fats through Al Embry.

In spite of the problems, skipped dates, and occasional lawsuits over Jerry Lee Lewis, we never lost any money other than missed commissions. Such, unfortunately, was not the case with Fats Domino.

Around the end of July 1985, our Northeast agent, Clyde Masters, made a deal with Monarch Entertainment Bureau for Fats Domino and Jerry Lee Lewis to appear at the Ritz Theatre in New York on October 18 and the Meadowlands in East Rutherford, New Jersey, the next day. I called Al Embry in California to get the two dates approved, since he was on the road with Fats Domino. Fats was to receive $10,000 plus a percentage at the Ritz. He was to earn $15,000 at the Meadowlands. In Concert sent contracts for Jerry Lee Lewis and Fats Domino to Monarch. The contracts were returned to us signed by John Scher of Monarch. They were immediately forwarded to Fats Domino for his signature. The contracts were returned to us unsigned by Fats with a note in Fats' own handwriting dated October 10, 1985, which said:

> Al, I am sorry, we did not come to an agreement on these dates. I did not o.k. these dates.
>
> Still your friend
Fats Domino
>
> P.S. Please stop the advertisement.

I tried to reach Al. Unable to get him, I decided to call Fats. In the meantime I phoned John Scher at Monarch and told him that there was a problem but that I was getting it worked out. I told him the truth, exactly what had happened, but he was not happy about it. When I finally reached Fats he said that Al had never mentioned the dates to him and that he could not play them. I explained the gravity of the situation, but he remained unmoved. He was nice enough about it, but he refused to play. It was that simple. I hoped that Al could persuade him to change his mind, but he couldn't.

I called John Scher and told him that Fats was not going to make his dates. He threatened to sue, as I knew he would. I told him that Fats was not coming because Monarch had failed to fulfill the contract by not sending cashier's checks for deposits. According to Al, this was the real reason that Fats was not going to do the dates. Scher said that his company checks were good and that we had received a 50 percent deposit on both dates as agreed upon initially. I replied that the contracts had called for cashier's checks. John Scher had taken the liberty of changing the contracts without authorization, a fact that was unacceptable to Fats Domino.

I did call my bank. The checks from Monarch had not cleared yet and there was no way of finding out exactly where they were within the banking system. I told him that Fats was not going to do his shows and that there was nothing I could do about t.

He again informed me that he intended to sue all of us. I told him that he was also in violation of the contract with Jerry Lee Lewis for the same reason, and that Jerry Lee would not take a company check from anybody. I told John that I would advance Jerry Lee the money from my own account to cover his deposit check, since there was not time for the check to clear the bank before the date of the show. If I had not done so Jerry Lee would have skipped the date. The contracts on both Jerry Lee and Fats clearly specified cashier's checks or bank wires.

The situation with Fats was beyond my control and I was very clear about that with John Scher. I did not feel that In Concert had been negligent. In return for advancing Jerry Lee Lewis his 50 percent deposit I told John that I wanted him to agree not to sue us over the situation with Fats Domino. I was really trying to help him, given the circumstances. His reaction, predictably, was not pleasant.

Fats did not make the dates but Jerry Lee Lewis did, solely as a result of my advancing him deposit money from the In Concert escrow account.

Monarch did sue In Concert International in the United States District Court for the District of New Jersey. They sued Al Embry, Clyde Masters, Fats Domino, and myself, individually. It also charged me under the RICO statute seeking treble damages.

I felt like shouting, "Now gimme some bass on those 88's." I had to hire an expensive lawyer to prove that I was not a gangster. Eventually the suits were dropped against all of us individually but only after spending around $20,000 on legal fees. Finally, my attorney advised me to settle out of court with Monarch.

I was reluctant to do this because I felt that legally we could beat Monarch in court since it had in fact violated the contracts.

I wanted the jurisdiction of the case moved to Tennessee but was unable to get this done. If I countersued I would most likely win, but under New Jersey law the most I could win would have been the lost commission of $2,500. To win this small amount would have cost me an additional $20,000. I believe we ended up paying Monarch around $12,000.

When the interrogatories began flying back and forth, Fats answered for the most part by saying that he did not know anything about the dates. He denied that there was any written or oral agreement pertaining to the shows in question. He said, "There was no binding agreement because Monarch Entertainment Bureau and John Scher changed the terms of my standard contract, refused to send a deposit by certified or cashier's funds, returned the contract late." He felt that he was justified in failing to appear because Monarch had changed the contracts and sent them back late.

Monarch alleged that Fats Domino never saw the contracts and never agreed to the dates. It was its position that we never had any intention of getting Fats to sign the contracts or play the dates. It never suggested any motives for our actions. How the hell were we supposed to make any money if the artists we represented did not perform?

The bottom line, in my opinion, was that Al Embry had dropped the ball out of sheer laziness. He told me over the phone from California that the dates on Jerry Lee Lewis and Fats Domino were OK, that he had asked Fats about them personally. Based upon his assurance we sent the contracts to Monarch. We certainly would not have sent them otherwise.

What I think really happened is that Fats forgot about the dates and that after he returned home to New Orleans he did not want to go out again for a while. By Al's own admission, Al never spoke to him or reminded him about the dates after the California tour was over. Knowing Fats, Al should have touched base with him. Al did not even speak with Fats about these dates until the contracts were returned unsigned. A couple of courtesy phone calls would have prevented the problem.

Al covered his ass by blaming Monarch for not sending cashier's checks for the deposits as called for by the contracts.

This was certainly true enough. Monarch had sent us company checks in the amounts of $5,000 and $7,500 as deposits.

The fact that the checks were good was not the point. When the contracts had first come back I told Clyde Masters to go back to Monarch and get it to send us cashier's checks because there was not sufficient time for its company checks to clear our bank before the dates were to play.

Representing Fats Domino had, in the final analysis, cost us money. After paying Al $7,500 up front and having to pay for what I felt to be Al's negligence, as well as 2 percent of our gross, we would have been better off financially never getting involved. On the other hand, in terms of my objectives for the company at that time, Fats Domino was an integral part of the picture.

As far as Al is concerned, I had an opportunity for revenge in 1990. Al had been hired as a talent coordinator by Hunter Mountain Resort in New York. This had been done over the objections of Eph Abramson, who had overseen the entertainment there for years. Al had promised Eph that he had secured dates on certain artists, but according to Eph, he had not received the majority of the artists' contracts that he had been promised. Among those artists was Barbara Mandrell, whom I was again representing at World Class Talent. Eph had put in an offer of $65,000 for Barbara but had not been able to obtain an answer and was tired of fooling with Al. I told Eph that I would sell him the date directly for that figure and he would not have to bother with Al Embry.

Al had put in the offer to World Class Talent at $60,000. In other words, by cutting Al out of the deal, our client Barbara Mandrell would have made an extra $5,000 and Al would have lost that amount, since Barbara would have received the extra money instead of Al Embry. Al threatened to whip my ass and started whining to agency president Joann Berry, who finally relented and sold the date to Al for $60,000, who then sold the same date to Hunter Mountain for $65,000, thus costing Barbara Mandrell $5,000. I did not care one way or the other, but it was fun watching Al squirm for a few days.

Chapter Eleven

Johnny Paycheck and George Jones

Johnny Paycheck was another wildman. When I was booking him at In Concert he looked a great deal like Charles Manson, with his long hair and SS tattoo. I set my first date on him for $1,300 at the Sundowner Club on Friday, November 26, 1976, in Salinas, California.

Johnny Paycheck had been a sideman musician in the late fifties and early sixties with Faron Young, George Jones, and others, and had also played bass for Ray Price at one time. Not content to remain a musician, he had gone on to become a very successful singer on his own. Johnny got his start as an artist on an independent record label called Lil' Darlin' and had even recorded an album at Carnegie Hall. The cover of that particular album is really funny. With his hair all slicked back, Johnny almost looks like James Dean.

When I started booking him the first time, he was on CBS, with hits like "Don't Take Her She's All I Got," and "Mr. Lovemaker" already under his belt. By the time "Take This Job and Shove It" became a hit, he referred to himself as being on his comeback.

He was always talking about being on his comeback, and

would eventually come back more times than he actually left. During this period Johnny was entering his outlaw phase. Formerly he had done well with the fancy hillbilly suits and a uniformly dressed band.

That's the way it was originally. The hillbilly singers dressed wildly in expensive and colorful suits, most of which were made by Nudie in Hollywood. Many of the country singers' suits were decorated in an individual way, reflecting some particular aspect of their career, a hit song perhaps. Ernie Ashworth still wears an atrocious but wonderful lip-covered suit. Porter Wagoner's suits are covered with wagon wheels. Performers were really more interesting then, and the audience knew they were in for a show. Now, with the exception of Marty Stuart and a few others, most of the country singers dress like the people in the audience.

In the late seventies, Johnny Paycheck wanted to be part of the new breed. His publicity photos from that period were taken in a jail cell and he had grown his hair longer. He was and is truly one of the great country singers of all time, but like most everyone else in this business, he is subject to the law of gravity. Whatever goes up must come down, and Johnny Paycheck was no exception.

In a two-year period he went from $1,200 to $10,000 a night. Eventually, he was dropped from CBS, supposedly as a result of the image that he had created for himself having caught up with him. He had a well-publicized and nasty split from his long-time manager, former Metropolitan Nashville trustee Glenn Ferguson, and was also sued by what was left of the Lavender-Blake Agency for $70,000 in past-due commissions. After these setbacks, Paycheck ended up back in my stable in early 1985.

By this time, he had a new manager, Charlie Ammerman, whom he called "Hammerhead." Ammerman had a financial backer, who served as his partner. Add to this stew the presence of road manager John Long, who did not like the partners, plus Paycheck himself, and the whole situation resembled a hillbilly comedy.

Paycheck would say that Ammerman was his manager one day, but then call me a week later, saying he had dropped

Ammerman and to ignore him if he called. John Long would tell us not to talk to Ammerman at all.

Ammerman was constantly seeking to protect himself from his partner, Paycheck, and John Long. He came by once and gave us a copy of his management contract just so we could see how things really stood, as if the contract meant anything. Eventually Ammerman's money-man left him holding the bag. With Ammerman out of the picture, things quieted down for about a week. Then Paycheck went to prison in Ohio over a barroom shooting he had committed, and that was the end of that.

I always liked Paycheck personally. He came by the office from time to time and it was always a treat to hear him discourse on the evils of whoever or whatever was on his mind at that particular moment.

He never had any money and lived from day to day, and yet he, like many other hillbilly singers, always had the ability to find some sucker to help him out in times of extreme need.

He generally performed great shows on the road and was not afraid of work. He was a real trooper and we worked him hard. The potential for lunacy always lurked beneath the surface. This could mean that he might get drunk and make an ass of himself, lose his false teeth, or anything else. His classic act of madness occurred when he collapsed in California a couple of days before the end of a very hard and lengthy tour. We got a call from Paycheck's road manager saying that Johnny was in the hospital suffering from exhaustion, and was in an oxygen tent. A couple of days later, when he was feeling better he lit a cigarette...in the oxygen tent. Well, what happened was a lot like the Three Stooges lighting a gas stove.

Paycheck is again out of the slammer and back on the road. His hair is short again, he has cleaned up his act, and he is singing as well as ever.

George Jones is regarded by many as the world's greatest country singer. Like so many other country music greats, he came from Texas. Born in 1931 in Saratoga to working-class parents, George developed his musical abilities early in life. The Grand Ole Opry, Roy Acuff, and Bill Monroe were his first and strongest influences. A successful recording career began in

1953 with Starday Records. From there he went to Mercury, then to CBS, and finally to MCA. He is a traditionalist in the strongest sense of the word, both as a honky-tonk singer and as a gut-wrenching balladeer.

Like Johnny Paycheck, George Jones was relatively easy to sell when we represented him at the Lavender-Blake Agency in the mid-1970s. He had a twenty-year string of hits and was further noted for his vocal duets and stormy marriage with country singer Tammy Wynette. But selling him was something I did not want to do. He had the habit of skipping dates with little or no notice. It finally reached the point where potential buyers were told that they bought George Jones at their own risk.

The agents at the office used to place bets on whether George would make his weekend dates. I felt fairly secure if I had several dates playing at one time but I frequently lost money as a result of my optimism.

One Monday morning, I reached my office to find a message from a hotel in Poteau, Oklahoma, the city George had played on Saturday night. I thought this was a good sign that he had made his dates, but figured he had probably skipped out on his hotel bill. I returned the call. Yes, he had left without paying the bill. I told the caller to send us a copy and I would see that the hotel was reimbursed.

I went on about my day and thought no more about the matter until later, when I called the buyer about selling him another act. The buyer was Dale Holcomb, a jeweler who ran a place called the Green Country Danceland. Usually when George skipped a date there would be several messages waiting for me as soon as I arrived at the office on the Monday following the weekend dates.

On this occasion, however, the buyer said George and his crew had indeed shown up and checked into the hotel. The buyer had seen the bus heading down the highway around lunchtime and figured that the guys were just going to get something to eat. That was the last he saw of them. George had decided to head on back home without notifying the hotel, the agency, or the club.

When show time came, the club was filled with patrons who had paid to see George Jones. His arrival was expected at any moment since many people had seen his bus earlier in the day. I thought that the buyer took it extremely well under the circumstances. He had not even called me to report that George had skipped on him.

George certainly earned his title "No Show Jones." His m.o. most of the time was simply to skip the date with no notice to anyone. He skipped June 3, 1977, at the Silver Dollar in Austin; June 4 at the Will Rogers Auditorium in Fort Worth; August 18 at the Western Swing in Houston; October 22 at the Lake Charles Civic Center; December 31 at the Palace in Lubbock; and July 16, 1978, at Randy's Rodeo in San Antonio.

There were many other dates that we had to cancel, usually at the last moment on the day of the show, when we actually received some advance notice, which was not that often. When this happened, Shorty Lavender always told me to explain to the buyer that George was sick. Nobody believed that excuse so I generally told the buyer the truth, that Shorty said to cancel the date. In most cases the promoter would go crazy, and with good reason.

As a result of having to cancel so many dates on George Jones this early in my career, I learned the procedure for canceling dates very well. The fact is that in such situations, the artist is not going to be there. All of the whys and should-haves do not make much difference at that point. The sooner the promoter can face this reality, the sooner he can do what he can to save himself.

One buyer bought a New Year's Eve date for the Possum, as George was nicknamed. I told him that I did not think George would show up. He said that he did not care one way or the other. He figured that since it was New Year's Eve and there would be other acts on the show, he would use George Jones' name to help sell tickets. If George appeared, fine. If George did not, then the buyer would have the benefit of advertising without the expense of having to pay George. If George did not show, he might have to refund a few tickets, but the majority of patrons would end up staying since they were already there. As the date approached I sent the buyer a letter informing him that in my opinion George was very likely to skip the date. Predictably, George did skip the date, and the buyer was foolish enough to sue the agency. Nothing came of it. He had been forewarned.

It was kind of funny in a way. It was less amusing to some people, however. I remember receiving a call at around eight o'clock one Friday night. The buyer was on the phone wanting to know where George was. I replied that I did not know, but as far as I knew, he was on his way there to play the date. He certainly should have been at the show by that time. I called Shorty Lavender but nobody answered his phone. I then called George Jones' number in Alabama and got him on the phone. He was obviously not at the date in Oklahoma. He dismissed the matter casually, saying that he had told Shorty on Wednesday that he was not going to make the date.

In other words, Shorty had known about it for three days but had intentionally withheld that information from me so that he would not have to hear me raising hell about it. Shorty had gone fishing and left me holding the bag. I called the buyer back and told her that George was not going to make the date. I did not tell her, however, that the agency had known about the situation and failed to protect her. She was crying on the phone, saying that she had borrowed money on her music store to do the show. There was nothing I could do to help her.

I did not have much use for George Jones as an artist or as a human being. He used to drive his car onto the steps of the Lavender-Blake building and hang around Shorty's office, wasting time and pretending to be drunker than he was. When Shorty Lavender died from cancer, George Jones, who had received so much from Shorty, did not even show up at the funeral.

The only time I ever got any insight into George Jones occurred one evening in 1978 or 1979 when George dropped by the office to visit Shorty. This was after the Lavender-Blake Agency had dissolved. Shorty was not there so I talked to George while we waited for Shorty to return.

George started the conversation by saying, "I bet you hate me, don't you?" I replied that I did not hate him but that I sure would like to understand him. He told me that he felt sorry for the people on whom he skipped dates. He said that he did not want to hurt anybody, but what about him? What about George

Jones? Nobody cared about him. Nobody cared what he had gone through. "I don't care whether I live or die. When I start feeling like that, I can't get on a bus and go play somewhere. I just can't."

He also told me that there was a warrant out for his arrest at that very moment and that he was hiding from the police even as we spoke. He said that they were after him for past-due child support to the tune of $40,000 for Georgette, the child he had with former wife Tammy Wynette. He said that he could pay it, that CBS would give him more than that sum as soon as he finished the album he was working on. I asked him why he did not just complete the album since he said that he could do it in a couple of days. He replied that he hated the record label and that the people there were just using him. He also said that he would die and go to hell before he gave any money to Tammy Wynette.

"Look at my eyes," he said. "I haven't slept in days." He looked tired and I felt sorry for him. As I looked at him, I began to notice that he really did physically resemble a possum. He was serious, and I believed him. Upon further reflection, however, I believe that while he no doubt meant what he said at the time, it was all just an extension of his act. After all, he was known as the Possum.

George continued to skip dates, but finally married someone good for him and has in recent years somewhat reestablished himself as a significant act in country music.

Chapter Twelve

Randy Travis and Lib Hatcher

Allen Whitcomb and I were complete opposites. I respected him and always had, but at the time he left In Concert I didn't like him very much. In looking back, I see that many of our problems were my fault.

Things were not going well for me in early 1985. It was the coldest winter on record, I had just broken up with my girlfriend, the company was almost out of money, and we were all at each other's throats.

I went to Haiti with a friend and spent a couple of weeks with two Spanish girls from the other side of the island. It was the first vacation I had had in quite a while. When I returned to Nashville, the problems still existed but I was in a much better frame of mind and was again ready to deal with things.

The winter months are always the worst for any talent agency. We all knew this and yet Allen and Linda Edwards would sit around, going over the books and scaring each other to death with dire predictions of gloom and doom. They were talking cutbacks but I really did not see where anything could be trimmed. It cost $50,000 a month to run the agency and that was that. The solution as far as I was concerned was to just do more business and make more money.

In any case, we got through the winter but Allen and I had some problems. Bruce had predicted that Allen would resign, but when it happened I was genuinely surprised.

I had always been irritated that Allen would not sign an employment contract with the company. He was one of the owners and I felt that he should have done everything possible to tie up any and all loose ends. I was glad that he was leaving, as soon as I made certain that he was not planning to start his own agency or work for a competitor. Since he had always been the responsible agent for singer Ronnie McDowell I suspected that we would probably lose Ronnie McDowell as soon as Allen left, which proved to be the case. I really did not know Ronnie very well; he was often referred to jokingly around the office as "The Elvis Impersonator." I frequently told prospective buyers that he was actor Roddy McDowell's son. It was all a big joke.

Allen Whitcomb left his job as vice president and part owner of In Concert International to open Hub Cap Heaven, which actually was a retail hubcap store. He must have really been sick of the music business. I was glad he was gone.

The hubcap business did not do very well, apparently, and before too much time had passed I heard that Allen was working as an agent for Joann Berry at World Class Talent, a smaller agency. I knew that this was a big step down and I felt sorry for him. On the other hand, Allen and I had not parted on the best of terms.

Furthermore, In Concert owed him commissions. He still owned around 12 percent of the company, he knew the inside scoop on all of us, and now he was working for a competitor. Since Ricky Skaggs had recently defected to World Class, I could not help but suspect duplicity, but then I didn't trust anybody. I did not know how aggressive Allen intended to be at World Class Talent, but I felt that he could do us some serious damage if he wanted to. I instructed Linda Edwards not to give him any further information about In Concert International. I did not care if he was a stockholder.

I called my lawyer and he said that there was nothing I could do about Allen's owning stock in my company and working for a competitor. This irritated me but it was beyond my control. The

next thing I heard was that Allen Whitcomb had gone off with
Randy Travis and was now his agent.

Shortly after Allen left us we took on an Epic Records act
named Keith Stegall. He had written "We're in This Love
Together," which was a big hit for pop singer Al Jarreau. Keith
got the big head very early in the game. It would have hurt his
career as an artist, if he had had one, which as it turned out he
did not. Keith's manager at that time was publishing magnate
Charlie Monk.

Charlie is a well-respected, well-known, and well-dressed
man. He talked us into going to see an unknown act named
Randy Travis who was playing as the house act at some tourist
joint out near Opryland, called the Nashville Palace.

Randy Travis, whose real name is Randy Traywick, is from
Marshville, North Carolina, and is the son of a farmer. Randy
was pretty wild as a youth and was supposedly rescued from jail
by club owner Lib Hatcher at age sixteen. She gave him a job
singing in her club and doing odd jobs. Eventually Lib and her
husband split. Perhaps he got tired of having Randy living in his
house. Ultimately Randy and Lib Hatcher moved to Nashville
and Randy was signed to Warner Brothers Records. His first
album, *Always and Forever,* was released in 1987 and spent
almost a year at the top of the charts. He is known as a
traditional artist.

I went with my new vice president, Lane Cross, to see Randy
Travis, largely as a courtesy to Charlie Monk. We were really not
interested in taking on any more new acts at that time. When
Lane and I arrived we said our hellos to Randy and to his
manager, Lib Hatcher, who looked as though she might have
been working in the kitchen that night. Lib Hatcher seemed like
a hillbilly version of Miss Kitty on "Gunsmoke"—in other
words, a redneck queen.

Randy Travis was nice enough, but had a blank look in his
eyes and seemed to be in another world. He was not drunk.
More like the light was on but nobody was home. His show
before a nearly empty house was boring and uninspiring. I had
no idea how Charlie Monk could possibly imagine that Randy
Travis would ever be a star. In fact, his show was so boring that

we would have sneaked out the back door if we hadn't already made ourselves known.

Well, Randy Travis became a big star and Allen Whitcomb made more money than he would have if he had stayed with us. In the next few years I would see Allen from time to time and we would speak briefly. Many things happened to all of us who had worked together at In Concert. One of the most significant things was that Allen had gotten a divorce and finally married his girlfriend after her own divorce came through. Inasmuch as things had worked out for him I would sometimes call and ask for advice, since I was myself involved with a married woman at that time. By then, Allen and I were on fairly good terms again. He knew the pain I was in and tried to help me.

Allen was very lucky. He was making plenty of money and had ended up with the woman he loved, against very great odds. Everything seemed to be going his way. Then, sometime during September of 1990, I heard through the grapevine that Lib Hatcher and Randy Travis had let him go. Here is the story.

Allen was driving home from work at World Class Talent one night in January of 1986 and heard Randy Travis on the radio. He was so impressed by Randy he was determined to find out more about him. The song he had heard was called "1982." He saw an ad in the Sunday paper that announced that Randy was playing at the Nashville Palace. He then remembered that Randy Travis once went by the name Randy Ray and that he was managed by Lib Hatcher.

On Monday, Allen called Lib from his office and arranged to meet her at the Nashville Palace that night. They struck a verbal deal and Allen brought Randy Travis to World Class Talent for agency representation. At that time Randy was playing only at the Palace. Allen thought that it would take some time to set dates. So Allen and Lib decided that it would be best to leave Randy at the Palace until March, at which time they would begin sending him out on the road as a single act. They would use backup bands wherever he played in an effort to keep expenses down until he could afford to put his own band together. In May of 1986 piano player Drew Sexton set up Randy's band.

In October 1986, Allen Whitcomb left World Class Talent and with Lib Hatcher started the Lib Hatcher Agency with Randy Travis as their first client. Allen owned no part of this new agency but received a straight commission of 5 percent. By the middle of 1987 Allen was being harassed by Lib Hatcher, who at times wadded up his paychecks and threw them at him. She felt that Allen was making too much money. This is standard hillbilly logic. Although the equation remains the same, the agent is suddenly getting rich. It never occurs to the artist or to the manager that they are making too much money.

According to Allen, Lib Hatcher "turned into a dragon" when she started to do well. This is interesting considering that she knew nothing about management and sought Allen's advice constantly on almost everything, frequently calling him at home late at night and picking his brain for hours at a time.

When Allen had called Lib with the first date on Randy Travis, she did not know whether to take the offer. She wasn't sufficiently knowledgeable to accept or decline the gig. In fact, Allen was the brains of the entire operation, to the extent that any existed. He arranged for the purchase of Randy's first bus. He booked the dates, drove the bus, served as road manager, and counseled Lib. He did it all, booking dates all week and then going out on the road during the weekend, returning home early Sunday mornings, and then starting all over again. Allen ate, breathed, and lived Randy Travis. He certainly earned his 5 percent.

When Allen left World Class Talent to work for Lib Hatcher she insisted on a one-year contract. The contract began in October 1986 and expired at the end of October 1987. As soon as Allen's contract was over, Lib Hatcher brought in Jeff Davis to promote dates on Randy "in house," meaning that Lib Hatcher's own company, Special Moments, would actually promote dates in some of the larger markets instead of selling them directly to a promoter.

Doing business this way is not an uncommon practice among the most popular hillbilly acts. What it means is that in cities where the artist's managers know for a fact that the performer is going to do very well, they rent the auditorium, pay the expenses themselves, and take all the money. This type of arrangement is good for everybody except the agent, who generally receives half or none of his regular commission.

The concert promoter and the club buyer do not generally appreciate this arrangement either. Often they have worked with an artist from the beginning, sometimes for years, losing money on him at first but hoping that when he became a big act he would show them special consideration. Not only does the promoter who had used the artist in the past lose his chance to make a lot of money, but now the artist comes into the promoter's backyard and directly competes against him. Despite all of the smiles and mock gratitude displayed to the public, the fact is that behind the scenes, in the real world, for most artists, people exist to be used.

Given Lib Hatcher's greed, Allen knew that self-promoted dates would soon be a reality. With this thought in mind he had tentatively struck a deal for that purpose with promoter Ben Farrell at Varnell Enterprises. Lib Hatcher, however, brought in Jeff Davis to handle the self-promotions without even mentioning to Allen she was doing this, knowing full well that discussions with Varnell Enterprises were already well under way. The fact is, she wanted it all—management, her own agency, and her own in-house promoter.

At this point Lib Hatcher made a management and booking deal with Texas singer Gene Watson. Gene is one of the true greats of country music. For years he has been working quietly, putting out hit records like "Love in the Hot Afternoon" and "Farewell Party." It is amazing that despite his genuine skill as a representative of his art, he has never been recognized by the Country Music Association. We had taken him on as a client at In Concert in late 1983 and had worked with him for several years. During that time he had caused very few problems and had been for the most part fun to work with. I liked him a great deal.

Some people at CBS Records, Gene's label at the time, speculated that he had a very large and secretly located cache of Vietnam-era bell-bottom jeans, since he wore them almost constantly and they were for the most part unavailable anywhere in this galaxy. He finally left us, thinking that he should be making more money. He went over to Jack McFadden, stayed there for a couple of weeks, and then ended up with Lib Hatcher and Allen.

Hatcher offered Gene opening slots for Randy Travis. This was a big boost for Gene, who had more or less been a honky-tonk artist. By that time Randy played large auditoriums in front of capacity crowds. By dangling the opening slot for Randy's dates, Lib was able to get him for management and booking. Of course, Allen would be expected to do all of the day-to-day booking when Gene was not out with Randy Travis. It was a good deal for Gene since it would advance his career and it was a good thing for Lib Hatcher since she had to have an opening act for Randy anyway. By using Gene Watson, who was now her own act, she could collect double commissions on him as well. There was no point in leaving any money on the table.

At this point, Lib Hatcher took Allen Whitcomb's 5 percent and gave it to promoter Jeff Davis. So Randy Travis was paying 10 percent to the agency on every date, plus another 10 percent of the net on self-promotion dates. From an ethical standpoint, since both companies were in-house, Randy should not have had to pay the agency anything on self-promoted dates.

In other words, Randy Travis was paying twice. While it is true that both the agency and the promotion company were owned jointly by Lib Hatcher and Randy Travis, it cost him an extra 5 percent personally every time he played a self-promoted date. This was on top of the management fee of 25 percent that he was already paying Lib Hatcher.

There were rumors of all types floating around town about Lib Hatcher and Randy Travis. Within the music community almost everyone knew that Lib and Randy were an item, but the all-pervasive question was "Why?" Why would Randy Travis want to mess with her at all? It was also rumored that she kept him under lock and key and that she paid him a pittance and kept all of the money herself.

It was true enough that nobody saw or talked to Randy Travis without first going through Lib Hatcher. Allen told me that the three of them were sitting around on the bus one night and Randy said how much he liked to shoot pool. Allen offered to take him out, but Lib put a stop to that very quickly and would not let Randy go. Allen and Randy liked each other, but were not permitted to be friends. Lib was with him constantly.

I believe that she married him not to stop the unfounded rumor that he was gay, but to keep him under control and to further confuse the financial picture so that if he ever split she would still come out on top. This is again strictly my own opinion, but having been around the music business as long as I have, I feel it to be fairly accurate.

The new arrangement with the in-house promotion company, Special Moments, was not so special for Allen. On the very day that his one-year, 5 percent contract with Lib ran out, she told him that he was making too much money and that he would no longer be on a straight 5 percent. Instead he would go on salary at $1,000 a week. This may sound like a pretty good salary to many people, but it was like cutting Allen's income in half. He was in effect being penalized for having done his job too well. They had a big argument about it, but Allen lost. He couldn't just go somewhere else and get a job for more money. He had invested all of his time and energy for the last several years giving Randy and Lib Hatcher the best of his lengthy experience. He had taken care of them both from day one.

After years in the business he thought that he would finally be able to put a little something back for the future, for his retirement. The public doesn't understand that for most people in the music business there is no pension or retirement fund. If you don't save some money now, you'll be destitute later. This applies to artists especially, but to almost everyone else as well.

Almost as soon as he was taken off commission and put on salary, his relationship with Lib Hatcher and Randy began to deteriorate. Lib would intentionally withhold information that Allen needed in order to do his job. This is a frequent practice employed by managers to keep the agent as powerless as possible. For example, Randy Travis would be on a television show and Allen would not even know it. A buyer or someone else would comment to Allen that he had seen Randy on TV last night. "Did you see it, Allen?" Allen had not seen it, however, for Lib wasn't telling him anything anymore.

As a conciliatory gesture Lib offered Allen 3 percent of Gene Watson. Allen understandably felt that this was like starting over again but accepted the offer since it was better than nothing. This was no great sacrifice or gesture of generosity on Lib Hatcher's part, since Gene Watson was not an easy act to sell. There was also no guarantee that Lib would not pull the same thing with Gene Watson that she had done with Randy Travis. As it turned out, Gene Watson and Lib Hatcher got into a fight, so Gene stopped paying commissions and Allen got beat out of his 3 percent anyway.

The dispute between Gene Watson and Lib Hatcher culminated in lawsuits, the first filed by Lib against Gene in Nashville on August 31, 1990. This suit claimed that Gene Watson had breached his management contract by failing to pay $61,414.38 in commissions for the time between September 17, 1988, and February 18, 1990. She also alleged that Gene had hired other agents and managers and thus made it impossible for her company to do its job.

Gene answered on October 3, 1990, with a counterclaim saying that he had not agreed to pay double commissions, meaning a management fee to Lib Hatcher in addition to paying her agency. He also said that he had not been given as many opening dates with Randy Travis as he had been promised. He sued her for reimbursement of management fees paid on dates booked by the Lib Hatcher Agency and also for another half a million for general damages.

I called Gene Watson and asked him some questions about the lawsuit, but he said that he could not answer since it was all still unresolved. He told me to ask Allen since he'd be right in the middle of it as a witness. Allen told me that both sides were counting on his testimony and that he knew enough of the inside story to "burn both of them."

On the Friday afternoon before Labor Day 1990, Lib Hatcher called Allen Whitcomb and administered the "Coupe de Ville," as we say. She was on the bus and Allen was at the office. She said to him, "This is the hardest call I have ever had to make." The fact is that she had been harassing Allen, wanting him to work all week and then go out on the road as well on weekends.

It was one thing to do this when he was on a percentage and making a great deal of money. It was another thing to do so for almost two-thirds less than he had been making before for doing the same work. She had also wanted him to "build the agency," something that he was understandably reluctant to do in light of the way he had been treated. It was obvious that Lib Hatcher wanted Allen out of the way. Perhaps he knew too much. Whatever the reasons, the day-to-day environment for Allen Whitcomb had become more and more inhospitable. He felt that she was trying to make things so bad that he would quietly resign. Nevertheless, he had determined to stay there until he could find something else.

Allen believes that promoter Jeff Davis hung him, that he knew Allen was looking for another job and that he told Lib Hatcher. Allen and Jeff had been friends for years, but the word "friendship" in the music business should always be viewed as conditional. Initially Jeff Davis would pick cities in which to do self-promoted dates. Allen, of course, would not be permitted to sell dates in those cities, so his hands were tied to a great degree. Toward the end, Jeff was starting to become involved in the booking of dates as well as in the self-promotions, and Allen knew that the end was near. Before it was all over, Allen would have to submit his dates to Jeff Davis for approval.

After all of his work with and for them, Allen was fired for having done his job too well. In less than four years he had taken Randy Travis from house band at the Nashville Palace to almost $60,000 a night plus percentages. That is the way things frequently end in Hillbilly Heaven. Greed and ego fuel the machinery that grinds up lives.

Is Allen bitter? Of course. He had booked the dates, driven the bus, served as road manager, sold concessions, and settled the box office. He had been available around the clock to Lib Hatcher to answer her questions. Allen had looked at this job as his retirement. Unfortunately for him, it turned out to be an early retirement. At forty-two Allen Whitcomb has had to start over, after seventeen years as an agent.

One day shortly after Lib Hatcher had taken away Allen's 5 percent, she told him to go get her car and bring it around front. "You know what?" she said, laughing. "I just figured out that I am a millionaire."

Chapter 13

Ricky Skaggs

One of the more unfortunate aspects of running any business is to have to compromise one's own ethics from time to time in order to keep the money coming in. For me, there were many ways in which this could happen; for example, selling a date to somebody I knew was going to lose money, but doing it anyway, or backdating a contract, as I did with Johnny Lee and Mickey Gilley. The worst thing of all was to represent people who were absolute jerks. Not only did I have to represent them, but it was necessary to lie to the buyers, telling them they were such nice people when I knew full well that the artist I was talking about was an asshole of the first magnitude.

It's truly a great feeling to get an artist more money than he is worth. A good agent continually seeks to get his clients more and more money. To do this for somebody you dislike takes away the pleasure of doing a good job. It's difficult after a while to keep telling buyers that so-and-so is such a great guy when you know that he is an idiot. You become a liar when you say that an artist is a pleasure to work with when you know that the buyer will encounter problems from the moment he can no longer back out of the deal. If you are good at doing this you book lots of dates and you become an agent of great renown.

Sometimes, however, after the day is over and you have a chance to reflect upon your activities, you feel like a hypocrite.

After a while, an agent becomes hardened and frequently laughs when he's able to make a big deal for an unpleasant artist. At other times the agent would like to be rid of a particular artist but fights to keep him anyway because he needs the revenue the commissions provide. As an agent, my problem was Ricky Skaggs.

Ricky Skaggs was born in Cordell, Kentucky, in 1954 and developed his musical skills on a variety of stringed instruments at an early age. With his friend the late Keith Whitley, Skaggs joined the traditional Stanley Brothers band at age fifteen and played bluegrass for two years. Beginning in 1972, Skaggs worked with a succession of different bluegrass bands, having his own band, Boone Creek, for a while. He did a stint as front man for Emmylou Harris before emerging as a successful solo act on CBS-owned Epic Records in the early 1980s.

Skaggs, while considered a strict traditionalist and a hedge against the pop infiltration of country music, has managed to make bluegrass music in particular more palatable to a large number of listeners. His use of electric instruments, his incredible virtuosity as a musician, and his pure tenor voice have made him the current bluegrass king. His style as a vocalist, while not original, is even more significant today in that he has expanded the range of bluegrass, which formerly had a much more limited audience.

Ricky Skaggs was a perfect example of an agent's nightmare. He prided himself on being called "Picky Ricky," as if it was cute to be a jerk. He complained and whined about everything constantly. Complainers are bad enough, but the whiners are the worst of all, and Ricky Skaggs was a whiner.

From an agency standpoint nothing was good enough for Picky Ricky, or Prickly Ricky as I called him. I didn't like him from the first time I met him at Dick Blake's office, and with good reason. He had the big head right out of the box, as if he were of any consequence in the universe. His manager, Chip Peay, seemed to be just as bad. We called Chip Peay "Chick Pea."

Chip came across as an ignorant yuppie who looked like he was fifteen. He was, however, intelligent and had a few good ideas from time to time. Mostly he seemed to me to be Ricky Skaggs' stooge and mouthpiece. In retrospect, I feel that Chip

Peay did a good job managing Ricky Skaggs, given what he had to deal with on his end, and it is a fact that Skaggs' career reached its zenith both with Chip Peay and In Concert. Ricky's best album on CBS was called *Highways and Heartaches*, and it was much better than his first CBS offering, *Waiting for the Sun to Shine*, which sounded to me like a eunuch singing with a clothespin on his nose.

That I did not like Chip was due primarily to the fact that he executed Ricky Skaggs' outrageous demands as if they were legitimate, which they were not. Thinking about it now, I realize that Chip had to do Ricky's bidding in order to keep his own job. Ricky was the type of guy who thought the world owed him a living, and if I sound a bit too harsh it is only because he was so difficult to deal with. I can usually handle that aspect of an artist's nature; in fact, many of us wonder if it's not to some degree necessary for an artist's success.

What I couldn't handle was Ricky's cutesy, goody-goody rap, when behind the scenes I had to clean up the messes he made for buyers. Ricky is talented and has made a lasting contribution to country music. That he has a big ego and did not handle it well is to some degree understandable. Nonetheless, none of us are that special, and Ricky Skaggs is no exception.

The thing that irritated me the most about him was his habit of talking about the Lord and parading his so-called Christian values. He claimed to be very moral and refused to play anywhere alcohol was served. He was also opposed to tobacco, but when Marlboro started paying him twice what he was getting at other dates he managed to force himself to play for it, although his doing so was "not an endorsement."

Behind the scenes he seemed greedy and unethical, not to say that I was any better at the time myself. But it bothers me, and always has, to hear someone talk about Jesus all the time with no regard for the people he deals with on a day-to-day basis. If somebody is a jerk, I can accept that and factor it into the relationship, but it's very hard for me to make God or Jesus a third party to his actions.

It is not my intention to demean or belittle Christianity in any way, but it has been my experience that the people who do their best to follow the teachings of Jesus really do not talk about it that much. They don't need to, since their actions generally speak for them.

In the music business, however, when somebody starts talking about Jesus or the Lord at an inappropriate time, it is a sure sign that it is time to hide your money. I prefer to deal with honest people, but in the music business it is not always possible. If somebody intends to cheat me out of something or beat me in a deal, I can at least respect him if he is man enough to take responsibility for his actions. We all make mistakes, and in retrospect I can only conclude that Ricky Skaggs did the best he knew how at the time, given his circumstances. It is not for me to judge him or to say what was in his heart, but his actions toward my company were anything but charitable and Christian.

On January 18, 1984, I set a date for Ricky Skaggs at the Jackson Coliseum with the singing group the Whites as the opening act. This date was approved by Chip Peay and contracts were sent out the next day for both acts. Ricky was to be paid $10,000 plus another 50 percent of the gate after allowing the promoter to make 15 percent. The Whites were to receive $2,500. A deposit of 50 percent on both artists was received the next day, and signed contracts were returned to the buyer. This was a good date, close to home and for good money.

On this occasion the date was canceled the Friday afternoon before his show on Sunday afternoon. In other words, the buyer was given two days' notice. Ricky Skaggs was allegedly sick, that is, he had a doctor's excuse. As I remember, however, ticket sales were not that good as the date approached, and Chip Peay had been telling me all that week that the promoter did not know what he was doing and that he was advertising on the wrong stations.

According to the promoter, there were advance sales of around sixteen hundred. The seating capacity as stated on the face of the contract was around five thousand. Ricky Skaggs did not wish to be embarrassed that close to Nashville by a poor turnout.

In any case the promoter was out almost $9,000, counting his advertising, lost auditorium rental, and other expenses. I had to cancel a date in Beaumont, Texas, that same weekend in order to make it look like the cancellation in Jackson was legitimate. If the cancellation had actually been made in good faith, the promoter should have been given another date at a reduced price. According to the promoter, Tim Jones, Chip was unwilling to give him any kind of financial break on a makeup date and refused to give him a Sunday as he wanted.

I am not saying that Ricky Skaggs was not sick on the dates in question, although any act can usually find a doctor to give him an excuse. Rather, as the agent who set the date, and as a party to the proceedings, I'm convinced that Ricky Skaggs canceled the date because he did not wish to be embarrassed by playing to an almost empty auditorium that close to home. Never mind that the buyer lost $9,000 on his first country show, or that the sixteen hundred fans who had bought tickets had to go to the trouble of changing their plans along with the inconvenience of obtaining refunds for their now useless tickets. The promoter instituted legal proceedings, which he says went on for two years before being dropped. It is hard to go against a doctor's excuse in court and win, but I feel that the promoter was wronged.

On December 13, 1982, I set a date on Ricky Skaggs with longtime Texas talent buyer Ray Sczepanik for a club called the Texas Dance Hall in San Antonio. The date tied in with two other dates that I had set for the same weekend, one for $10,000 and another for $15,000. Two days before this date in San Antonio was set to play, I received a call from Chip Peay telling me to cancel. Ricky had decided that he did not want to play where alcohol was being served, nor did he wish to perform anywhere people would be dancing instead of giving him their undivided attention. There are many country acts who mistakenly feel that their music is so significant and important that it must be heard, and consequently get upset when people fail to listen and pay attention. This was the case with Ricky Skaggs.

I called the buyer, a perfect gentleman, and told him the situation. My main concern at that point was to protect him from my own artists. Ricky Skaggs did not care that the date had been set for two and a half months, that the buyer had advertised at great expense, or that the buyer had fulfilled the contract to the letter. Nor was he concerned with his fans or show any respect for the work that the agency had done on his behalf.

I sent a telegram to Ray Sczepanik, as Chip Peay had instructed, telling him that the date was canceled due to his breach of the contract. This telegram was both insulting and absurd. The buyer had not done anything wrong. I told Ray that his best move would be to send me a telegram refusing to accept the cancellation and threatening to sue. He was certainly within his rights.

When Chip and Ricky realized that they were not going to be able to mistreat this buyer and get away with it, they finally agreed to play the date, but not before they made some more outrageous demands. Ricky insisted that the buyer put up a five-foot barrier around the stage so that Skaggs would not come too close to the riffraff. Ricky also wanted the buyer to forbid people to dance at the show, but Ray could not have prevented dancing even if he had wanted to. In Texas people dance. So what should have been an easy show was turned into a major pain in the ass for the buyer and for me because of Ricky Skaggs' ego. It was not the only time this happened.

They did the same thing to Sherwood Cryer at Gilley's on December 10, 1982, but Sherwood stood up to them and they backed out of the date with little notice. He really wanted to sue them and would have, had I not been able to talk him out of it. In retrospect, I wish that he had sued. He most likely would have won and it would have served them right. Time passed, and Sherwood tried hard to get me to sell him a date on Ricky— not that he liked Skaggs, but he felt he could make some money on him even at the price of $40,000 he was offering. But the place was not good enough for Picky Ricky.

Eventually we lost Ricky Skaggs as a client, and as generally happens to all artists sooner or later, his price dropped. What goes up must come down. One day Sherwood called me and told me that Ricky's new agent had called and was trying to sell him Ricky Skaggs for $12,500. I told him to pass on the deal and he did.

We were never in a very good position with Ricky Skaggs from an agency standpoint despite the incredible job we did with him, taking him from $1,000 to $40,000 a night in the several years we represented him. This was due to the fact that we did not have a signed contract. When Blake died we inherited him. I have no doubt that he would have left us before he did were it not for the presence of the Marlboro dates, which were very desirable and high-paying shows. Ricky was always crying poverty, and when this kind of thing starts happening, the agent who does not have his act under contract is usually in for trouble.

In Concert was no exception. Ricky Skaggs had us where he wanted us and he knew it. We were a new company and could not afford to lose any acts so early in the game. It came as no surprise when Chip Peay showed up one day and wanted us to drop all commissions on the self-promoted dates and to drop from 10 percent to 5 percent on the Marlboro dates. According to Chip, the band had threatened to leave Ricky and there was no way he could pay them more money with what he was making at that time, unless we would help him out.

This was an insulting thing to do, especially since we knew what he was actually making then. I would have really liked to throw Chip out of the office, but we had no choice in the matter. It was either accept his nicely worded ultimatum or lose Ricky as an artist. The question of loyalty never came up. I graciously accepted his generous offer with the provision that all of the Marlboro dates continued to be contracted by our office as they had been in the past. One would think that such a sacrifice on our part might be appreciated, but it was not.

What happened instead was that Skaggs, having succeeded in beating us in the first instance, decided to do it again on a grander scale. He cheated us out of all of our commissions on the last series of Marlboro dates, and other dates as well.

The Marlboro dates were the most desirable of all possible shows for a country act. I talked to British rock promoter Harvey Goldsmith for three years to work out the details of this corporate sponsorship, which even to this day has not been equaled in country music. Harvey had obtained a financial commitment from Marlboro for this extensive public relations project. Marlboro wanted the package to play auditoriums with a minimum of ten thousand seats, but the auditoriums could not be on university or college campuses. I think that this decision had something to do with its corporate policy. Each act would do one show and money was no object. The shows were understandably an artist's dream.

Harvey Goldsmith was now ready to do some shows, but was not really sure where to start. I notified promoter Ben Farrell of Varnell Enterprises that I felt discussions between myself and Goldsmith had reached the point where we needed to make some definite decisions as to where to play a couple of trial dates and with which artists. It was my desire to use Ricky Skaggs as the opening act, followed by Ronnie Milsap, and then ending with Barbara Mandrell as the headliner. Varnell Enterprises would promote the dates.

I put Ben in touch with Harvey Goldsmith and between the three of us, we decided to play Dallas at the Reunion Arena as the first date. When the details were all worked out, Varnell Enterprises was to receive $10,000 as a consultant's fee. There was no risk involved for Ben and Varnell Enterprises since Marlboro was paying for everything associated with the shows. All Ben had to do was select appropriate cities, auditoriums, and dates that would not conflict with other shows in the same markets.

Harvey Goldsmith had originally intended to work with regional promoters, thus spreading the money around and helping local promoters in their own areas. In other words, he did not wish to generate any backlash by coming into a promoter's backyard and dumping a big show on top of him. This was really a very good idea, and it was fair, but I killed it as a favor to Ben Farrell because I considered him a friend and felt that I was in a position to help, and should do so. I told Harvey Goldsmith that Marlboro would have to use Farrell on all of the dates or he would not be able to get Mandrell, Milsap, and Skaggs. I had no idea that Ben would eventually cut me out of the picture altogether, but that is what happened.

The first show was set in Dallas, as I suggested, with Barbara Mandrell getting $100,000, Milsap $40,000, and Skaggs $15,000. It was the most money that any of them had ever made up to that point on a single date, with perhaps an exception here and there. I know that it was the most Barbara Mandrell have ever received for one performance.

I flew to Dallas in the middle of negotiations with Ronnie Milsap and his concessions salesman, Tommy Kerkeles, about going with them to start our own agency. There were some delays in the show, but it went fairly well.

A second Marlboro date was set in Tulsa at the Assembly Center. Instead of using Mandrell and Milsap, Marlboro hired Hank Williams, Jr., and Merle Haggard, with Little Wings as the promoter. Ricky Skaggs was also on this date. He did something for Opryland that morning and we flew up to Tulsa for that show on the Lear Jet of NLT, the company that then owned Opryland, and came back to Nashville as soon as it was over.

Marlboro apparently liked the first show better and I ended up using the original package of Mandrell, Milsap, and Skaggs from that point forward, using Ben Farrell as the promoter on all of the subsequent dates. The first set of multiple dates was agreed upon and I did a million and a half dollars' worth of business in one afternoon.

I decided not to go with Ronnie Milsap to form his own agency and he left the Dick Blake Agency shortly thereafter, justifiably angry with me for having backed out on him at the last minute after having already agreed to join him.

After Blake died, Barbara Mandrell started her own agency, Skaggs stayed with us, and the Marlboro dates went on. By the time the second series of dates had been set, Harvey Goldsmith was out of the picture and Ben Farrell had more or less taken over the whole thing, still using Mandrell and Milsap, but not through my company. By then, I was too busy with In Concert to worry much about it. I simply trusted Ben Farrell to handle things for me.

When the time came I took down the information and sent the contracts directly to Entertainment Services in New York, which was handling the project for Marlboro. They were always slow in sending contracts back, and often the cities would be changed, but after several months the contracts would invariably come back signed with everything in order. By the time the second series of Marlboro dates was set on Skaggs I was getting him $20,000 a night. On the 1984 dates I brought him $22,500 for each show. When the fall 1985 dates were set he was receiving $40,000 a night, over twice what he was getting everywhere else, and ten times more than he was worth in my estimation.

I remember one day I came into Allen Whitcomb's office and found him in a heated phone conversation with Chip Peay. We were about to lose Ricky Skaggs. I had told somebody that Ricky Skaggs was getting $40,000 a night on the Marlboro dates, and Chip was mad about that. Allen acted as if it was a big deal, that it was my fault and that it was some kind of big problem. It seems that somebody did not want Marlboro to know that it was paying such an excessive sum for Ricky Skaggs.

I do not think that this was the case at all, I think that it was just more of Ricky Skaggs' horseshit. Allen was angry about the situation, and blamed me since he did not want to lose Ricky Skaggs. I was outraged and said that both of them could go to hell. I was proud of the fact that Skaggs was getting such a ridiculous amount. It was a tribute to our ability as an agency. I had put the entire Marlboro tour together and made them a hell of a lot of money. Their attitude was infuriating. I was really on the verge of telling them to hit the road.

I had personally obtained over a million dollars' worth of business for Ricky Skaggs and never received as much as a thank-you call. He was the worst artist I have ever represented, including James Brown. He nauseated me, literally.

After nearly four years of representing Ricky Skaggs, and putting up with his whining and complaining, the end came fairly quickly. We had Ricky playing some dates in California in September 1985, among them the Concord Pavilion, the Universal Amphitheater, and a date in Modesto. I remember the date at the Universal in particular because it had taken some time to find an appropriate act to appear with Ricky. The buyer for Universal at that time, Larry Vallon, had suggested doing the show with Roy Orbison. I thought that this was a great idea but Chip said that Ricky Skaggs would have to close the show if Ricky agreed to work with Roy Orbison at all.

As I mentioned earlier, the artist who closes the show is generally considered to be the main attraction or the "headliner." This position in the scheduling of the show is considered to be the place of honor. That Chip or Ricky Skaggs had the audacity to imagine in his wildest dreams that Roy Orbison should ever be expected to open any show for Skaggs, anywhere in this world, was beyond belief, but Chip told me that that was the way it would have to be. In an effort to solve this problem, I called Roy's wife, Barbara, who understandably refused even to consider such an absurd and insulting suggestion.

In fulfillment of the famous Murphy's Law, there was a problem with the September 13 date in Modesto. Neither of the two deposits had come in and the date had to be canceled after Ricky was already in California. It was an obvious oversight on agent Bruce Shelton's part. Such things do happen from time to time, although not that often. It was the first time in my recollection that anything like that from our end had ever happened with Ricky Skaggs.

In such cases the artist is always angry about it but realizes that even the best agent makes a mistake every once in a while, and generally there are some kind of extenuating circumstances to lessen the degree of fault. In this case the buyer was well known, had a good reputation, and had been doing shows for years. As a result, Bruce consequently had let things slide with this particular situation longer than he should have, but he had been in constant contact with the buyer and had been told that everything was all right with the date.

On September 19, we received a terse letter from Chip Peay with an enclosed check to In Concert for $283.84 as payment in full for Ricky Skaggs's August commissions to In Concert. He and Skaggs actually owed $15,634.84 by their own admission. In the letter they said that they were deducting $12,500 for Ricky Skaggs's alleged losses associated with the canceled Modesto date. I would have paid their actual out-of-pocket expenses such as hotel rooms and meals or other costs.

But it was clear that they were trying to pick a fight. My belief is that this was an attempt to work themselves up into self-righteous indignation in order to lay a smokescreen for their next move, which was to cheat us out of the commissions we would be owed on the upcoming Marlboro dates, scheduled to begin in October and continue into November. Sensing their duplicity, I checked on the contracts for the upcoming Marlboro dates. I'd sent them months before and they had yet to be returned.

In the past I had not worried about Marlboro's late contracts, but now, in light of Skaggs' most recent actions, I had good reason for alarm. I called Regis Boff's office at Entertainment Services in New York to inquire as to why my contracts had not been returned, and was told that he had been instructed to disregard our contracts and that another set would be forthcoming.

I was furious and phoned Ben Farrell. I did not act as if there was anything wrong at first and just went over the cities and dates to make sure that I had them right. Ben gave me the updated schedule as he was accustomed to doing. It was obvious to me that he was unaware that Chip and Ricky intended to cheat us out of our commissions on these dates.

After I was certain that I had the correct schedule, I told Ben what had happened and asked him to intervene on our behalf with Chip and Ricky in the name of fairness and common decency. Instead of helping me, he said that it had nothing to do with him and that since he liked us both he could not get involved.

Ben had sounded honestly surprised when I told him what had happened, but he refused even to mention the situation to Chip or Ricky. It was incredible to me that after all of the money I had made for him by giving him the Marlboro shows, he would not protect me at all.

I was angry, but sadly not surprised, by the actions of Ricky Skaggs, Chip Peay, or Ben Farrell. I refused to cash Chip's $283.84 check and still have it to this day as a memento of the real Ricky Skaggs, and of how he sought to and succeeded in defrauding In Concert. It is just this kind of thing that makes me very happy that I don't have to fool with people like him anymore.

I contacted my attorney, Peter Curry, the man who had solemnly vowed to defend me to my last dollar, and made preparations to sue Skaggs immediately, although I didn't think that I could actually do anything about the commissions on the Marlboro dates until after they had been played.

In the meantime I received another letter from Chip Peay

exactly like the first one, along with another check for the same amount as the one he had sent before. I never understood this, not that it mattered then or now.

My attorney did not respond until November 7, after the eight Marlboro dates had been played. Skaggs countered by offering to deduct $6,000 from what he and Peay owed us instead of $12,500 as they had originally attempted, but added that our acceptance of this proposal would be in "exchange for a complete release of Mr. Skaggs...with respect to any and all claims that In Concert may have or may claim to have now or in the future arising out of booking or other transactions..."

If I had accepted this offer I would have automatically been out the commissions due on the Marlboro dates, which so far had not been mentioned by either of our attorneys.

On December 12, my lawyer refused their offer and informed them that they owed an additional $16,000 for the recently played fall Marlboro dates.

On December 31, their attorney responded by saying that since we had refused their "fair and reasonable proposal," we must "therefore bear the consequences." He then addressed the situation with regard to the commissions due us on the Marlboro dates:

> With respect to the claims asserted by In Concert with respect to the engagements which were part of the fall Marlborough tour, please be advised that Mr. Skaggs has absolutely no obligation whatsoever to In Concert arising out of those engagements. In Concert neither secured nor contracted those dates and performed no services in connection with those dates. Mr. Skaggs' verbal nonexclusive agreement with In Concert was terminated prior to the time that the Marlborough tour performances were contracted. To avoid any misunderstanding with respect to this issue, at the time the agreement between Mr. Skaggs and In Concert was terminated, Mr. Skaggs' manager, Chip Peay, confirmed with then president Allen Whitcomb, that the agency would not be entitled to any commission with respect to the fall Marlborough tour engagements.

In the first place, their attorney, Mike Milom, was unfortunately unable to spell "Marlboro." I was willing to overlook this mistake on his part since he was not only a lawyer, but perhaps was a nonsmoker as well. I was even further prepared to forgive the fact that he referred to Allen Whitcomb as "then president of In Concert International," but that was as far as I was willing to go. I had always been the president of In Concert. Allen left In Concert on March 13, 1991. He has no recollection of any such conversation with Chip Peay regarding the Marlboro dates. I seriously doubt that any conversation of that nature ever transpired.

It would seem that since In Concert had set all of the Marlboro dates from the very beginning and had issued all contracts on every date, Chip would have notified us of any changes in writing on something that important. At the very least he would have phoned me, as president of the company and as the one who had originally set up the dates, if he were acting in good faith. He didn't call.

We filed a complaint with the intention of suing them for what they were trying to steal. As any good attorney (please excuse the contradiction in terms) will tell you (after he has received his fee, of course), the minute that you have to start defending your interests you are already at a loss. This proved true enough.

This underlines the need for a legal contract when dealing with people like Ricky Skaggs. It makes it harder for them to get away with this type of thing. When Dick Blake died, Skaggs was already a big act and didn't have to sign anything. At that point I had the choice of either working with him without a contract or not having him as a client at all.

Skaggs' attorney attempted to get us out of court and into arbitration through the American Federation of Musicians, no doubt figuring that these hearings would take years to conclude and that they would wear me down. My attorney confirmed this view and said that I should get what I could from them and be done with the matter. As a result of these suggestions we offered to settle with them for an immediate payment of $15,000. They countered with an offer of $12,500, which I reluctantly accepted simply because I did not wish to be bothered about the matter any further.

On October 17, 1986, I signed a release protecting them from any further legal actions and they signed a similar release. Shortly thereafter we received a check for $12,500. The settlement was considered to be a compromise in which neither party admitted any kind of liability at all. I signed the release as president of In Concert. I would never have signed it personally.

Despite my acceptance of the settlement, I know what happened and what their intentions were, and they do too. Since I don't believe in hell, I don't have to worry too much about ending up there, but if I were Ricky Skaggs I would stay away from lightning. I still keep a copy of his checks around as well as a couple of photographs in the off chance that one day I might need some toilet paper.

After seven years Ricky disposed of Chip Peay as his manager. I heard that it was the result of his moral outrage over allegations that Chip had become involved with some girl in New York. Whether this was merely a rumor is impossible for me to say. Chip was subsequently divorced from his wife. In all probability, like most artists, Ricky figured that since he had become famous he could save himself some money by getting rid of Chip Peay. In any case, Ricky Skaggs is no longer getting $40,000 a night. In fact, it would be extremely rare for him to get half that amount. I think, as he might say, that he is now paying the price for having "gone above his raising."

Chapter Fourteen

James Brown

I had always been interested in black music, and when In Concert was started it was a lot like giving a kid the keys to the candy store. I had money to play with and, finally, the opportunity to do what I wanted. I had a vision, not only for my company, but for Nashville as well. I wanted Nashville to be truly "Music City U.S.A.," a center and base of operations for all types of music.

As a result of my aspirations, black music at In Concert had become a high priority for me. We had picked up Lou Rawls as a client. I had been with him on several dates in different parts of the country and had begun to feel fairly secure. My relationship with his manager, David Brokaw, had improved as well and I hoped that he and his brother, Sandy, would steer more clients my way.

Since we were representing Lou Rawls, I spoke to David Brokaw daily. Apparently, James Brown had asked Dick Clark to suggest a possible manager, and Dick had suggested David Brokaw as a candidate.

The King of Soul, Soul Brother Number One, The Hardest-Working Man in Show Business, Mr. Dynamite, and the God-father. These are but a few of the titles bestowed upon singer James Brown by an ardent public whose adoration he has enjoyed for four decades.

Born in Barnwell, South Carolina, in 1933, raised in poverty by an aunt, James Brown worked as a shoeshine boy and danced in the street to get money for groceries. He was influenced musically by what he heard on the radio and what he saw in church. He developed his skills on the keyboard by practicing on a church piano. Moving with his aunt to Augusta, Georgia, he did his first talent show at age eleven. Eventually he formed a group called the Famous Flames and was signed to King Records in 1956. James Brown rose from total obscurity to become one of the most musically influential artists of this century. His ability to work an audience into a frenzy, combined with his wild dance steps and screaming vocals, has made him one of the most respected and imitated figures in music.

At this time, late 1985, James Brown was represented by Universal Attractions in New York, which had been his agency for years. Universal Attractions was no threat, in my estimation. I was feeling my oats, having successfully stolen Mickey Gilley, Johnny Lee, and Lou Rawls from large West Coast agencies. I had definite plans about black music at In Concert but had no way of knowing how strong the relationship really was between James Brown and Universal. In my ignorance I perceived Universal Attractions to be an old folks' home, with probably no more than three agents, none of whom was less than a hundred years old.

When I had represented James Brown for a brief period at Dick Blake International, he had not worked any of the dates I had set, even though they were generally for more money than he was making at the time. I had received his phone number through a mutual friend. I called James, told him who I was and what I wanted and that I would be glad to come to Augusta for a meeting. He said to come on down, so agent Dave Barton and I took one of Dick Blake International's Beechcraft Barons and flew there. We were met at the airport by Al Garner, his manager, who took us to a hotel for some drinks and then over to James Brown's house outside of town.

I thought Al Garner to be kind of strange in that he did not display the confidence and authority that I was used to with most managers. In addition, he kept referring to James Brown as "Mr. Brown." That seemed rather formal considering the extent of their relationship, which went back over fifteen years according to "Mr. Garner."

James Brown met us by the pond just inside his front gate. I think that he was planning to see us briefly as a matter of courtesy and then get rid of us. Instead, we hit it off and he wanted to show Dave Barton and myself his office.

On the way there, we discussed his music, Nashville, and other matters. I had met James Brown several years before when he had played on the Grand Ole Uproar as a guest of Porter Wagoner, who had been managed by my sister at that time. I asked him about jazz organist Hank Marr, who had been a label-mate on Cincinnati-based King Records, Brown's first label, during the early 1960s. He said "What choo wanna know bout him for?" which translated meant, "Why would I possibly be interested in any other organ player when I was in the presence of the world's greatest jazz organist."

I had discovered Hank Marr at a used-record store and wanted to find out if he was still alive, and where he lived. His album *Live at Club 502* was one of the best live jazz records I had ever heard. I admired his bold style of playing and felt that perhaps I could do some business with him, if he could be located. I thought that maybe James Brown and Hank Marr were friends and that James might know where to reach him. James Brown apparently had not seen him in years and I felt that he did not want to talk about the matter, so I moved to something else.

It was kind of funny, because we drove to his office just as two of his workers were sneaking off, figuring that he was gone for the day. When they saw us arriving in his van they slinked back to the office like dogs expecting a whipping, which I believe they escaped due to our presence. It was a strange scene, with everybody referring to each other as "Mr." and "Mrs." The place was nice enough, but seemed disorganized to me. Nobody had a correct booking schedule or any publicity. Anyway, we struck a verbal deal with James Brown, and I returned to Nashville, feeling elated that I finally would be able to work with an artist whose music I actually liked.

I called in favors owed from buyers all over the country as a result of dates they had received or wanted to receive on the

Statler Brothers, Barbara Mandrell, and others in order to get
James Brown dates. Several good dates were set and approved
by James Brown, and contracts were sent. The contracts were
returned signed by the buyers along with deposits, and then
sent to James Brown for his signature. None of the contracts
ever came back from James Brown and all of the bookings had
to be canceled. It was all very strange, especially in light of the
fact that most of them had been for more money than Brown
had been getting.

I did not wish to see a replay of that situation, but felt that
with David Brokaw acting as manager, perhaps we could make
some money with him.

"Living in America," from the soundtrack of *Rocky IV,* was
moving up the charts at this time and it looked as if James
Brown's career was again on an upswing. We had been given
authorization from David Brokaw and Brown's attorney, Buddy
Dallas, to solicit dates for him. We had taken out a full-page ad
in the 1986 *Cavalcade,* an industry "yellow pages," announcing
exclusive worldwide representation. We were receiving and
submitting offers on this artist, and yet the same sort of
problems existed as before.

It was difficult to obtain a correct itinerary. I obviously did
not wish to call Universal Attractions and get his schedule from
them. Neither David Brokaw nor Buddy Dallas was certain of
the correct schedule of his dates. What everyone did know was
that James Brown was definitely playing at the Memorial
Auditorium in Chattanooga, on November 22, 1985.

I felt that a visit in person from me would make everything all
right, that he and I would be able to sit down to dinner and that
I would tell him exactly what I wanted him to do and that he
would do it. With as much experience as I had at that time, it
seems strange now, in looking back, that I could have imagined
that things would work out that way. They never do, and they
never will.

These artists never do anything they are told. In the first
place, they resent being told anything, and in many cases, not
without good reason. Life on the road produces its own logic.
Playing two hundred cities a year and traveling tens of thousands of miles provides the artist with a sense of perspective that

only that particular artist can ever truly understand. Furthermore, many so-called managers quite frequently give bad
advice.

I am going to digress and give the finest example of stupid
advice that I have ever heard from the standpoint of management, even though it has nothing to do with James Brown.
There was an act named the Thompson Brothers, consisting of
two brothers by the names of Harry and Larry Thompson.
They haunted the streets of Nashville, seeking their fame and
fortune around fifteen years ago. I remember them particularly
because of their unusual stage attire, which consisted of heavy
floor-length fur coats, and for their guitars, which had been
made from toilet seats. They lived in an old apartment building
next door to my office at the Lavender-Blake Agency.

At noon during the tourist season, they would begin their
short walk to the corner of Sixteenth and Demonbreun, where
they played outside every day. They performed in the blazing
sunshine wearing those coats. They were well known to all of
the music people in town, since we saw them on the streets
constantly.

Finally they succeeded in putting out an album on an
independent label and were kind enough to give me a promotional copy for my review. The music itself was as good as much
of what the major labels are producing these days, but their
vocals were somewhat slurred. I was told by one of the two that
this was due in all probability to the fact that both of them had
been to the dentist and had all of their teeth removed. They had
been advised to do this by their manager, who had determined
they needed some sort of gimmick to further their careers. It
was fortunate that they had not mistakenly wandered into the
office of a urologist.

Getting acts to do what they are supposed to do is especially
difficult in cases where artists like James Brown and Jerry Lee
Lewis are involved. These acts have been there since the
beginning of their art form, have weathered its many changes,
and are still standing. Such persons have been almost everywhere and done nearly everything, and usually to great excess.
They have been adored by the masses, and their egos have
evolved to an insane degree. These acts are referred to by the

public as "living legends." To the people behind the scenes, those of us involved with them on a day-to-day basis, they might be more appropriately called "living nightmares."

Of all the entertainers I have ever met, known, or dealt with, James Brown is the worst, with the singular exception of Ricky Skaggs. He truly believes that he is the father of rock and roll. No, "father" is not strong enough. He calls himself the Godfather. He knows that he is greater by far, and certainly more universally acclaimed, than Elvis Presley, or anyone else for that matter. According to him, his is the only face that can be recognized worldwide, by anyone, anywhere on earth. "Besides," he adds as an afterthought, "Elvis never played Africa!"

Bruce Shelton and I drove to Chattanooga on Friday morning the day of the show, hit a couple of junk shops, and settled into the Read House Hotel for a little rest before greeting James Brown. I called the promoter and told him that I would meet him at 4:00 P.M. at his place of business on Market Street, about half a mile from where we were staying.

It was cold outside and I felt somewhat depressed even though I was at the height of my career. Things were going well at In Concert. We had weathered the storm, had plenty of money, and were moving ahead. Everything was beautiful on the surface, as usual, but my life was not going so well on a personal level. I knew that things would get better, but I was beginning to wonder when.

At the hotel, I read for a while and took a shower. It was time to visit the promoter. We took Bruce's big Cadillac and drove to 405 Market Street to some toilet that passed for a teen club. The joint consisted of some graffiti-covered walls, a front and rear door, and that was about it. The promoter, Charles Locke, was about thirty years old and looked like a yuppie.

We discussed the situation. The promoter had bought the date from Universal Attractions based upon the projected success of the single "Living in America." He claimed that he had been promised radio interviews by James Brown's agent and that he had been unable to get any. He felt that he had done everything he could to promote the date and that he had received no help from either the artist or the agency. He had advertised on the appropriate stations and arranged a welcoming committee, as well as a highly publicized reception at the Martin Luther King Center. In addition, he had paid for the act's rooms at the Chattanooga Choo Choo Hotel and arranged for limousine service for the Godfather and his court.

Tickets at the forty-eight-hundred-seat facility were not selling very well. I think there was an advance sale of around three hundred, which was not very good at all. The promoter appeared to be high on something, and under the circumstances, I can't say that I blame him. He was lamenting his fate, feeling abandoned by the gods. He said that although it was his first show, he had rolled the dice knowing full well that it was a high-risk situation. He was, so he said, man enough to deal with things on that basis.

The lack of help from the artist and the agency, however, placed him at an increased risk, which he was not prepared to accept. Consequently, he felt somewhat bitter about the lack of ticket sales, more so than he would have if he had received the help that he said he had been promised. I did not know whether his allegations were true, but I had reason to believe they were.

What I did know was that the show would be a disaster. In addition, the tickets were overpriced. They should have been priced at $10 instead of $15 to $18. When a show has such a poor advance, it is very seldom saved by a last-minute walk-up crowd. I attempted to comfort the promoter, but the handwriting was on the wall.

We got into the limousine and headed over to the airport to greet the Godfather upon his arrival. There was a small group of fans, mostly black, waiting for him. Among those gathered was one man I recognized, a black disc jockey named Bobby-Q Day. I reminded him that we had met back in June when Lou Rawls played the Riverfront Festival. He remembered me vaguely and we talked about the upcoming show. Bobby-Q explained that the promoter had done his homework, meaning that the show had been properly advertised.

In a few minutes, Mr. Dynamite, the King of Soul, the Godfather himself came walking through the gate arm in arm with his new bride. There were a few faint screams from the crowd. It was certainly not the welcome he would have received ten or twenty years ago. James Brown sported a fur coat and a large pair of emerald-green sunglasses with convex lenses.

I walked up to him and reintroduced myself. I had not seen him since the night of a fund-raising show for disc jockey John R. at the Opry House two years before. I said, "Hello, Mr. Brown, nice to see you." He mumbled something in reply that I took to be favorable, and we proceeded down the corridor. There was an anteroom somewhere in the airport in which a TV interview took place. The questions were asinine and offensive, although not intentionally so. I found it commendable that James Brown showed such restraint.

However, his impatience soon surfaced and he became irritated as the interviewer kept asking him age-related questions, such as "What are you going to do when you get old?" "Do you plan to retire soon?" and so on. James Brown told the reporter in all seriousness that he would never get old. Questions of a similar nature kept coming and I sensed there was going to be trouble. This was fortunately averted by the arrival of his bride as she walked up, on her knees, to the chair in which he sat.

The promoter asked me to speak to James Brown about visiting the Martin Luther King Center, where a reception was waiting. He declined to go, notwithstanding that this was a black organization honoring him and that it would look bad for him if he did not show up. I explained the situation to Bobby-Q and he graciously interceded with Soul Brother Number One, persuading him to stop by the center for a cameo appearance. On the way over, I sat in the front seat of the limousine next to the driver and the promoter. James Brown and his lovely bride sat in the back of the car.

I mentioned to James Brown that I understood that he had a new manager, referring to David Brokaw. He did not know what I was talking about, so I rephrased the statement, this time mentioning David Brokaw by name. He quickly replied that David Brokaw was not his manager, but that they might "do some things together from time to time."

James Brown then asked about the advance sales for the show that night. The promoter told him the truth, but this did not seem to bother him. He told the promoter not to worry, that plenty of people would show up. He was not very talkative. I knew this would be an unpleasant night.

Bruce and I arrived at the Memorial Auditorium about fifteen minutes before show time. The place was virtually empty. I located the promoter, who was understandably frantic. He said that the auditorium manager had warned him not to use James Brown. He was angry that so few tickets had been sold. He did not know what to do about any of it.

The opening act was some terrible car-wreck band that was managed by the promoter. I ran into the promoter again backstage. He had thought about the situation a bit more and had reached some definite conclusions. He gave me a quick rundown of his expenses. I asked him if he had settled up with the building manager, and he informed me that he had.

"What about James Brown?" I asked.

He had not yet paid him the other $7,500 that he was owed, and did not want to. He felt that James Brown had been totally uncooperative throughout the entire charade, and he had reached a decision that he wanted me to explain to the performer.

There were two options that the promoter was prepared to offer: First, Brown could keep the $7,500 deposit that had been sent to Universal Attractions, and he could go ahead and play the show. The promoter did not wish to pay him any more money. Second, James Brown could keep the $7,500 deposit and not do the show, in which case the promoter would refund the ticket money to the people in the auditorium.

I asked him if he had the other $7,500 that was due James Brown and he replied that he had the money in his pocket. I had driven down from Nashville and I wanted to see a show if possible. I felt sorry for the promoter to a certain degree. He was obviously in way over his head, and had most likely done this, his first show, because he was a fan of James Brown. The promoter, despite his inexperience, had acted honorably and had done what he was supposed to do.

He had promised the auditorium manager, Clyde Hawkins, that he would have the rest of the money he owed James Brown in cash. If he refunded the ticket money he would end up with nothing. In addition, I feel that an artist should be worth his selling price. In this particular case, it was obvious that James Brown was not. I told the promoter that I would go talk with Mr. Brown. I had learned from his former manager, Al Garner, that the Godfather insisted on being called Mr. Brown. I had also noticed on this present outing that he had to put on a dirty white glove before he could shake hands with anyone. What a pretentious bunch of horseshit.

When agent Dave Barton and I had visited him in Augusta five years before, James Brown had seemed to be a pretty nice guy, given of course that he was an egomaniac. He might still be all right in a one-on-one situation, but add to that a third person, anyone, and he had to play the part of the heavy. What a shame. It requires so much more effort to be a jerk than it does to be nice, especially to people who admire you to begin with.

I knocked on the dressing-room door and was admitted by Danny Ray, the man who has covered James Brown with the traditional cape and helped him off stage for almost thirty years. I explained the situation very concisely, offering both of the options that the promoter had outlined, neglecting to mention that the promoter actually had the other $7,500 in his pocket.

If I had expected an intelligent response, I was disappointed. Mr. Brown said that God would take care of it. I thought that perhaps I had misunderstood him, or that he had misunderstood me, so I ran through it one more time. "God will handle it," he mumbled.

The choice was clearly up to him and I felt like saying, "Well, you imbecile, how would you like for God to handle it?" It was obvious that I wasn't getting anywhere. The opening act had already finished their so-called show. Whatever was going to be done needed to be done quickly.

The dressing room was hot as hell, so I started to remove my sport coat. James Brown turned to me quickly and said, "Mr. Faragher, your coat. This is my dressing room." I wondered what could possibly happen next. In the meantime, I put my coat on, excused myself from the dressing room, found the promoter, and told him what had happened.

We went back together and tried again. When the promoter

explained that he had not been granted any of the interviews he had been promised to help promote the show, James Brown acted as if it was all a surprise to him. When the promoter mentioned that he had called James Brown's office in Augusta and had spoken to his secretary, Mrs. Blanchard, several times, I knew that he was telling the truth. James Brown had been told about the calls—he just had not wanted to go to the trouble to do the interviews.

"I have worked my ass off on this show," the promoter said. He was immediately reprimanded by Soul Brother Number One with the words, "Watch your language. My wife." I looked over at his wife. She sat there with a big smirk on her face and said nothing. When the promoter again mentioned the two options available to the Godfather, he responded in much the same fashion as he had before, only now, in addition to saying that God would take care of it, he also tossed out phrases like "The people!" "This great American nation!" and "Only in America!"

We were getting nowhere. I left all of them in the dressing room and located Clyde Hawkins, the auditorium manager. I had known him for quite some time. He had been the manager of that auditorium as early as 1971, back when I was in college in Chattanooga. He seemed very nervous to me, much more so, I felt, than the circumstances actually warranted. I explained the dilemma to him in much the same way as I had explained it to Mr. Dynamite, but this only served to upset him further. "This happened once before, with Wilson Pickett," he said. "It was just like this, a small but volatile crowd. They wrecked the place."

I escorted him to the dressing room, which now contained James Brown, his wife, the promoter, the auditorium manager, and myself. Under the circumstances, I felt as if I was the only normal person there. Clyde Hawkins asked James Brown what he intended to do. Once again, James Brown started with "The people!" and "This great American nation!" The auditorium manager was not interested in hearing any of that horseshit and cut him off immediately.

"I just want to know whether or not there is going to be a show, and if so, when?"

"Now!" James Brown replied.

Clyde Hawkins left the room, followed by the promoter and myself. The promoter asked me what he should do with the other $7,500 that he had in his pocket. I asked him what he wanted to do with it.

"I'd like to keep it," he said. "What should I do?"

I told him that if I were him, I would leave through the nearest door as soon as possible, and not return. As far as I was concerned, he could keep the money. James Brown had wasted my time in the past and seemed to be wasting it now. He had been completely irresponsible and could have helped the promoter but had chosen not to. Furthermore, all of that pretentious crap about putting on his dirty white glove before he could shake hands and not letting me take off my jacket in his room really irritated me.

There was another factor that influenced my decision to let the promoter walk away with the money. The date had been set by Universal Attractions, and they had been representing James Brown almost forever. James Brown would no doubt be furious about not getting paid, and he would be angry with Universal Attractions. A fitting end to a long relationship. James Brown would think of me in the back of his mind as the one who had been there and had tried to work things out. I had been courteous and had humored the aging Mr. Dynamite by calling him "Mr. Brown," even though he had conducted himself like a moron. After this night's insanities, I realized once again that he would be a major problem, but I was used to that. Another day, another dollar.

The show itself was horrible beyond words. The band played for over twenty minutes, if it could indeed be called playing, before the star of the show hit the stage. He was flammably attired in some hideous polyester jumpsuit of the type that had been discarded by the fashion world a decade before.

His wife sang backup, using a microphone placed behind the curtain at stage left so that she could not be seen by the audience. I could not help but wonder about that arrangement. I was standing about eight feet from her and I could not hear her. I don't think that the microphone was even plugged in.

The horn section blasted away, but in an undisciplined manner. Each musician appeared to be playing to himself, without regard to the other band members. It was dreadful. At one point during the show, James Brown moved to the keyboard of his Hammond B-3 organ to offer a display of his virtuosity. The Hammond B-3 is a beautiful instrument with a nice walnut finish. It somewhat resembles a coffin on four legs. This one had been completely covered in a Mexican-looking red-swirled padded vinyl. Boldly emblazoned across the front of the instrument in black vinyl letters were the words THE GODFATHER.

I was standing on the side of the stage behind some curtains, about five feet away from the organ. Almost the entire time that James Brown played his lengthy organ solo, he stared at me as if to say, "I'm bad!" Indeed he was. He swept the keyboard from side to side without any particular purpose as the horn section blasted away. He is truly an excellent organist, but his performance on this occasion gave no indication of his abilities.

James Brown did his two encores after having been helped off the stage draped in his famous cape. It was very unconvincing, and I was anxious for the show to be over. At this point he was presented with the key to the city. His band had already left the stage.

After the presentation, Mr. Dynamite turned with his hand on his hip and stood facing in the direction of the dressing rooms. He did not tell anyone to summon the band. Instead, he sought to bring them back to the stage with telepathic rays. He intended to subject the small audience to yet one more encore. He stood motionless in this fashion for a full five minutes before the band members returned to their posts. It appeared to me that they were all back in their places, and yet the Godfather continued to stand there silently for a few more minutes until at last the missing musician went past me, cursing. "That son of a bitch."

Bruce asked me what had happened with the money and I replied that I had told the promoter to keep it. "Hell," he said, "you should have made him give you a couple thousand."

I had no doubt that I could have done so, but I was not interested in doing anything that might come back to haunt me later. Besides, I was making enough money already. Bruce and I returned to the Read House, glad that this horror show was over.

And so it ended with James Brown the second time much the

way it did the first. I came into the situation as a fan, looking forward to doing business and having a good time with someone I really admired and respected, but left the brief relationship feeling otherwise. I was sorry that we had not become friends, but the Godfather doesn't want friends. He wants to be worshiped, and that's not my style. As far as doing business is concerned, it was not possible.

I finally called up the president of Universal Attractions, told him who I was, and actually apologized for any trouble I might have caused him. As far as I was concerned, he could keep James Brown.

I think that now is a good time to mention briefly the relationship between the artist and the fan. While their relationship seems simple enough on the surface, there are a number of complex psychological factors that come into play. Among these are the artist's sometimes desperate need for approval and the fan's need to project his unconscious psychic contents upon a suitable object. Without the fan, the artist has no career. The fan also needs the artist. The artist in many instances provides a role model or hero for the fan to admire and to emulate. In many, if not most cases, the fan assumes that the star is probably a great guy, someone the fan would really like if they ever met. In cases where the artist and fan are members of the opposite sex, the projection factor can be stronger still, with the fan imagining that he or she is in love with the star.

Many times a fan buys every record an artist releases, attends concerts, joins the fan club, and supports the artist in a number of ways. This can go on for years. In most cases this is all fairly healthy and normal, and everybody benefits. But what happens when a fan finally meets a star? Generally the fan tells the artist how much he or she enjoys his music, gets a photo or an autograph, and everyone is happy.

Most fans never meet their idols, but when they do the way it is handled by the artist is very important. A fan may have waited literally years for an opportunity to speak to an artist. If the artist is short or discourteous in that brief instant, he can lose a lifelong fan.

At the same time, many fans actually believe that the object of their adoration is a public property and owes them something for their support. As a matter of consequence, fans are often rude and inconsiderate, interrupting the artist in public and intruding into his private life at inappropriate times.

From my standpoint as an agent, it was really interesting and exciting to sometimes represent acts I admired, especially when they turned out to be genuinely nice people. This was rare enough, but it happened. I only wished James Brown was one of them.

The Jamaican group The Itals. The Temptations meet the Twilight Zone. Incredible harmonies. They were nominated for a Grammy in 1987. (Author's collection)

The I Threes, with the author. Rita Marley, Judy Mowatt, and Marcia Griffiths were the three most prominent women in Jamaican music. This was taken in Kingston, Jamaica, in 1987 after the Lou Rawls concert. Sly Dunbar, Yellowman, and The Itals also showed up for Lou's performance. (Author's collection)

In the Blue Mountains of Jamaica with Joseph Hill, the lead singer of the group
Culture. Dem a payaka. (Author's collection)

Ronnie Milsap. His associates suspected the author of
hoodoo, devil worship, and
black magic. (Courtesy of
RCA Records, Nashville)

The author, Waylon Jennings, and Jess Colter, Nashville 1974. The Outlaws were just breaking onto the scene nationally. At Chuck Glaser's Nova Agency, our clients were Waylon, Jesse, Tompall Glaser, and David Allan Coe. (Herb Burnette)

The marquee at Gilley's, the "World's Largest Honky Tonk." For more than a decade, everybody who was anybody played Gilley's. The club was torched on July 5, 1990. Mickey Gilley and Sherwood Cryer each thought the other had had the place burned down. (Author's collection)

The author and Mickey Gilley in Hollywood, November 1984. I wouldn't have been smiling if I knew what was about to happen. Still, we had four good years together. (Courtesy of *The Tennessean*)

Sherwood Cryer, the brains behind Mickey Gilley and Johnny Lee. He had a reputation for violence but was well liked by almost everyone in Nashville. One of my best friends, and one of the greatest men I have ever known. (Author's collection)

David Brokaw, one of the prime movers in the *Urban Cowboy* phenomenon. He tried to stop Gilley from leaving the William Morris Agency and joining In Concert, but eventually we won him over. Gilley brought us Lou Rawls. (Author's collection)

Billy Ray Cyrus. "Elvis on Steroids," that's how he was described by a club manager in Austin at the South By Southwest Festival in March 1988. RCA passed on him. So did Curb Records, and so did Mercury. (Peter Nash, courtesy Mercury Records, Nashville)

The new Kentucky Headhunters, one of the most interesting acts in country music. Many of the oldtimers complained that they weren't country. The public thinks otherwise. (Alan Messer, courtesy of Mercury Records, Nashville)

The ———— Brothers, Ricky Lee and Doug Phelps, left the highly successful Kentucky Headhunters during Fan Fair in 1992. They ran a contest to decide the name of their new group. I thought they should call themselves "The Foolish Brothers." (Courtesy of Mercury Records, Nashville)

Left to right: Jack Coe, David Allan Coe, and the author at the Exit/In, Nashville, 1974. David Allan Coe called himself the Mysterious Rhinestone Cowboy. One of the true enigmas of country music. (Bob Shanz)

Ray Price is one of the most successful country music entertainers of all time, a pioneer whose career spans four decades. His band, "The Cherokee Cowboys," once included country greats Willie Nelson, Johnny Paycheck, Buddy Emmons, Roger Miller, and Johnny Bush. Ray is again recording for Columbia Records. (Courtesy Columbia Records, Nashville)

Chapter Fifteen

Live From Jamaica

I was fortunate enough to have seen Jamaican artist Bob Marley perform live in my own hometown at Vanderbilt University on December 8, 1978. Unfortunately, however, some idiot had selected the Memorial Gymnasium as the venue. The acoustics were terrible and it was therefore one of the worst shows I have ever attended, although it was not the artist's fault. There was not much reggae in the Music City during those days. Very few record stores carried anything other than the big three: Bob Marley, Peter Tosh, and Bunny Wailer. Most stores didn't even carry their music.

In early April of 1982, I was pleased to see posters announcing a Jamaican Reggae Festival at some short-lived club on Second Avenue South called Under the Bridge. The acts scheduled to appear were the Itals, the Roots Radics, and Don Carlos. The ticket price was $9, and the face of the ticket read "Top Secret Agency Presents." I had been an agent in town for nine years by then and had never heard of that company. I looked forward to seeing the performance and meeting the agent who had set the date.

The place was sold out so there was no place to sit. The show, which was scheduled to start at 9:00 P.M., didn't get going until about 10:15 P.M., a practice that I subsequently found to be standard procedure at most Jamaican events. I had expected to see a Hammond organ, banks of amplifiers, and a large number of drums and other equipment on the bandstand. Such had been the case with Bob Marley. His organ player, Earl Lindo, played a Hammond C-3, with four Leslie tone cabinets. Marley had used two keyboard players, three backup singers, several percussionists, and a row of horns. This band, however, consisted of four musicians with about the same type of equipment we had used in our high school bands.

The Roots Radics opened the show. When the song "Young Lover" started to play, I realized that the singer was Bingy Bunny, formerly a vocalist with a group called the Morwells and one of reggae music's foremost guitar players. After about twenty minutes, the band was joined by singer Don Carlos; and later a vocal trio, the Itals, closed the show.

The influence of music on our lives is far greater than we realize. It is almost impossible to get away from it. We hear so much music, in fact, that many times we cease to be aware of it at all. Supermarkets, restaurants, department stores—it is everywhere; and it affects us even when we don't consciously hear it. I was exposed to reggae in much the same way.

My first experience of Caribbean music came to me in the form of Harry Belafonte's album *Calypso*, which was played at quiet times in my third-grade classroom. It was our favorite record. The music was subtle and compelling and it touched me deeply the first time I heard it.

In the early sixties, a song entitled "My Boy Lollipop" by Jamaican artist Millie Small received heavy airplay. Millie Small was sixteen years old and the music was known as "Ska" or "Blue Beat." The song was really a novelty tune, but it did well. It is interesting to note that this record was produced by Chris Blackwell, who was later to produce Bob Marley and would also found Island Records.

In September 1968, Johnny Nash had a hit on the American market with a reggae-flavored tune called "Hold Me Tight." He followed with another Jamaican-flavored hit, "Stir It Up," which was written by Bob Marley. One afternoon, while I was in navy boot camp, I saw a TV show featuring Johnny Nash. He talked about having recorded in Jamaica and made it sound like a happening place. The impression stuck.

In 1969 another Jamaican artist, Desmond Dekker, had a smash hit called "The Israelites." I had no idea what the song meant. The lyrics were mostly unintelligible, but the music itself was quite distinct. In 1971 a Jamaican duo named Dave and Ansell Collins had an instrumental hit called "Double Barrel." In 1979, Deborah Harry of the group Blondie had a successful record with a remake of a song called "The Tide Is High," originally done by a Jamaican group known as the Paragons. Like most American listeners, these were my only experiences of the music that would eventually become known as reggae. At that time, I had no idea that the term "reggae" even existed, and yet slowly, subconsciously perhaps, the music took hold.

This all changed for me in 1978, when a friend from out of town made a surprise visit. He had been in Jamaica a few months and was passing through town. In the tape player of his old Cadillac convertible was some of the strangest music I ever heard. At times different instruments would suddenly cease to play without warning right in the middle of the melody. It was difficult to understand the singer at all. He would sing awhile, and then talk some as the music continued. I had never heard anything like this in my life. The beat was primitive and erotic. The horns served mainly as a backdrop to a heavy bass and chopping, staccato guitar. The horns sensually soothed and caressed, while the indistinct vocals lulled and intoxicated. It was the most emotional and purely sexual music I had ever heard. The singer was named Big Youth, the music was Jamaican, and it was called reggae.

I subsequently learned that this music represented its own genre. As I began to seek more information about it. I found that the music had evolved from calypso. Reggae's style had originally been a Caribbean interpretation of American soul music. Within the class of reggae music, there are several subdivisions. The vocal groups such as the original Wailers, the Heptones, and Paragons were my favorites. Their smooth harmonies are exquisite and most of their early music dealt with romantic themes.

As the music progressed, the themes changed to some degree. Where calypso had been a happy and sometimes ribald music, its child, reggae, had become increasingly political. Some of this music was all right, but the political side of reggae had no relevance for me. I do not feel myself to be a "Down Presser," and I have never owned any slaves. I think that this political base has hurt the music overall.

For the most part, black America has bypassed reggae. The Rastafarian is not a particularly snappy dresser; he is not likely to be driving a Mercedes or manifesting any other aspect of a lifestyle that American blacks would care to emulate.

Most of the American audience for Jamaican music consists of predominantly white college kids. It is always interesting to see students dancing and jumping around at these shows as the music spreads its message that Babylon must fall. These students are the children of the "Babylonians" and most often will soon enter that world in pursuit of wealth and prestige, the very things Rastafarianism detests. The extent to which reggae music has been commercially successful in the United States is proportionate to the degree that it has been relevant to the white, twenty-to-forty-year-old record buyer.

If reggae is ever really going to succeed in America, it must sacrifice a certain vital part of its nature in order to do so. Perhaps Bob Marley's commercial success was due to the fact that his music was not strictly message music. He mixed his political songs with a reasonable amount of love songs. Genetically, he represented the fusion of two completely opposite cultures in one man (his father was white and his mother was black) and was therefore uniquely qualified to speak to and for both races. He also opened the door for the music as an art form worldwide. The music has failed on the whole to take advantage of this opportunity by harping overly on political issues.

American rap music is nothing more than an adaptation of Jamaican "yard style" or "dub" music that has been changed to suit the black American palate. Jamaicans should have owned this form of music, since they created it. The world market was lost commercially because the Jamaican creators of rap music failed to understand that the majority of Americans do not care what happens in Jamaica or any other Third World country.

This applies equally to black America as well. Most black

Americans realize that success comes from pursuing the same things that white America seeks: prosperity, ease, and comfort. These things are available for black America to the extent to which they can become a part of the white-dominated system in America. Although racial prejudice still exists, most white Americans are very anxious to see the black population successful in both their business and personal lives.

I am not sure that this is the case in Jamaica, and this perhaps accounts for the intense musical preoccupation with the destruction and fall of Babylon, meaning primarily white society as we know it. Reggae music may already have had its heyday. I hope not. My feelings about the reasons why Jamaican music, reggae in particular, has not come to full fruition are strictly my own. I have no doubt that some musical scholars will take issue with what I have said, and could go as far as to say that reggae music is political by definition.

Back to the show. The Roots Radics and Don Carlos were both incredible, but it was the Itals who really knocked me out. These three, with their long, matted hair, reminded me of "The Twilight Zone"'s answer to the Temptations. They were amazing, and it was an evening that I will never forget. This show, with these acts, in this dumpy bar, with minimal equipment, was without doubt the best show of any kind I had ever seen in my life.

Several months later, another reggae show came to Nashville and played at another short-lived club called Roosters, which was actually the upstairs portion of an old mustard factory known as the Cannery, a place in which I had worked for a couple of weeks one summer during my college years. This show consisted of the Gladiators, featuring vocalist Albert Griffiths and singer Yabby Yu. I had no idea that in a very short time I would be in Jamaica and would be representing the Itals, the Gladiators, and other Jamaican acts.

After the November 1985 Chattanooga show with James Brown, I went to Columbus, Ohio, to hear jazz organist Hank Marr play. I had gone to considerable trouble finding him, and after a nationwide search had located him playing a place called the Coventry Inn. It was indeed a treat getting to hear him play.

He is a master of the Hammond B3 organ and one of the great jazz organists of all time. Saxophonist Rusty Bryant was accompanying him that night as well. It was a wonderful experience.

The following evening I again went to hear the Gladiators, who also happened to be playing in Columbus. This was the fourth reggae show I had attended. I was by this time hooked on the music and wanted to be involved, but I did not know if there was enough public awareness or demand to be able to make any money fooling with it. Furthermore, I did not personally know any of the people involved in the music or what it would take to do business with them. I decided to put reggae on the back burner for a while.

It was only November, yet it was already very cold in Nashville, so when the opportunity to go on a sea cruise presented itself, I took it. One of our clients, CBS artist Mark Gray, was scheduled to go out aboard the SS *Emerald Seas* for a Nashville Network special, along with the Whites, Ricky Skaggs, and Reba McEntire.

Formerly a singer with the group Exile, Mark had been the fair-haired child at CBS for a brief time. He had cowritten "The Closer You Get" for the group Alabama and "It Ain't Easy Being Easy" for Janie Frickie, among others. Despite a tremendous expenditure by the record label, a great deal of hype, and the release of three albums, nothing had really happened for him as an artist, even though everyone who heard him readily admitted that he was great. He was subsequently dropped by the record label, but that was still in the future at the time of this cruise.

The ship went to Freeport, St. Thomas, and Nassau. It was in Nassau that I finally decided what to do with reggae music. It was blasting from doorways and car windows. I determined then and there that I would take over reggae and eventually control the world market. This was a lofty undertaking and would no doubt require a great deal of work. Despite the fact that I did not yet know the inner workings of the reggae scene, I felt that I was in a position to reach that goal.

In the United States there were only a few agencies dealing with that type of music at all, and none of them were major companies. I had the experience, the money, the manpower, the reputation, and the desire to get the job done. I also felt that the heavyweight black acts on my roster would give me all the credibility I needed with the Jamaican artists, as well as with talent buyers in America. There was absolutely no doubt in my mind that within a very short period of time I would be able to step into the reggae marketplace and take anything I wanted. And I wanted it all.

I called Sherwood Cryer and told him what I had in mind. He was pleased with what was happening with the other black acts I was handling and asked me how I intended to accomplish my aims with the Jamaicans. I replied that it was my intention to go down to Kingston in person and line up the artists I wanted to work with. I knew from reading the magazine the *Reggae Beat* that artist Dennis Brown would be playing the auditorium there on December 28, 1985. That seemed like an appropriate time to start my mission. It was by then the end of November, so there was not much time to prepare for my trip, but I had made my decision.

Sherwood wished me well and, as usual, told me to do what I wanted to do. What I really wanted to do was to build an agency the size of William Morris, Triad, or ICM. I wanted it based in Nashville, with offices eventually in New York, Los Angeles, and Europe. Talent agencies in Nashville traditionally had very limited goals. I was certain that such an agency would one day exist, based in Nashville. I just wondered if I was sharp enough personally to put it all together. I was not intimidated by the West Coast or anything that happened there. I did respect those agencies' unquestionable sovereignty in television and movies, but those areas were not on my agenda this early in the game, and I doubted that we would ever be able to beat them in that branch of the business.

As far as personal appearances were concerned, however, I knew that we could whip their asses. I was proud of my company and of the work we were doing. We were the first and only agency in Nashville that had any black artists at all, and even though we only had three at that point, Lou Rawls, James Brown, and Fats Domino, those few were all in the living legend category. When it was all over, several years later, and the dust had settled, I proved to have been at least fifteen years ahead of my time.

Kingston has a reputation for being a rough place, and though I first intended to go to Jamaica by myself, as the time for departure approached I realized that it might be a good idea to take somebody with me since I had not been there before. I selected agent Jeff Nunnally, who was very pleased with the assignment. After making the necessary arrangements, we left Nashville on December 27, 1985, anticipating a great adventure.

I had done my homework, having made a number of calls before we left Nashville, and had a fairly good idea whom I wanted to meet when we arrived. My perception of Kingston at that time was much the same as the average country music fan's perception of Nashville. It was the capital of reggae music, and I expected to see famous Jamaican artists dining in fashionable restaurants and walking around town.

Unfortunately, I already knew that some of the artists I would have liked to see were living elsewhere. I had read that Leroy Sibbles, former lead singer of the Heptones, and vocalist Ken Boothe were both living in Canada. I was told that Jimmy Cliff had not been to Jamaica in a while and that Dennis Brown was living in London. There were, however, many other artists living in and around Kingston whom I did wish to meet. Bunny Wailer, Peter Tosh, Gregory Isaacs, the Mighty Diamonds, Big Youth, and Culture were all acts I was interested in who were still in Jamaica. It was my intention ultimately to represent all of these acts and more on a exclusive basis.

I planned eventually to run these acts just like I used to run country acts in the Southwest. I imagined having three or four reggae acts touring simultaneously in different parts of the country. I wanted to crisscross them and keep them working constantly. This was certainly a logical plan and I saw no reason why I could not put it into action. I attributed the fact that it was not being done this way already to the feeling that reggae had been handled in the past by amateurs or by companies operating on a shoestring budget. It should have occurred to me that there were other, more significant reasons why reggae had not really made it in the United States.

We had flown Eastern all the way from Nashville so I was not surprised when our baggage failed to arrive, since the same thing had happened to me with Eastern in Haiti. We waited around the airport for a while before we gave up completely. It would have been nice if there had been someone there to help us, but such was not the case. We had left a cold Nashville and were now in a tropical paradise, so there was no need for alarm. We could pick up our rental car, check into the hotel, drive around for a while, and then check back at the airport and see if our baggage had showed up.

There were no rental cars available and we were unable to get one the entire time we were there. The fact that I had made the arrangements for the car to be waiting before we left Nashville, and that I had received a confirmation number, meant nothing. Jamaica. No problem! This was my first introduction to business in Jamaica. Very few people concern themselves with details or considerations about time. A two o'clock meeting, for example, might or might not mean two o'clock. "I will give you an answer on Thursday" might mean a week from Thursday, or perhaps not at all.

This general attitude is very irritating to outsiders who are accustomed to dealing in specifics, and the only way to keep from going crazy is to establish quite clearly at the outset that two o'clock means precisely two o'clock. Having made this absolutely clear at the beginning, intelligent people should then adjust their own attitude so that when the inevitable happens they will not be upset.

I should also mention that the promise to do something does not necessarily mean that it will be done. A promise is just that, a promise and nothing more. There are most likely several reasons for the prevalence of such a casual attitude on the part of the general population of Jamaica. In the first place, poverty and unemployment seem fairly high in some areas. In addition, there is not much to do down there after a while. Life goes on pretty much the same from day to day, so the life of the average Jamaican is unlikely to change much one way or the other whether he or she is punctual or not. Since few opportunities exist, there is little to be gained from being unusually diligent. The heat and constancy of the climate also produce a certain indolence and apathy, which are further exaggerated by the frequent and widespread use of marijuana, at least among the musicians.

We finally took a taxi to the Pegasus Hotel, checked in, and decided to go out for a stroll through the district known as New Kingston. We had not traveled far before we encountered two rather seedy street youths who offered to sell us some herb. This sounded good to me, although I felt somewhat uneasy when the four of us stepped into an alley and the ugliest of the two, "Tex," produced a knife. I could tell that Jeff did not care for this arrangement either, and wanted to get out of there and back on the main drag. I was prepared to fight if necessary and figured that we could take both of them if we had to, although that was not my desire.

Tex used the knife to cut up some of the buds and we transacted our business. He was a very shrewd, calculating type of guy and asked a great many questions about why we were there and what we were doing. I explained briefly and he said that he could put us together with anyone we wished to see. I doubted that, but then, reggae is, after all, the music of the streets. Perhaps he could be of some help later, so I told him that any help he could provide would be appreicated, and Jeff and I went on our way.

We returned to the hotel and then took a cab over to a club called Epiphany, where we were at first denied admission because of our tennis shoes. We finally talked our way into the place and found ours to be the only white faces there. I danced with some of the local girls and had a wonderful time while Jeff stood at the bar and watched.

The next morning I was on the phone bright and early, attempting to locate a rental car. The yellow pages were loaded with advertisements from car rental agencies offering to deliver your car to the hotel. There was not one rental car available in the entire city of Kingston, and there was not going to be. As soon as I accepted this, my attitude improved considerably. Our baggage finally arrived and everything again seemed to be under control.

When it was time for the Dennis Brown show, we went to the auditorium in a taxi with two girls we had met at the pool. There was a long line to buy tickets but we waited patiently, standing outside in the warm and sultry night air. It was truly incredible. Here we were, two hillbillies from Nashville, Tennessee, with two Nubian queens, prepared for a night of intoxicating music and sensual pleasures.

Once inside, we were surrounded by a sea of probably eight thousand black faces. I think that I saw one other white boy in the whole place. In standard Jamaican fashion, the show started an hour and a half late. I reflected that there was no way that many American blacks would have waited that long and that quietly for any show. About the only disturbance consisted of a few people dropping large packs of firecrackers off the balcony onto the floor below. I gathered from the frequency with which this happened that it was a standard and accepted procedure at such events.

The show itself was magnificent in every way, and featured artists Half Pint, 809, Ziggy Marley, and Dennis Brown. After Dennis Brown performed, I left Jeff with the girls and went backstage. Dennis Brown was so intoxicated that conversation was impossible. There were many other famous Jamaican artists in attendance and I was fortunate in getting to meet Manley Buchannon, a.k.a. Big Youth. I should mention at this point that reggae artists have some rather unique and unusual stage names, as did their predecessors who sang calypso music. Most of the calypso artists used professional names that began with titles of nobility, such as "Duke," "Lord," or "Earl." The reggae artists had dropped the titles of royalty in favor of more stylish names such as Dennis Alcapone, Prince Far I, Clint Eastwood, Half Pint, U Roy, I Roy, Tenor Saw, and a host of others.

Jeff and I spent several days soaking up the sun and walking around in Kingston. The following Monday we got down to business and visited Harry J's studio, where we met famed producer Harry Johnson, who ran the place. He was very helpful and had arranged a meeting for us with Dennis Tomlinson, manager of singer Pablo Moses, an artist in whom I was particularly interested. We talked for a while and then went over to Channel One, the most famous studio in Jamaica.

Harry J's had been a fairly nice place, if somewhat primitive. Channel One, however, was like nothing I could ever have imagined. The place was in the heart of the ghetto and did not look like any recording studio I had ever seen. Viewed from the front, it resembled what it must have originally been, an automobile service garage with four service bays, each of which was permanently sealed with heavy sheets of corrugated metal. The second story of the cement building was a pale pink surface interrupted by three bar-covered sets of double windows. There was no entrance as far as I could tell.

Jeff did not wish to be there at all and suggested that we leave. It was indeed an unfriendly-looking place. At my insistance we left the taxi and entered through an adjoining door into a small, dark room with iron bars over two interior doors. I am not talking about nice, decorative wrought-iron doors, I mean steel doors about three inches thick, with heavy steel bars over the small openings that passed for windows. It reminded me of a prison cell. The place was littered with paper and greasy motorcycle parts. There were also shelves that had boxes of 45-r.p.m. records intermingled with motorcycle parts.

This closet-sized room was indeed the office of Channel One Studio. As soon as its inhabitants were satisfied that we were indeed who we professed to be, another door, this one a hinged sheet of solid steel, opened and we were premitted to enter the actual studio itself. Inside the studio we met Clifford and Franklin Irving, the two brothers who ran the place. They were very cordial and showed us around.

For some reason, I had expected to find absolutely state-of-the-art equipment in this place. So many famous artists, such as Eric Clapton, Paul Simon, and the Rolling Stones, had recorded there (in Jamaica) that I just imagined that that was the way it would be. Channel One had a very nice new Yamaha piano and a partial set of Simmons electric drums. There was also a beat-up old Hammond organ of some kind with wires hanging out of the back. There was one old Fender bass amp in addition to the above-mentioned equipment, and that was it.

I told them that they had a nice place but wondered how anyone could record in a place like that. The worst country music artist would refuse to cut a record in any studio so ill-equipped. What I learned from this experience was that as poor as the studios were, the Jamaican musicians, artists, and producers were such masters of their art that they were able to overcome these circumstances. Perhaps it has been adversity that has forced the Jamaican artist to excel. Whatever the reasons, Jamaican music is unique in the world, and seeing this and other shrines was for me a rewarding experience. It might do some of the artists in the United States, who take so much for granted, a lot of good to see some of these studios.

After the visit to Channel One, Jeff and I returned to the hotel and I made some more calls to set up several appointments for the following day. Later that evening I received a call from Clifford Irving at Channel One, who wanted Jeff and me to come hear a band on New Year's Eve, the next night, over at a club called the Blue Marlin.

On Tuesday morning we took a taxi to 20 North Parade, which was the address to Joe Gibbs' studio. North Parade passes through the center of downtown Kingston. Twenty North Parade faces a town square or park of some sort that is teeming with vendors of all types hawking fruits, clothes, sunglasses, cigarettes, and anything else they can sell. It is perhaps the busiest part of the city. At the address we were given we found not a recording studio, but a small supermarket. We were at the right address, but confused. As it turned out, the entrance to the studio was through an unmarked door in the rear of the grocery store. I had called producer Errol Thompson before I left Nashville and asked for a meeting with him.

My intention initially had been to get to Dennis Brown, an artist he had produced for Joe Gibbs Records. After having seen how incoherent Dennis Brown had been at the concert on Saturday night I did not feel that I would be able to do any business with him. Errol Thompson also produced a group called Culture and had made an appointment for us to meet Joseph Hill, the lead singer of the group. We met Errol, who said that Joseph Hill had called and said that he was running a bit late.

With that, Jeff and I went for a walk and found our first Jamaican record store down the street. I received a major shock when I saw the type of music that was stocked there. There were no records by Madonna, Huey Lewis, Hall and Oats, or other current major American pop acts at that time. Instead there were albums by artists like Eddy Arnold, Jim Reeves, Marty

Robbins, and other mostly American country singers. Along with these were the records of older American soul artists like Dorris Troy, Joe Tex, and Fats Domino, but traditional country records were predominant. There were also Jamaican artists represented, some whom I had never heard of, but it was strange to me to see Opry singer Skeeter Davis on the shelf next to reggae singer Yellowman. It was this way at every other record store we visited in Jamaica. The older American country artists were held in veneration.

By the time we returned to the studio, Joseph Hill of the group Culture was waiting. Errol had also invited bassist Lloyd Parks of the band We the People. In Jamaica, very few artists have their own bands per se. If the artist secures an engagement it is usually necessary for him to put together a band for that particular show or to persuade another band already there to play backup. My idea was to find a band and two artists who would in my estimation provide a complete show, both in terms of drawing power and actual length of time. Whatever band we used could play a short set and then play backup for the opening act and the main attraction as well. Errol Thompson seemed either very quiet or uninterested, since he did not stick around for the meeting after we got started.

When the meeting was over, Lloyd Parks went his way and Jeff and I had lunch with Joseph Hill at some Chinese restaurant. He wanted us to go up into the mountains with him and see his place, an offer that I was only too ready to accept. On the way up the mountain, we stopped at the house of a friend of his, and in a moment Joseph emerged with some marijuana.

It took us about forty-five minutes to reach his place, which was a small hut in the jungle. Joseph started to roll a joint for me on the hood of his car, mixing marijuana with cigarette tobacco. Once, in Copenhagen, I had smoked some hashish this way and subsequently became very nauseated. I told him this and he rolled me a straight one without tobacco. I seldom smoke marijuana, and when I do, it is usually in moderation. But to have elected not to smoke some herb under those circumstances would have been to refuse the hospitality of our host.

We sat on a log amid heavy tropical foliage, smoked reefers, talked philosophy and business, and refreshed ourselves by chewing on sugarcane stalks. After a while we walked down to the bank of a stream and inspected his marijuana plants. Joseph gave a loud shout and in a few moments a couple of his herbsmen appeared out of nowhere with machetes in hand.

When evening began to fall, we started back down the mountain. As we drove, we remained quiet for the most part, reflecting on our afternoon together. I felt this incredible sense of peace. It was almost transcendental. The words and melody of Jamaican singer Burning Spear's song "Throw Down Your Arms and Come" kept running gently through my mind. I was not high on marijuana, for I had not smoked that much. I was high on life. It was incredible. Music is indeed the universal language.

It was New Year's Eve, but I did not wish to go anywhere. I wanted to have a quiet dinner at the hotel, read a little, reflect upon the wonderful afternoon we had enjoyed, and then go to sleep at a reasonable hour.

When we got to the room, however, Tex had called several times, and Clifford Irving had left word that he would pick us up at nine o'clock to take us over to the Blue Marlin Club to see his band. Jeff and I cleaned up, grabbed a sandwich downstairs, and then waited in the lobby for Clifford to show up.

The Blue Marlin was a small club with a fenced-in patio where the band was to perform. The band was actually a group of high school kids with very inadequate equipment and only one microphone, which did not work most of the time. They were talented enough, but the sound system was so bad that it was really difficult to tell.

On Wednesday morning I read about the death of Rick Nelson in the *Daily Gleaner,* Jamaica's main newspaper. Just the past August we had booked some dates on him and had used him to open for Fats Domino in California. Our agent Bruce Shelton had even flown with him on the same plane from San Bernardino to Las Vegas. I had never seen Ricky Nelson perform, but I had met him at the Orpheum in Memphis at a show with Roy Orbison and Carl Perkins, whom I had been representing at the time. I could not believe that he was dead.

Like most everyone else my age, I had grown up with him, watching him on "The Ozzie and Harriet Show." His death was a great loss.

On Thursday morning we went to visit Bob Marley's operation, Tuff Gong. We were greeted by his widow, Rita Marley, who introduced us to a man named Franklin Williams. Franklin was pushing singer Half Pint, whom we had seen at the auditorium the past Saturday night, and female vocalist Carlene Davis. We stayed there about an hour, made an appointment with him for dinner that night, and then headed over to Dynamic Studio, which proved to be a waste of time.

Later in the afternoon we again met singer Joseph Hill and went with him to the offices of his new record label, Blue Mountain. There we were offered artist Tenor Saw, who was also on Blue Mountain Records. I had been reading quite a bit about Tenor Saw lately and was unfamiliar with his music, but since he had not previously toured the United States, I felt that he would be an excellent addition to the bill. With his presence, along with Culture and We the People, we now had a complete show, one that should sell tickets. With our first show arranged, our business in Jamaica was for the moment completed, so we decided to return to Nashville the next day.

Later that afternoon Jeff and I went for a walk and encountered Tex's minion, Andy. Our conversation started out well enough, but when we told him all of the people we had seen and what we had accomplished, he became angry, talking about all of the trouble he and Tex had gone to setting up appointments for us. He then became abusive and started saying that we were in the CIA and other such horseshit. I really do not enjoy such scenes, and I do my best to avoid fights wherever possible. There comes a point, however, at which I cross some unseen line, and unless my antagonist backs off there will be a fight.

Andy must have sensed this change on my part, because he started to tone it down a bit. He finally left, and I felt sorry for him. Living on the streets and hustling is the only way many people get by. They are not necessarily bad people, it's just that given their lack of education and opportunity, they pursue whatever means are at hand. One cannot resent Third World street hustlers, and yet it is necessary to keep in mind that many of them have no hesitation whatever in slicing you up if they feel like it. As Andy walked away, he became bolder, shouting something about going home to get his gun and blowing our heads off.

On our last night in Jamaica we had dinner with Franklin Williams from Tuff Gong and Tommy Cowan, manager of singer Carlene Davis. After dinner, the four of us went over to Carlene's house for a visit.

The next morning we said good-bye and put our girlfriends in a taxi home. They seemed rather forlorn at the prospect of our return to Nashville. Life for them after we left would again be monotonous and uneventful. Jeff and I, however, were pleased to be getting back home. Before we could get out of the hotel, Joseph Hill showed up and needed some money for gasoline. We gave him twenty dollars and he said that he would pay us back later. We returned by taxi to the Norman Manley Airport and bid a fond farewell to Jamaica.

Our first reggae tour did not work out for several reasons and ended up getting canceled at the last moment. We really did not know what we were doing. We had thought that we would book the tour like we would book any other artists, but it did not turn out that way. The demand for those artists was not as great as we had anticipated. Nor could we get any pictures or publicity from the record company in Jamaica.

There were problems with work permits, travel arrangements, equipment, and ground transportation in America. It all turned out to be much more of a hassle than it was worth, so we abandoned the project altogether. I was sorry about this, but it could not be helped. It was not a priority for my agents, and just did not work out.

I had reluctantly given up on reggae, but received a call in spring 1986 from Robert Schoenfeld that persuaded me to reconsider. Robert, a St. Louis–based entrepreneur and owner of Nighthawk Records, a small independent label, was recording and promoting Jamaican music in the United States and had produced such Jamaican acts as the Gladiators, the Ethiopian, and the Itals. He asked why I had dropped out of the reggae business and I explained that there had been too many problems with too little potential for making money.

His chief concern was the Itals. He wanted them on tour in support of their forthcoming album on his label. I was persuaded to fly to St. Louis to see them perform at the Adam's Mark Hotel on August 29, 1986. As a result of that trip we decided to do business, and In Concert brought over the Gladiators, featuring Albert Griffiths, in 1987, and later the Itals, backed by the Roots Radics, Jamaica's premier studio band.

These shows were successful in that they actually happened, but that was about it. By the time we bought equipment for them, worked out their transportation arrangements, and cleared their work permits, it was all more trouble than it was worth. We lost time and money and it was not that much fun. The Jamaicans were hard to deal with, constantly threatened to go home in the middle of the tour, and always thought that everybody was trying to cheat them. These two tours were the end for me, and as the masons say, I threw in the trowel.

Chapter Sixteen

Lou Rawls

W hen I traded my prized possession, a Budweiser clock, to cadet Clay Yager for Lou Rawls' *Soulin* album in military school, I had no idea that I would get the chance to meet Lou Rawls, let alone ever be his agent.

Chicago-born Lou Rawls grew up on the city's South Side. Heavily influenced musically by both the church and the famous Regal Theatre, he joined legendary soul singer Sam Cooke in a touring gospel group known as the Pilgrim Travellers. He left the group for a tour of duty in the army. After completing his time, he rejoined the group but was almost killed in a car accident with the Travellers that left one of the band members dead.

He recovered from the accident, signed with Capitol Records, and began a long and distinguished recording career that has resulted in almost sixty albums, as well as major hits like "You'll Never Find (Another Love Like Mine)," "Love Is a Hurting Thing," and "Wind Beneath My Wings." Lou Rawls is also known for the millions of dollars he has raised for the United Negro College Fund through his annual telethon.

At the end of December 1986, Lou Rawls called, saying that he would like to visit me in Nashville on the way back from his date in Jamaica on January 18, 1987. He had left us and moved to the Norby Walters Agency a few months before and it seemed that things had not been going that well for him over there. This was an unexpected call, and I was quite anxious to have him visit me in my own territory. The fact of the matter was that we had done a good job selling him in spite of many obstacles. We had started booking him at the end of 1985.

In 1986 we made about $45,000 in commissions, which was not bad considering we were limited in the dates we could obtain for him. In the first place, my deal with his manager, David Brokaw, excluded all casino dates, as well as any dates he worked for the Fairmont Hotels. I also received no commissions for any dates that had anything to do with Anheuser-Busch. In 1985, for example, these dates comprised eleven weeks of his schedule, and it was just about the same in 1986 and 1987.

To acquire Lou Rawls as a client, I had to make these concessions. I was not pleased about this, but I had no choice in the matter. It was important to me to have Lou Rawls as a client in terms of both income and prestige, since he was an internationally known act. It was also significant that we had stolen him from Triad Artists, one of the West Coast giants in the entertainment field. I am sure that its loss of Lou Rawls meant less to it than getting him meant to us.

From the artist's standpoint, there is a reluctance to pay an agency commissions on preexisting accounts. Lou Rawls had been playing the Golden Nugget in Las Vegas, for example, for years before he met me or came to In Concert as a client. David Brokaw merely answered the phone and said, "Yes, how many weeks do you want?"

Why should Lou Rawls have paid me any commission? I had nothing to do with setting up that account originally. I understood this and could live with it. The same circumstances existed in connection with Anheuser-Busch and the Fairmont.

From an agency's point of view, however, things are a bit different. If an agent has to work very hard most of the year making cold calls for an act that is hard to sell, he should get some of the gravy. If there is an occasional call-in date, he should be paid for that date as a reward for his work and as an incentive. Both positions are equally tenable, and it generally boils down to which side of the fence you happen to be on in any particular situation.

Lou Rawls was a hard sell. His price was $20,000 a night, which was difficult to justify, considering that he had not had a hit record in quite a while, and for that matter did not have one the entire time he was with In Concert. In addition, any buyer who used him had to hire nine horn musicians to work with Lou's band. The musicians were selected from the local musician's union by Lou's conductor in whatever city the performance took place. These extra musicians had to be paid for their rehearsal time and for their performance on the night of the show.

If airfare was required, the buyer had to provide that as well, and it was not as simple as just writing a check. Lou's band members lived all over the country. The promoter had to make their flight arrangements and pay their airfare also. A date on Lou Rawls could be quite expensive before it was all over with. Lou's price was, as I mentioned, $20,000, and yet he refused more dates at that price than he accepted.

Lou did not wish to play up north in cold weather. He had refused to play Jamaica for me because it was too hot. He would often refuse to fly on commuter jumps. The list went on and on. I soon learned that the best way to book Lou Rawls was to get $25,000 per night plus hotel rooms and airfare. Even then, there was no guarantee that I could get a date approved.

Our biggest problem at the agency with Lou Rawls was his manager, David Brokaw. David seemed to me to be a yes-man as far as Lou Rawls was concerned. To an artist who surrounds himself with such people, there are both advantages and disadvantages. The advantage is that the artist is always right, nobody contradicts him, he gets his way and becomes a big wheel in his own mind. The downside is that the artist seldom hears the complete truth. At best, he is told what the yes-men think he can handle. At worst, he gets what they think he wants to hear. No major problem will occur as long as things go smoothly.

When events take a turn for the worse in the artist's career, however, the artist has nothing to fall back on except his or her own character, which is seldom of much help, since an artist who hires people who agree with him or her usually lacks character in some significant way. Yes-men are very little help to any artist, and yet their numbers are legion. The more insecure an artist, the greater the need for constant self-affirmation from outside sources.

From a manager's standpoint there are several factors to consider. A manager who argues with his client usually does not last long. The artist invariably feels that his knowledge exceeds that of everyone around him and when he makes a decision to do something, it is unlikely that he will permit himself to be dissuaded by anyone. The wise manager, in order to keep his job, will seldom disagree with his client, even if he knows that the client is wrong. This is where the manager fails his client but keeps his job. Ideally, an artist should have a manager whose knowledge and experience exceed his own, someone whom he trusts to act in his best interests and who is not afraid to stand up to the artist when circumstances warrant a confrontation. All in all, I feel that David Brokaw was a good manager for Lou Rawls, but he was often rude and unnecessarily abrupt to others.

The Brokaws themselves are a strange bunch. David is an agent's nightmare, always trying to take something he does not need. He told Sherwood Cryer that he wanted the commissions on Mickey Gilley's Harrah's casino dates, a request that Sherwood refused. The Brokaws held themselves to be Mickey Gilley's managers, which they were not—they had been hired as his publicists. From time to time, someone would call them and ask about getting a date for Mickey Gilley or Johnny Lee. Instead of referring the caller to the agency, they would try to set the date themselves, then call the artist directly to talk him into letting them have 10 percent commission on the date. They would also actively solicit dates in their area, California, from time to time for Mickey Gilley, trying to beat out the agency instead of minding their own business and doing what they were supposed to be doing. I had Gilley's situation so well covered that they seldom succeeded.

It was different with Lou Rawls. David Brokaw was so protective of his client that his own brother and business partner, Sandy, did not have Lou Rawls' date sheet. David would do anything he could to beat the agency out of a commission. A classic example involves "A Salute to Lou Rawls" in the December 23, 1985, issue of the *Hollywood Reporter*.

The way these salutes and special tribute editions work is as follows: Some marketing wizard, in an effort to take in more advertising dollars, decides to pay tribute to a particular artist. Everyone who does business with the artist is obligated to buy some type of congratulatory ad. The solicitations for these advertisements are made by the sales staff of the magazine. The issue itself runs with the standard format, but includes some laudatory and heartwarming tales about the artist and his many accomplishments.

It is good for the publication, since the tribute edition brings in some extra money and can be run with a different artist whenever extra revenue is needed. This special edition serves the artist from the standpoint of publicity and ego gratification. It is, however, a great pain in the ass to those who feel obligated to buy ads.

In the case of the *Hollywood Reporter*, the publication sells the cover. In other words, whoever the spotlight issue is about has to pay to have himself featured, or someone can buy the cover on his or her behalf. The purchaser then provides leads to people who are likely to buy ads. These people are then contacted by the sales staff of the magazine.

With regard to the Lou Rawls spotlight issue, here is what happened. I received a call from David Brokaw saying that the *Hollywood Reporter* wanted to pay tribute to Lou Rawls and that it would be a good idea if we took out a full-page ad. The cost of the ad was around $1,000. David said that he knew someone who could handle the artwork for us for a small fee. I wanted something that would clearly indicate that In Concert was Lou Rawls's agency.

We finally decided that we would run an ad that featured the agents' signatures and a letter with a few congratulatory re-marks. I secured the autographs of my agents on a sheet of paper and sent it to David Brokaw's office in California. David said that he would take care of everything, and indeed he did.

When the Lou Rawls edition of the *Hollywood Reporter* appeared, our ad featured our letterhead and signatures just as they had been sent with the message "We are proud of our association with Lou Rawls and congratulate him on his distinguished career." It was a trashy-looking ad that said nothing about the fact that In Concert International was Lou Rawls' booking agency. The real killer was that the bottom of the page read, "For further information call the Brokaw Company," and listed its address and phone number below. Nowhere could a reader find the line "For bookings call In Concert" or any indication that In Concert was Lou Rawls' agency. In other words, In Concert bought a $1,000 advertisement for David Brokaw. The significance of this affront will be more clearly understood when its intent is explained.

In the situation with Mickey Gilley, the Brokaws sought to set dates in order to pick up some extra money, a thousand or two here and there. Even though their efforts sought to beat the agency out of its rightful commissions, at least a tangible motive existed, that of making money. In the case of Lou Rawls, however, David Brokaw would set dates so he could say to Lou Rawls, "Look what a good boy I am. Through my great skill and hard work, constantly seeking to serve and protect your best interests, I have secured a date for you and it will not cost you any commission."

If David had made Lou Rawls pay him commission on the date it would have been irritating, but at least understandable. As it was, David Brokaw took from the agency merely to make himself look better. This type of activity is unfortunately all too common, and serves to substantiate the ancient maxim, "A blind hog will find an acorn every once in a while."

Everybody wants to be an agent. A manager gets a call-in date and instead of referring the caller to the agency, he seeks instead to try and steal something. The problem is compounded because the would-be agent will frequently accept a date in some out-of-the-way place, keep the commission himself, and then expect the real agency to find other dates to go with it. Incapable of seeing the overall picture, these managers nickel-and-dime an agency to death, ultimately demoralizing the agents to the extent that they cease to consider it worthwhile or profitable to put forth their best efforts on the artist's behalf.

The Brokaws were among the worst I ever met. They would

drop by from time to time when they were in town and use our offices, spending hours on the phone at our expense. I never complained, and was glad to be of assistance. If one of us, however, chanced to make a couple of calls from their offices in L.A., we were told to be sure and put them on our credit cards. I guess that years of doing business with guys like those two helped make me really sick of the music business.

Another interesting point about the Brokaws is that they have developed this "good guy, bad guy" routine. In this game, David plays the role of the bad guy and if someone finds him too abrasive, they can go to his brother, Sandy, and ask him to intercede. Nevertheless, I still owe the Brokaws a debt of gratitude. Had it not been for David, I would never have had Lou Rawls as a client. I genuinely like both of them and we had many good times together in Nashville, L.A., Memphis, Las Vegas, and elsewhere. There is nothing that I have said in this chapter that I would not say to either of them directly. They are astute, aggressive, and capable.

I was anxious to have Lou Rawls as a client again. His brief time away from us had been long enough. I really did not know where I stood with David Brokaw. If I told David that Lou had called me and wanted to come to Nashville, there was a chance that David Brokaw might get in the middle of things and persuade Lou Rawls to go back to Triad or to the William Morris Agency.

On the other hand, if I failed to mention to David that Lou had called me, and David knew about the call, it might look as if I were trying to make a deal with Lou behind David Brokaw's back. Even if I had been able to do so, it would have been foolish on my part. On a day-to-day basis, David Brokaw's approval and help were essential in representing Lou Rawls. I called David and told him that Lou had called me. Apparently Lou had not mentioned this call to him.

As always, I felt that it was urgent to strike while the iron was hot, and I did not feel like waiting around on the chance that Lou Rawls might visit me in Nashville. I decided that I would make a surprise visit to Lou Rawls at the Wyndham Hotel in Kingston. I wondered whether I should tell David Brokaw about my plan. I thought about the situation and decided that in consideration of the depth of David's relationship with Lou, it would be best to enlist his aid if possible, rather than trying to work behind his back. There was no way I could have undermined that relationship even if I had wanted to, which I did not. David Brokaw and Lou Rawls had been working together for fifteen years in one capacity or another. I told him that I intended to pay a surprise visit to Lou. David Brokaw wished me well.

The idea of returning to Jamaica appealed to me a great deal, especially that winter. The sunshine and balmy temperatures have always served to clear my mind and improve my outlook. After all I had been through in the previous weeks, I knew that a brief vacation would do me good.

I arrived at the Norman Manley Airport in Kingston on Friday, January 16, 1987, and took a taxi to the Wyndham Hotel. As soon as I checked in I called Robert Schoenfeld, the president of Nighthawk Records. He came from St. Louis and was staying at the Wyndham Hotel annex. He was in Kingston producing another album for the Jamaican trio the Itals, his pet project. I visited him and discussed plans for the upcoming tours I had scheduled with the Gladiators and the Itals. Albert Griffiths and the Gladiators were scheduled to start touring the United States in March, with Leonard Dillon as the opening act. I met with the Gladiators and we took some publicity shots and talked about the upcoming tour.

Lou arrived that night, but did not know I was there. The next morning I surprised him by showing up unannounced at breakfast. As a result of my being there, we struck a deal and he was once again back in the In Concert fold. My motto has always been, "Anyplace! Anytime!" I have never lost a deal with anybody, anywhere because I was unwilling to spend the time or the money to be somewhere I needed to be.

The show took place outdoors at the hotel pool on Saturday night. It was a beautiful, tropical night in Jamaica. Many of the reggae greats were there, like Yellowman, the I-Threes (Rita Marley, Judy Mowatt, Marcia Griffiths), Sly Dunbar, and the Itals. The crowd was calm and appreciative as Lou Rawls brought his unique, uptown music to the people of Kingston.

The next morning we were all at the airport bright and early on our way back home. As it turned out, Lou did not come to Nashville after all, but returned to L.A. I might have gotten him to return to In Concert without having personally made the trip to Jamaica, but going there myself cemented the deal. I returned to Nashville, then flew out to L.A. on Wednesday at Lou's request for a dinner meeting to discuss tour plans.

Lou Rawls was the next to last major client to leave In Concert. By the time he departed, I did not care one way or the other; I was tired of the music business altogether. Lou Rawls was always a gentleman and it was both a pleasure and an honor to be able to work with him.

As for the Brokaws, David taught me at least one very important lesson. I used to badmouth the competition constantly, and I learned from him that when trying to sign an artist, it is much better to talk about one's own strengths rather than a competitor's weaknesses.

Chapter Seventeen

Ronnie Milsap

Of all the artists I have ever worked with, Ronnie Milsap is probably the most gifted. His voice is powerful, distinctive, and immediately recognizable. As a performer, Ronnie is frequently credited with having the best show in country music. He is a big man, over six feet tall and weighing around two hundred pounds. During his show, I have seen him jump from the floor to the top of his grand piano at point-blank range. Few entertainers would attempt this feat, especially in light of the microphones, wires, and cables. One would never suspect that Ronnie Milsap is blind.

Milsap was born in Robbins, North Carolina, on January 16, 1944. Abandoned by his mother, he was raised by his father's parents. Blind from birth, he started school at age five at the North Carolina School for the Blind.

As soon as Milsap picked up his first musical instrument, it was obvious where his real talents lay. He quickly mastered the violin, piano, and guitar. His first formal training musically was in classical music, a style he still enjoys today. As a teen, he experimented with rock and roll and formed a band called the Apparitions that played local dances.

Although Milsap enjoyed music, he saw no real future there and decided to pursue a career in the legal field. He completed two years at Young Harris Junior College in Atlanta and was offered a full scholarship at Emory. By this time, however, Ronnie had become known for his recording studio work in the Atlanta area, and decided to follow his muse.

He went to Memphis in the late 1960s and tried his hand at blues-flavored music before finally moving to Nashville in the early 1970s and returning to his true musical roots. He has said that country music is all he heard on the radio during the first five years of his life, and it obviously left the greatest impression.

I set my first date on Ronnie Milsap for $6,000 at the Rising Sun in Trinity, Texas, in March 1977, as an agent for the Lavender-Blake Agency. At that time, Ronnie Milsap was hot and getting hotter. Having come to Nashville via Memphis, he had established himself as an artist of note by playing at a lounge called The Roof atop what was then known as Roger Miller's King of the Road Motor Inn. By the time I was booking him, he was on the road quite a bit with Dick Blake's pet act, the Statler Brothers. Ronnie Milsap opened, followed by Tammy Wynette, and then the Statlers finished. By the time he made his last run with this package he was receiving $5,000 a night.

Ronnie also had a stream of hit records during this period, culminating in 1977 with the CMA's Album of the Year award for *Ronnie Milsap Live*. In that year, he also won Male Vocalist of the Year, an honor he had already won twice before, in 1974 and 1976. The biggest prize of all came in 1977 when he received the CMA's Entertainer of the Year award.

The Lavender-Blake Agency had been responsible to a great degree for Ronnie's awards by having placed him in front of so many country music fans prior to the 1977 voting period. At the time he received those awards, he was making $6,000 to $7,000 per night, with the exception of the $5,000 he had been getting on the package shows with the Statler Brothers and Tammy Wynette.

Almost as soon as he received Entertainer of the Year he moved to the William Morris Agency. His move was a big letdown to all of us at the agency since we had worked hard for him and had done a great job. We were told that the William Morris Agency had promised him one hundred dates at $20,000 per night. This was quite a substantial raise over what he had been making, but his growth with us had been measured and steady.

This is a classic example of what happens when a big agency puts the pitch on an artist who does not know any better. It all sounds good, but in this case Ronnie Milsap did not receive any dates that I know of at $20,000 a night. No matter to the agency, however; after it wins over the artist, it will make money whether or not it can deliver what it has promised. After an act has made a highly publicized move, inertia sets in, and the act has a certain reluctance to move again for a while.

The William Morris Agency did, however, charge as much as it could get for him during this period, with the result that many buyers were overcharged and lost money. I do not have any specific figures or dates to back up my allegations, since I do not have access to the William Morris files from that period. What I do know for a fact is that Ronnie Milsap returned to Dick Blake in February of 1980, two and a half years after winning the Entertainer of the Year award, with his booking page in a shambles. I think that he had perhaps three dates on the books for the forthcoming year.

At the same time that Milsap left the Lavender-Blake Agency he also got rid of his manager, Jack Johnson. As a manager, Jack Johnson was well respected around town, having brought Charley Pride to an unprecedented level for any black artist in country music, a level that has still been unequaled by any other black singer in this field. As manager for Milsap since 1973, Jack had loaned him the money to move from Memphis to Nashville. Jack got Ronnie Milsap his recording deal with RCA and had done everything possible to further Ronnie's career.

As a result of his efforts, and after having taken Ronnie Milsap to Entertainer of the Year, Jack was sued by Ronnie Milsap for mismanagement. Suits of this nature are frequently filed when an artist starts making real money and wants to dump his manager. When the news hits the streets, an erroneous charge of mismanagement is better for an artist's public image than for the public to think that the artist is greedy and unappreciative. This particular situation never went to court. Ronnie Milsap paid Jack Johnson a substantial but undisclosed amount, and as a result of his actions succeeded in disposing of his manager.

Jack Johnson still speaks highly of Ronnie Milsap and told me that he is not bitter about the situation and that he is "too old to hold any grudges," but I feel personally that this was the biggest disappointment of Jack Johnson's long and illustrious career. In essence, Jack Johnson was fired for having done his job too well, a fate suffered frequently by both managers and agents. How could he not be bitter?

Jack Johnson subsequently sued Lavender-Blake for interfering in his contract with Ronnie Milsap. He blamed Dick Blake personally for all of his troubles with Milsap, alleging that Dick Blake had talked Milsap into working the Statler Brothers–Wynette package shows for $5,000 per day after Jack, as Milsap's manager, had told Blake that Milsap would not work them for any less than $10,000 per show. Dick Blake had been more concerned with the Statler Brothers than he was with Ronnie Milsap, and saving them $5,000 per day was more important to him than making Milsap an extra $5,000 per day.

I was there, and this is what had happened. Jack Johnson was acting in Ronnie Milsap's best interests, but Blake had gone around him and talked to Milsap directly. The matter went to court but Jack Johnson lost due to lack of evidence. Although he could not prove in court that Dick Blake had interfered in his relationship with Ronnie Milsap, Blake had. After court, Jack and Dick Blake had lunch together and remained friends until the end.

In Nashville, business and personal relationships are often intertwined to an astonishing degree, and a bitter fight between parties over a business issue seldom destroys a long-standing friendship as it would in another line of work. Here, anyone who is successfully involved in the music business is part of an extended family. Disagreements are resolved, and in time things return to normal.

At Dick Blake International we began rebuilding Ronnie Milsap's career and raised his price from a low of $8,500 in 1980 to an average of $20,000 per night, where it remains to this day. I became the responsible agent for him at Dick Blake International and set around 250 dates between 1980 and 1983, at which time he left to start his own agency, Headline International Talent.

I felt that Ronnie Milsap was an easy enough act to book and wondered why his booking page was almost empty when he joined us at Dick Blake International. In my opinion, the William Morris Agency had taken the most lucrative years of his career, made as much money as it could off him, and then more or less abandoned him and moved on to another project. I do not believe this to have been an intentional policy on the part of the William Morris Agency, but feel that when interest began to wane, it shifted its priorities to other artists. It exhibited the same behavior with Mickey Gilley before I took him away in late 1983.

By the time we got Ronnie back in 1980, he had acquired a new manager, Dan Cleary, who was then with a West Coast management company, BNB, which at that time managed the O'Jays, Natalie Cole, and others. Dan Cleary is a charming and well-mannered West Coast type who resembles Roger Moore. He was smooth-talking and polite, but obviously knew nothing about country music. Dan was concerned with protecting his own interests and did not want Ronnie Milsap at Dick Blake International. He was understandably uncomfortable with our previous relationship, as well as with the fact that we were literally across the street from Milsap, while he was out in California. Dan was good for Ronnie to some degree, but we fought constantly.

All of Milsap's dates were approved by Dick Blake at first. Any agent getting an offer would write up the information and turn it in to Dick, who would then discuss the matter with Dan Cleary, who would then discuss it with Don Reeves, Ronnie's brother-in-law. Don would then discuss it with Ronnie and call Dan Cleary with an answer. Dan would then call Dick Blake and he would in turn notify the agent whether or not the date had been accepted. This was a slow enough process under the best of circumstances, but with Dick Blake on the road with the Statler Brothers constantly, it made it difficult for us to get dates approved at all.

One day I had a date that needed an immediate answer. Dick Blake was out of town, so I just called Don Reeves myself and got the date approved that afternoon. Dick was angry about it at first, but got over it soon enough. After all, I was making him money. During this time I would sometimes get dates approved through Dan Cleary, through Don Reeves, or through Ronnie himself.

I became unhappy at Dick Blake International because I felt that I was not making enough money. I had talked to Dick about this and he had given me several raises, but none of them was sufficient. The company was handling the Statler Brothers, Barbara and Louise Mandrell, Merle Haggard, Ricky Skaggs, Brenda Lee, Ronnie Milsap, and others. Matters finally reached a peak with me and I went in and told Dick Blake that I had to have more money or I was gone. I had all of my facts and figures with me, showing how much money I had made for the company and how much I had made personally.

Blake did not want to talk about it and said, "If a man can find something better to do, he should do it."

I told him that I did not wish to leave but I wanted to be paid what I was worth. I also added that if I left, Ronnie Milsap would most likely be right behind me. He said that he seriously doubted that.

Two weeks later I went in to tell Blake, "Today is my last day." In the meantime, Blake had found out that I had made a deal with Ronnie Milsap and that we were going to start our own agency. On this occasion Dick Blake's attitude was much improved and he offered me generally whatever I wanted. I told him that it was too late and that he should have listened to me two weeks ago. He finally turned me around by giving me a large sum of money, a raise, and a Cadillac.

This put me in one hell of a situation. If I stayed with Blake, I lost Ronnie Milsap's respect. I would most likely lose him as a client also. If I left Blake and went with Milsap, I gave up the safety of numbers that working at Dick Blake International afforded, as well as a fairly easy job and my cars.

I decided to stay with Blake. He wrote me a check. I cashed it and then called Ronnie Milsap to tell him what had happened. It was a call I dreaded making, especially since none of this had been necessary at all. Milsap was understanding, but I felt that he would leave the agency anyway since I had used all of my considerable skill as an orator and after-dinner speaker to persuade him to leave in the first place.

I was angry at Dick Blake for having put me in that position and told him that Ronnie Milsap would probably leave the agency. Blake replied that he would rather have me as an agent than Ronnie Milsap as a client if it came down to an either/or situation. This was the highest compliment I ever received as an agent.

Dick Blake took care of the matter with Ronnie Milsap by calling him and dropping his commission for the next six months from 10 percent to 5 percent, an expensive gesture that would have been unnecessary if Blake had listened to what I had to say to begin with. In other words, it cost Dick Blake about $200,000 to tell me to kiss his ass for two weeks.

When the six months were up, Ronnie Milsap moved to a New York–based agency called APA or Agency for the Performing Arts. It was at that time handling Johnny Cash, the Gatlins, and a few others. I openly referred to it as "APE." I think Ronnie stayed there about a month before I flew down to a date I had set in Montgomery, Alabama, and persuaded him to come back where he belonged.

In retrospect, I believe the brief and fruitless move to APA to have been Ronnie's idea. At the time, however, I felt that Dan Cleary was responsible. I determined to do my best to get him out of the picture once and for all. He had Milsap under contract, so he had to be paid. I told Ronnie that Dan Cleary was a big mistake and that it was one thing to have to pay him, but it was another to pay him to screw things up. I did not care personally whether Ronnie Milsap had to pay Dan Cleary. I wanted Ronnie to pay him if he had to, but to keep him out of our business. I did not want to fool with Dan Cleary at all and felt him to be a hindrance to my work.

In 1982 life got weird again at Dick Blake International. The company was making an incredible amount of money, and we kept taking on more and more acts. There was no incentive for any of the agents, since we were on a fixed salary. I wanted all of us to have a base salary and a percentage of the overall business, to be divided monthly among the agents. By this time, Blake's health had grown worse and I felt that he was losing control of the situation. I felt that if I could talk Dick Blake into putting all of us on commission, we would all be making so much money that the chance of any agent taking some artists and leaving would be greatly reduced. Furthermore, there would be no further need for me to fight with Blake over money. I could determine my own income by the amount of work I did, which is all I really wanted anyway. He again refused to listen to what I had to say, not having learned anything from the $200,000 mistake he had made the last time.

I again talked to Ronnie Milsap, Tommy Kerkeles, and Don Reeves. They had been irritated when I backed out of our deal the last time, but had gotten over it and were ready to talk about opening our own agency. I went to Blake one more time to try to work things out, but made no progress. Feeling that the situation had become impossible, I got the ball rolling with Tommy, Don, and Ronnie Milsap once again. This time Blake pulled the same thing, waiting until I had already made my deal with Ronnie Milsap a second time.

I fully intended to leave, but a conversation with Dan Cleary changed my mind. He was on the way out as a result of my constant efforts to have him removed, and for other reasons. Ronnie Milsap finally bought back his contract from Dan Cleary, but Dan's final words to me were to the effect that I was stepping into a volatile family situation and that one day, sooner or later, I would invariably do something to irritate Kerkeles, Reeves, Milsap, or Ronnie's wife. I would not be able to get any of them on the phone and would find myself out of a job.

I guess that somewhere in the back of my mind I felt that what he had told me was absolutely true. With these words of warning, and Blake's acceptance of my demands, I chose to remain with Dick Blake a second time. On this occasion, as a result of Dick Blake's head games, we lost Ronnie Milsap as a client. It was a foolish and unnecessary loss, Ronnie went ahead and started his own agency, Headline International Talent, taking Charles Dorris, a rookie agent of ours, to run the place. Charles stayed there until the spring of 1986, when he and Tommy Kerkeles got into a fight and Charles was fired.

At this point, Tommy Kerkeles hired agent Eddie Rhines to run things. I did not think that Eddie had enough experience to last very long with such a tough bunch as Tommy Kerkeles and Don Reeves. I was right, and in February of 1987 I made my move.

Headline International had done much better than I ever expected, and in addition to Ronnie Milsap had represented Steve Wariner and Reba McEntire. Those acts had left Headline International, but still had quite a few dates remaining to be played. I had been called by Eddie Rhines for a lunch meeting and as a result knew there were problems.

Armed with this information, I phoned Tommy Kerkeles and told him that we should make some kind of a deal to bring Milsap to my company. I could not see any point in him and Reeves spending the money that they had coming in from commissions running a place that was about to collapse.

I told Tommy that he should let me have Milsap, shut down Headline International, and keep the commissions that were already on his books. He replied that Halsey and William Morris had both made him offers, but that he was getting ready to sign some big acts. To listen to him, Headline International was doing great. I knew what it cost to run an agency and doubted he was telling the truth. I felt that he would think things over and give me a call sooner or later.

I did not have to wait long. One afternoon I received a call from Tommy asking me if I would like to add Ronnie Milsap to my roster. He wanted me to pay him $50,000 for that privilege, which included the purchase of Headline International. As a result I would get Ronnie Milsap as a client. I met with Tommy and Don Reeves and we struck a deal. For my $50,000 I was to receive all of the physical assets of their company, plus all of the accounts receivable. I did not want to be responsible for collecting money from people I did not know in order to pay Tommy and Don.

I made a counterproposal in which I suggested that they deduct their accounts receivable from the purchase price. Whatever commissions were owed to them, they could keep for themselves. They agreed, with the result that the selling price of Headline International dropped from $50,000 to $22,000. I would have paid them that much in cash in order to get Ronnie Milsap as a client. I agreed to pay them $10,000 in cash and another $12,000 plus interest before December 31, 1989. In return, I would take immediate possession of all their property.

This deal sounded good enough, but there was a definite

downside. I was not to receive any commissions on any dates that Ronnie was scheduled to play with singer Kenny Rogers, since I had not been involved in those arrangements. Instead of 10 percent commission, I would receive only 5 percent on Ronnie Milsap. Last but not least, Ronnie would not be under contract to my company. I did not care for these provisions but accepted them anyway, feeling that if I showed any hesitation at all, they would make a similar deal with one of my competitors. I asked them to give me a day or so to work out the details.

I called Sherwood Cryer in Texas, explained the situation to him, and asked his opinion. Again, he told me to do what I wanted. I was feeling good about the company and business in general as a result of having gotten back Lou Rawls from the Norby Walters Agency in January and having patched up matters between Sherwood Cryer and Mickey Gilley. Life was looking good again, despite the fact that I had lost my most important agent, Lane Cross. I told the company secretary, Linda Edwards, to write Reeves and Kerkeles a check, and on February 27, 1987, I was again representing Ronnie Milsap. That news would certainly shake things up around town. In Concert International was at its zenith. I had no idea that beginning in May things would quickly start falling apart.

The situation with Milsap on this occasion did not work out from the very beginning. First of all, there was the problem with the Kenny Rogers tour. Ronnie was scheduled to play spring and fall dates with Kenny Rogers. It was bad enough that we were not getting commissions for these dates, but what was worse is that we never got a correct schedule of these dates or in which cities they would play. We would bring Tommy an offer for Milsap and he would turn it down, saying that we could not set a date in that particular city because he thought that Ronnie might be working there with Kenny. We tried booking dates at different times and that did not work out either.

When Mickey Gilley left the agency in May due to his continuing disputes with Sherwood Cryer, Milsap followed suit. I received a letter from Ronnie Milsap dated June 26, 1987, firing In Concert. This was another confirmation of the late Shorty Lavender's famous statement, "When that tap is turned on it doesn't turn off until the tank is empty." Translated, this means that when an agency loses a major client, it will almost invariably lose several others as well. This had always been my experience.

This time around, the situation with Ronnie Milsap was hardly worth the trouble. I was tired of fooling with all of the hassles and irritations of fighting what seemed like everybody in the world. By the time Milsap left the agency I did not care anymore.

After we shut down In Concert, at the end of 1988, I took some time off, but after a few months began to run out of money. Not long after I decided to look for work I gave Tommy Kerkeles a call at Ronnie Milsap's office, and took him and Don Reeves to lunch. We had not spoken in quite a while and had in fact ended our relationship on a sour note.

In Concert International still owed them around $10,000 plus interest, which was due by the last day of 1989. I knew that they would go to lunch with me, if for no other reason than to harass me about that money.

During lunch, I approached Tommy Kerkeles about the possibility of again starting our own agency. I could tell that the thought appealed to him. He and Don and Ronnie were still irritated with me over the fact that I had agreed to go with them twice before then backed out at the last possible moment. I had high hopes for things working out with them, but matters dragged on for several months without a favorable resolution. Finally Tommy said that it did not look like Milsap would leave the Halsey Agency because it was doing a good job. I had to admit to myself that the Halsey Agency *had* done a good job with Milsap. I really did not think that I could do any better.

I kept pressing Tommy and Don, feeling that their desire to collect the money In Concert owed them would keep things moving, but matters did not look very promising for me. Several deals were discussed but nothing came of them. It was finally decided that I should go on the road with Ronnie and see if I could put a deal together with him myself. I felt that if I got him alone I would be able to work things out. With this in mind, I met his two buses at the Nashville airport at around eleven-thirty one Thursday night in early May 1989, and settled in for the long ride to Dallas.

It is always strange boarding a tour bus if you have not been out in a while. It is somewhat like stepping into someone's house as a stranger. Everybody there has his or her own space more or less already lined up. The presence of an extra person on an already crowded bus is not particularly welcome. Ronnie's band was nice enough, and I already knew most of them, but I still dreaded the long haul to Dallas.

We arrived at about eleven-thirty on Friday morning, and I had a business lunch with Ronnie Milsap and his wife, Joyce, on their bus. I have always liked Ronnie Milsap personally. He has an excellent sense of humor and a true appreciation of irony. He sometimes acts like an angry child when things aren't exactly his way, but unlike most artists, he knows what he is talking about as far as the technical aspects of his own show are concerned. He knows precisely how the stage should be arranged, what the levels should be on the various instruments, and how the monitor system should be mixed. Musically, he is a genius.

Ronnie had talked to Tommy Kerkeles back in Nashville and Kerkeles had told him that the Halsey Agency was flying a couple of people down to the show that night to cover the date, since they knew I was going to be there. I did not like this at all and felt that Tommy Kerkeles should not have told anyone at Halsey that I was going to be on the road with Ronnie Milsap, but then Tommy received a great deal of pleasure from watching Jim Halsey and his assistant, Judy Seale, squirm and grovel.

I went to the club for sound check at two-thirty in the afternoon. There had been some kind of fire in the kitchen so the sound check had been delayed. Milsap was in somewhat of an unpleasant mood as a result and so, realizing that the timing was not right, I did not discuss any business.

Milsap was playing a Texas honky-tonk called Cowboys. It was one of the nicest clubs I have ever been to, and a good-size crowd had shown up to see him. The house band was excellent and a good time was had by all except Ronnie Milsap, who did not like the sound system, and Halsey agent Ron Baird, who had for the most part been ignored by Ronnie. Milsap later told me that Ron was probably a nice guy but that he did not know him and consequently had nothing to say to him.

The next morning we left Dallas at about ten in the morning. It was hot as hell outside and we had no sooner left the hotel than the air conditioner on the bus broke down. The windows would not open at all so we rode in the intense heat all the way to Midland, Texas.

After the show everybody loaded up and left. This is one aspect of performing that is intolerable. It is terrible to get on a bus at two or three in the morning after having been up all day and then start the long trip home. I guess that they get used to it, but I never have.

We arrived home on Sunday. I was in a very good mood and felt that I was close to a deal and would be representing Ronnie Milsap again very soon, for the fifth time.

On Monday morning I called Tommy Kerkeles and the elation that I had felt was quickly destroyed. Billy Coren, Milsap's traveling companion and stooge, had been assigned to the hotel room with me on Friday night, and he had caused some problems.

Billy reminds me of Friar Tuck. His face is perfectly round and he is a bit chubby. He used to handle stage pyrotechnics for Milsap, but from what I gathered was now paid by Ronnie for doing nothing, somewhat like a housecat. He rode on Ronnie's private bus and received preferential treatment. At the motel, he had taken the liberty of opening and going through my briefcase to see what he could see. What he had seen were two books by the so-called "Black Magician," Aleister Crowley. I read constantly and always take several books on the road with me. I had not read Crowley in years and these two books were small and fit easily in my briefcase.

I had also been accused of wearing a "devil ring," which was actually a German Viking ring with horns coming out of each side of the helmet. This is, of course, the manner in which Vikings are most frequently depicted.

Anyway, it seemed that my undeserved reputation as a practitioner of the black arts had again surfaced. It became necessary for me to take the offending books as well as the "devil ring" to Tommy's office. He kept my books overnight and showed them to Grand Inquisitor Don Reeves, Ronnie's brother-in-law.

"Shit, son, those books scared Donald so bad that he didn't want 'em in the building," Tommy said.

It became necessary for me to provide the right, although not necessarily correct, answers to such questions as "Who is Jesus?" and so on. I felt saddened that I had to answer such questions. I felt them to be a violation of my privacy as a person. I gave them the answers they wanted, but I started to get angry. I finally said that if I were Ronnie Milsap I would be much more concerned about having some fat toady snitch in my organization than I would be about what somebody happened to be reading.

"Ronnie don't care," Tommy said. "He thought it was funny." They then speculated that Ronnie Milsap had a great day of reckoning coming himself when the "roll was called up yonder."

"It's me and Donald you got to worry about. It ain't funny to us. Weez Christians. Donald and I used to be afraid to come to your office over there with all that voodoo shit. Charles Dorris told me that you were sticking pins in a Tommy Kerkeles doll. He saw you do it!"

To make a long story short, I acquitted myself of the erroneous charges of voodoo, black magic, and devil worship, but I still did not have a job.

We decided that I should go to work at the Jim Halsey Agency for a few months in order to get my feet wet as an agent again. At In Concert, most of my time had been consumed by administrative matters. Then, if it seemed desirable, we could start our own agency. This was not exactly what I wanted at the time, but it sounded reasonable enough. The only problem was that Halsey had not hired me.

My initial meeting with Jim Halsey was not impressive. This was all extremely urgent to me, but nobody else seemed to be in any kind of hurry. I was tired of fooling around and did not particularly like the attitude of the Jim Halsey Agency anyway. I knew that I was a better and more experienced agent than anyone over there. I was ready to take Ronnie Milsap and do my own thing. To hell with all of them!

One Thursday morning I was over at Milsap's office visiting Tommy when Ronnie showed up. He asked Tommy if Halsey had hired me yet. Tommy replied that Halsey was going to give me an answer on Monday and then we could see how it went.

"There is only one way it can go," Ronnie replied, meaning

that unless I was hired, Halsey would be fired. This made me feel somewhat better, but I was still irritated that Ronnie had to force them to hire me. I wanted just to take him myself and do our own thing.

I again met with Jim Halsey. He was much more receptive on this occasion and told me that I came highly recommended. This time he hired me. We agreed on a salary base of $40,000 a year plus some kind of undetermined bonus at the end of the year. Since I had existed on $150 a week for the previous six months, his proposal sounded great. Jim was quick to make certain that I understood that I was not being hired as a result of any pressure from Ronnie Milsap and that he could not permit any artists to determine his company policy. This was pure horseshit and I knew it, but I sensed that it was important to Halsey to feel in control.

It felt really strange being the low man on the totem pole, especially after all that I had accomplished. I determined to make the best of a bad situation, but be that as it may, it was still the worst place I have ever worked.

There were closed-door meetings all of the time, and despite Jim Halsey's talk of "synergy" and the strength of the group, the fact was that everybody was more or less working for themselves and stepped out of their office only when absolutely necessary. It was not a team effort and there were no team players. It was instead a place of closed doors, whispers, and ass-kissing.

The Halsey Agency was like a ship that was slowly filling with water. In this case the ship was costing $150,000 a month to float, and that amount was clearly not coming in. The recent signings of acts like Mark Collie, Zaca Creek, and Cee Cee Chapman did nothing to alter the overall picture. Revenues were down. Halsey assured us that he had no intention of selling the company, but the fact was that Ronnie Milsap was not happy as a client, and neither were Waylon Jennings, T. Graham Brown, Pat Boone, Earl Thomas Conley, the Bellamy Brothers, and others. Part of this unhappiness is just the nature of the business. Acts are almost always unhappy about something and they generally use their alleged dissatisfaction as a weapon with which to threaten and intimidate their agency. It is as if to say, "You are not treating me right. So-and-so has more dates than I do and if you don't put me first then I am going to take my ball and go home." In most cases, these artists are only as happy as they think they are anyway. Their displeasure with the agency is usually the result of some drop in their career, but they take it out on the agency.

Waylon Jennings was unhappy because he did not have enough dates. His price was supposedly $25,000 a night with his band. Reality was, however, another matter altogether. In my area of the country, experience taught me that he was worth around $15,000 a night on average with a little less money in some situations and a bit more in others. It was my opinion that he should not turn down any dates at $12,500. As it is with most artists, nobody had the courage to tell him the truth. As was the case in olden times, the messenger bearing unpleasant news is frequently dispatched. This is especially true in the music business, and yet it is only by sitting down and accepting the situation as it is that there is the possibility of changing it in the future.

Waylon decided that he would again try his one-man show. This was to be more or less a hillbilly version of "An Evening With Cary Grant" and was entitled "A Man Called Horse." It was priced at $12,500 a night, with a minimum price of $10,000. This show was not that easy to sell in my area. Tom Bene, owner of Club Bene in Amboy, New Jersey, had it scheduled but it was canceled because of Waylon's heart attack. "It was a good thing that Waylon had a heart attack," Tom said, "or I would have lost my ass." Advance ticket sales were poor.

Then there was Mark Campana, who booked the Six Flags park in Jackson, New Jersey. He told me that the last time Waylon was there he only did a twenty-five-minute show. He did not want him back. Buyers do not care for that type of thing. Waylon also decided that he no longer wished to play places where alcohol was served, and consequently turned down dates that he should have taken if he was in fact truly anxious to work.

T. Graham Brown, the guy on the Taco Bell commercials, thought that he was worth more money than he was getting. Some of these artists are really out there in terms of the fees they wish to charge. They arbitrarily decide that some figure they have more or less pulled from a hat is what they ought to be getting. Usually the more unrealistic this figure is, the more they attempt to justify it. They make comparisons to other artists, saying things like "I blew him off the stage at that show we did last week!" or "I know for a fact that at least two-thirds of that crowd was there to see me and not so-and-so!" Despite beliefs to the contrary, many country music acts leave a trail of financial death and destruction for promoters. They tend to overlook this in their own lives and say that the promoter did not advertise properly, or say that nobody showed up because it was cold outside, or too hot, or too wet, or use any other excuse that blinds them to the truth that nobody cared whether they were playing in town. In any case, most of the acts at the Halsey Agency at that time were unhappy for one reason or another.

It was strange working there for other reasons as well. Everybody was from out of town. They did not know who I was or what I had done. They were all newcomers to Nashville. I was infinitely more qualified than anybody in the whole place with the possible exception of Jim Halsey. It was a truly humbling experience taking instructions from persons with less knowledge, experience, ability, and intelligence than myself. It was very strange to have to explain where I was going to some stooge or dimwitted secretary. In spite of all of this, however, I felt thankful to have a job and I accepted the situation without complaint, feeling that I was in this purgatory for some reason, probably as a result of my past actions. I sensed that if I handled myself well during this period that fate would provide me with something better at the appropriate time.

There was, I felt, a conspiracy of sorts at the Halsey Agency to keep me from gaining any power. It was as if all of the ass-kissers protected each other. Any new acts signed to the agency were given to Bob Kincaid, Ron Baird, or Terry Cline.

Tommy Kerkeles had wanted me to be Milsap's responsible agent, but longtime Halsey employee Judy Seale whined and moaned so much that she succeeded in remaining Milsap's responsible agent. This really did not matter that much to me since I consequently did not have to be under the constant harassment and pressure that job entailed.

On January 15, 1990, the Jim Halsey Agency sold out to the

William Morris Agency, another West Coast giant. This was a complete shock to most of the agents. This move was hailed as the creation of a "superagency." It turned out to be something else.

Jim Halsey had been fighting and winning for three decades, had built a great business, and was, in my estimation, too tired to fight anymore. There was no way that the agency could afford to continue financially at its present level of operations. In the six months that I had been there, the agency had lost the Bellamy Brothers, Patty Loveless, Earl Thomas Conley, Carl Perkins, and Pat Boone. Prior to my arrival, it had lost Dwight Yoakam, the Judds, Reba McEntire, Lee Greenwood, and Merle Haggard.

These setbacks, along with the defection of several key agents, had left the Halsey Agency weak and vulnerable. The mystery and mystique that the company had enjoyed while based in Tulsa had been lost when it moved to Nashville. The salvation that had been hoped for with the sale of the Halsey Agency to West Coast giant ICM had failed to materialize when that deal fell through. Jim Halsey had fought hard, made money, introduced many new acts, and expanded the frontiers of country music worldwide. He was tired and it was time to rest.

The supreme irony is that Halsey ended up selling out to the William Morris Agency. He openly hated them and spoke ill of them constantly. It was his feeling that any approach in dealing with them was acceptable. He frequently explained to us how the William Morris Agency duped hillbillies with its TV and movie rap:

"What they do," he said, "is invite them to California for a meeting. They then introduce them to some famous movie directors and producers, who tell them that they would be thrilled to do a movie with the artist in question. There is just one problem, however, and that is that an artist of that caliber will require the perfect project. It will not do to put out a film just to put one out. It will take time to find the right script. The artist is then fully hooked by his own credulity, and the William Morris Agency has another client."

When Halsey sold out to the William Morris Agency, this

transaction was called a merger. What it really was, was a successful attempt on the part of the William Morris Agency to get rid of a major competitor once and for all. It was a great credit to Jim Halsey that he was able to sell a company the size of William Morris a sinking ship.

The William Morris Agency in Nashville is regarded by many as a group of outsiders. It was in its best interests that the deal be seen in a favorable light within the music community. The *Tennessean* article of Tuesday morning, January 16, talked about the superagency resulting from the merger of the two companies. My first reaction was that now the country music business was totally in the hands of outsiders. The record companies and the publishing companies were the first to go, and now the talent agencies as well. So much for Music City. The atmosphere of open competition and respect for one's rivals was gone. The spirit of zestful exuberance and that hopeful expectancy that anything could happen had been devoured along with the small companies. It was now strictly business. It was about money, and all that counted was the bottom line. The corporate giants would henceforward determine who made it and who did not. The public would be force-fed whatever music these few companies decided it should hear. It would all eventually evolve into a generic stew. Amerikan Music. Easy come, easy go. Careers, music, artists, lives—all disposable.

These were my first thoughts. Perhaps I just felt left out of the big party. This is probably true to some degree, and yet upon further consideration, I think not. Country music as it existed is being devoured slowly by the corporate giants. This is happening now, and will continue.

On the other hand, there will always be those individuals who believe in themselves and their abilities, people who will persist in their efforts despite having doors closed repeatedly in their faces by the big companies. These people will find each other, as they always do, and out of their struggles new music will evolve, as well as a new spirit.

Large companies are not by their nature evil. It is rather than in time they tend to be controlled by people who look at the bottom line only. To them an artist is a number in the computer.

The artist's personality, his personal goals and dreams, are not something to which they relate at all. That is just the way it is.

In the final analysis, Jim Halsey was an outsider himself. He sold the William Morris Agency a pig in a poke, a most fitting and appropriate revenge on a company that had caused him so many problems.

It did not require very much time for things to start shaking at the new so-called superagency. Reports came back of dissension between the absorbed and the absorbers. The Kentucky Headhunters left the stew almost immediately. They were followed by the Goldens, David Lynn Jones, Waylon Jennings, Michael Martin Murphey, Roy Clark, Ray Price, and finally Clint Black, along with a host of lesser luminaries. The William Morris Agency explained some of this by saying that it had "trimmed its roster" so that it could better serve its other clients.

I took Ray Price and David Lynn Jones. Michael Martin Murphey moved to World Class Talent along with the Goldens. Waylon Jennings went to the Buddy Lee Agency, and Roy Clark went out on his own with former Halsey agent John Hitt.

Ronnie Milsap ended up at the William Morris Agency once again as a result of the merger, and appears to be happy. He continues to exercise his musical genius and remains at the top of the charts.

Of the four agents and three secretaries who made the trip from the Halsey Agency to the William Morris Agency, only one agent, Bob Kincaid, remained a year later.

It is fun looking back at all of the media hype about the so-called superagency. At least some of the objectives so highly touted by the parties involved were met. The William Morris Agency got rid of Jim Halsey as a competitor once and for all. In addition, they made some money before most of the clients they acquired in the deal left for greener pastures. Jim Halsey got out from under an agency that he was tired of fooling with and got the last laugh from having, in a sense, snookered the great William Morris Agency. As for the so-called superagency, it turned out to be just another country-style crock of horseshit.

Chapter Eighteen

Mickey Gilley and Sherwood Cryer

On November 14, 1986, I flew to Miami and checked into the Hyatt Regency Hotel. Mickey Gilley and his crew were scheduled to arrive that evening and we were all to board the SS *Norway* the next morning for a week-long cruise in the Caribbean. Gilley and his group did not arrive until almost 11:00 P.M. They had been in Boca Raton all afternoon at a party at talent buyer Vic Berry's house.

I found Gilley in the lobby and we went up to his room while he changed clothes. Gilley was almost drunk, and the subject of his alcohol-induced rage was his manager, Sherwood Cryer. He had expressed his dissatisfaction with Sherwood many times in the past, but this was the first time I had actually seen him in a blind fury. I immediately suspected that someone had been talking to him, trying to get him upset. The more successful an artist is, the more his manager and agency have to worry about a behind-the-scenes attack from some competitor who wants a piece of the action.

In this case, it did not take long to figure out what had happened, or who was behind it. Gilley had played some ill-fated Las Vegas type of showroom in Kissimmee, Florida, on the Monday through Thursday preceding his arrival in Miami.

These dates had been set by In Concert vice president Lane Cross, who had sold them to Jimmy Jay. Jimmy Jay started as a bus driver for Loretta Lynn and had worked his way up the ladder the hard way, finally becoming the president of United Talent, a major competitor in the talent agency business in the seventies. United Talent had been owned by Conway Twitty and Loretta Lynn, but Jimmy Jay left the company in 1983, taking Conway Twitty with him and starting a new company called Jayson Promotions that consisted of Jimmy Jay and his two sons.

At United Talent, Jimmy Jay had booked Mickey Gilley for several years, as well as honky-tonk singer Gene Watson, who was now on our roster at In Concert. Since Jimmy Jay's main agent had recently quit, I knew that he was looking for someone to take his place. I should have been suspicious therefore when Lane Cross asked me if he could fly down to Kissimmee and keep an eye on Mickey Gilley. Advance sales had not been going that well, but then nobody in his right mind would have expected them to in a town that small on weeknights. While I suspected that the dates would be a bust from the outset, I figured Mickey Gilley could pick up an extra $40,000 in a period when he would not normally be performing.

Situations like this turn up frequently. Some wheeler-dealer wastes a great deal of money on a project that everyone but himself knows is going to lose every cent. The money-man usually enlists an agent in Nashville to secure all the talent for him. The person hiring the talent knows in his heart of hearts that the project is going to be a disaster, and makes sure he gets his money up front, while there is still some in the pot. He encourages the money-man to spend as much as possible, his own fee being based on a percentage of the talent costs. When the situation proves as disastrous as expected, as it always does, the people who have made all of the money scratch their heads in mock disbelief and then look for another impresario, leaving the skinned buyer alone in the ruins of his folly.

Since I trusted Lane Cross, I had no problem letting him go down to Florida for a few days, even though Gilley and Jimmy Jay were both there. To tell the truth, I was glad to get Lane out of the office. By the end of 1986, he had become a major pain in the ass to everybody in the office.

We had hired Lane in 1983, not long before Dick Blake died.

When we formed In Concert and Joanne Berry tried to employ him, we had to match her offer. He had gotten his butt kicked when his pet act, Exile, left the agency in early 1984. His ego was greatly deflated, but at least he was man enough to acknowledge what had happened. I thought that he had learned his lesson.

Eventually, in late 1985, he became CBS singer Mark Gray's manager. In any case, I let him manage Mark and keep his job at the agency. This arrangement would never have been permitted by any of my competitors.

I felt that Mark Gray was an incredible artist and that he really had a shot at making it to the top. Mark had either written or cowritten many major hit songs, such as "Take Me Down" and "The Closer You Get" for Alabama, as well as "It Ain't Easy Being Easy" for Janie Fricke and "Nice Girls" for Melissa Manchester. Mark had a unique, raspy, and powerful voice and had made a couple of albums. Like so many others before him, Mark had been the record label's darling before the buzz and the hype died down and he parted company with CBS.

Lane was spending a couple of days a week on the road with Mark and as a result began to miss work with increasing frequency. I did not have his salary cut on a prorated basis, nor did I hinder him in any way. I wanted all of the agents to be happy and comfortable with their circumstances as long as they took care of business. Lane Cross' ego had grown again as a result of sporting the title "manager," although there was to my knowledge no contract to back it up. Managing an act without a contract is a very risky business, and rather foolish as well, since very few artists display any loyalty at all. When it became obvious that Mark Gray was not going to make it as an artist, Lane's attitude took a turn for the worse. I should have suspected he was up to something.

Anyway, Mickey Gilley raised hell throughout the cruise about Sherwood Cryer, but it was more than that. He was also irritated that he did not have any "pussy" with him. He complained, "It always seems like if you have some, then you don't need it and if you need it you don't have it." I asked him about his girlfriend of seven years, Connie Moore, and he explained that their affair was over. He was still upset about her, saying that she had been the love of his life. I had been with both of them quite a few times in public and considered her to be foulmouthed and trashy. In my opinion, however, she was infinitely preferable to his wife, Vivian, who was universally considered to be a shrew of the first magnitude.

Gilley fancied himself a real ladies' man, and I guess he was. When we were abroad the *Norway* the first time, back in May 1986, Gilley had scored with one of the showgirls on the ship. We called her Cleopatra, since that had been the part she had played with the troupe of entertainers. She had been fairly attractive, unlike some of the roadhogs I had seen him with from time to time, while Cliff Wildeboer was his road manager.

Cliff and Gilley were always up to something. Cliff told me about a mother-daughter team they sported with from time to time. The best story of all involved one of Gilley's former girlfriends who had actually stayed at Gilley's house masquerading as the road manager's girlfriend from out of town, under the very nose of Gilley's wife. Gilley's main squeeze, however, was Connie Moore, also known as "Fluff" because she had once remarked that her "fluff was sore" after a night with Gilley. Almost everyone called her that, including Gilley, Sherwood, and the Brokaws.

Mickey always bragged about his conquests. He wanted everyone to know about them except, of course, his wife. Sherwood Cryer frequently intercepted love letters and other intimate mail meant for him that might otherwise have ended up on Vivian Gilley's desk at Mickey's office in Pasadena, Texas.

On the Wednesday of our week at sea, Gilley called me to his stateroom for a meeting. His rage over Sherwood Cryer was undiminished and he wanted some definite answers. I knew that the time had come to lay the cards on the table. Gilley had been in Florida with Jimmy Jay and I could guess that Jimmy had been trying to create some mischief. With Lane Cross, as vice president and part owner of the company, along, supposedly acting in our interests, I felt that Jimmy Jay would not be able to do too much damage.

A big issue around town was who actually owned In Concert International. This was a matter of extreme importance to Mickey Gilley as well. I felt that it was none of his business, but he was my number-one client and I had to humor him. I told Gilley that I had borrowed the money from Sherwood Cryer to start In Concert and that I had given Charmin, Inc., 51 percent of the stock as collateral for the loan.

I further told him that to the best of my knowledge Minnie Elerick, Sherwood's woman, was the sole owner of Charmin and that he could check that out there since it was a Texas corporation. While it was true I ultimately had to answer to Sherwood Cryer, he never actually owned any part of In Concert at all. This seemed to appease Gilley to some degree.

I was not particularly concerned about Gilley leaving the agency, but I felt that his growing rift with Sherwood Cryer needed to be closed before a serious problem developed later. I did not think that Gilley would leave us, for several reasons. In the first place, we had done an incredible job for him. We brought his price back up to $20,000 a night and kept it there, long after the *Urban Cowboy* phenomenon was over. In addition, the building that In Concert occupied had been purchased by Sherwood Cryer on behalf of Gilley Enterprises, a company that was jointly owned by Sherwood and Mickey. The rent that In Concert paid covered the note on the building. As far as I knew, Gilley had no money invested in the property at all, other than half of the down payment, if even that. Sherwood was seeing to it that the notes were paid and Gilley was receiving cost-free equity in the building. It would be foolish for him to leave the agency.

On the other hand, for the last several months, every time I had been around Gilley he complained about Sherwood Cryer. Since Gilley surrounded himself with yes-men and drinking buddies, he was always grandstanding on their behalf, bad-mouthing Sherwood in front of them. In their capacity as court jesters, they constantly sought to gain favor with the king by agreeing with him and egging him on. To listen to Gilley, one would think that Sherwood Cryer was the cause of all of his problems. He blamed Sherwood for everything that was wrong in his life. I cannot say whether Sherwood did anything criminal to Mickey Gilley. I do know that Sherwood did everything possible to promote both Mickey Gilley and the club that bore his name. Since I was in the middle of the situation, I will present the two sides of the issue, and then tell the way it really was.

Mickey Gilley's side: Gilley's club was an embarrassment to him. He complained that fans approached him at shows and told him that they had been to his club and were disappointed by how dirty and nasty it was. The sound system was bad. The restrooms were so filthy that some patrons close to use the parking lot, which itself was full of potholes. The club was the most famous nightclub in America, having won the Academy of Country Music's Night Club of the Year Award in 1979, 1980, 1982, 1983, and 1984. In addition, other artists complained to Gilley that the place was a dive, that the dressing rooms were primitive, and that he really should fix the place up. In addition, the club crawled with Sherwood's hired thugs and other unpleasant riffraff.

The Nashville property proved just as irritating to Mickey as the club was, perhaps even more so, since due to its prime location in the tourist district it was seen by more people. It was a large, decaying house that had been purchased by Sherwood Cryer on behalf of Gilley Enterprises. Sherwood had fixed up the inside of the place, but the outside was horrible. Gilley felt that the presence of this building within the area of the local music community made him look like white trash and that it caused the people in the music business to think of Gilley personally in that manner. He even went so far as to say that the presence of this eyesore caused him to suffer such a loss of reputation that it cost him his record deal with CBS.

And then there was Sherwood Cryer himself. According to Gilley, Sherwood was a low-class, ruthless tyrant with redneck women all over town, some of whom had carried his children. To make matters worse, Sherwood had failed to pay at least one artist who had played at the club, with the result that the club started to get a bad reputation among performers as well as the general public. Since artists and fans alike thought Gilley owned the club, it made him look bad. He also thought that both the recording studio and the publishing companies that they jointly owned were a joke.

Sherwood Cryer's side: Sherwood felt that he was largely responsible for the *Urban Cowboy* phenomenon that had really put Mickey Gilley on the map as an artist. Sherwood owned and operated Gilley's and felt that the club was what it had always been, the largest honky-tonk in the world. If the club was in fact a dive, it had been good enough for Mickey Gilley at the time of the *Urban Cowboy* craze. The club had not changed; Mickey Gilley had.

Sherwood had worked hard to push Mickey Gilley, publishing a magazine that promoted Gilley, Johnny Lee, and the club. He had made a deal with the Spoetzel Brewery to have Gilley's Beer produced and available to the public. He had initiated a Gilley's line of clothing featuring jeans, hats, and boots. He had also syndicated the radio show "Live from Gilley's" through Westwood One. He had come up with the mechanical bulls and built the rodeo arena at the back of the club. All Gilley had to do was sing, act decent, and help the overall effort. Sherwood believed Gilley had done everything he could to oppose him. Gilley had been against the mechanical bulls. He had not wanted Sherwood to hire the Brokaw twins to handle public relations. He had fought the construction of the rodeo arena. According to Sherwood, Gilley's wife, whose office was in the recording studio, had been so unpleasant to customers that nobody wanted to record there. He also felt that she instigated trouble between Gilley and himself.

There is some truth to both points of view. The club was definitely a honky-tonk, in the truest sense of the term. People came there to get drunk, dance, raise hell, listen to music, and hopefully get lucky. Sherwood should have had nice dressing rooms constructed, especially since the top acts in country music played there on a regular basis. He should have updated the sound system, remodeled the restrooms, and paved the parking lot. These measures would not have altered the character of the place. I tried repeatedly to talk him into doing so, and so did Mickey Gilley and the Brokaws.

I always received the same response, that everything was fine the way it was. "I don't tell Gilley what to do on the road, or how to sing," Sherwood would reply, "and he don't need to be telling me how to run the club." Sherwood resented the fact that Gilley wanted to change the club and felt that he had been spoiled as a result of playing places like Harrah's and the Desert Inn. I would explain that these things were important to Gilley and that he ought to tend to them.

On the other hand, the club was largely responsible for Mickey Gilley's success, and when he received complaints, Gilley should have defended the place, explaining it had always been a honky-tonk. Sherwood would listen to what I said, but he remained inflexible. He maintained that if he did what Gilley wanted then Gilley would complain about something else two weeks later. He may have been right, but he never found out. He refused steadfastly to change anything, and never did, even until the end.

As far as the building in Nashville was concerned, it was the same thing. All of the other souvenir shops and tourist traps looked great. The building at 117 Sixteenth Avenue South was indeed trashy-looking and a bad reflection on Mickey Gilley. In the music business, image is all important. The public expects its heroes to be bigger than they are. In Gilley's defense, it would have been far better for him to have had no building with his name on it in Nashville. A negative image in this case was worse than no image at all. The building had truly gone from bad to worse.

Once when I asked Sherwood to paint the building, telling him of a scheduled meeting with singer Johnny Rodriguez, he said that I should tie a goat to the door so that Johnny would feel "right at home." Sherwood Cryer was referring to the manner in which Johnny Rodriguez got his career start. He had been arrested for stealing a goat and was "discovered" singing in his jail cell.

The building had the best location on Music Row and could have been a showplace instead of the eyesore that it was. Sherwood again would not budge.

As for the studio, Gilley felt that it was fine for demos and other similar projects but was inadequate for turning out master-quality recordings. I think he felt that nothing good could come from Pasadena, Texas. The studio was quite adequate for any project, and having been there, I do believe that Gilley's wife was the problem. I was told by insiders that she and

Gilley both categorically opposed everything that Sherwood wanted to do. It was almost as if they wanted the studio not to work.

I had been at Gilley's fiftieth birthday party at Gilley's club in April 1986. Things seemed to be fine between Sherwood and Mickey at that point, and Sherwood staged a big birthday celebration at the club, followed by Gilley's performance. I spent that night at Gilley's house and the next day we boarded his plane, a twin-engined King Air, and flew back to Nashville where he performed a couple of songs with the Nashville Symphony. He was in a good mood then, as I visited with him and his girlfriend Fluff, who was backstage.

Gilley performed at his annual arthritis telethon in Nashville at the end of April, and we went out for our first week on the SS *Norway* in May.

By the following November, before the second cruise had ended, Gilley wanted a complete break with Sherwood. Gilley proposed to divide the property as follows: Gilley wanted the airplane, the buses, the Nashville property, and the removal of his name from the club. Above all, he wanted to be free of Sherwood Cryer forever.

I felt that this was a hell of a lot to ask, especially since Sherwood had been making all of the payments on the Nashville property from the very beginning. It was a large old house in a prime location. A souvenir shop was located in the front of the building, and the offices of In Concert were located in a Breeko Block structure affixed to the back of the house. Despite the shabby outside appearance of the property, it was worth several million dollars, and had been a good investment. I was surprised that Gilley felt he owed Sherwood nothing. He was willing only to relinquish his half ownership in the jointly owned property upon which the rodeo arena had been constructed.

His desires seemed insane to me. It was a hell of a deal for him but left nothing for Sherwood. All I wanted was to keep him as a client, so I humored him. He had been reasonable with me up to this point, and I felt that when I got back to the office I could call Sherwood and explain the gravity of the situation. I assumed that he would at last take the necessary measures to get things squared away between them.

When I returned to Nashville, I immediately called Sherwood and gave him a complete rundown on the conversations between myself and Gilley. He was not particularly upset and said something to the effect that he had Gilley under contract and that he was not worried about it. I had an uneasy feeling when Johnny Lee got away from Sherwood so easily, and I think that the ease with which he accomplished this opened the door in Gilley's mind for him to do the same thing. In spite of Gilley's fiery words, I still honestly felt that things could be worked out between them easily enough.

On December 19, 1987, Lane Cross resigned as vice president. He said he had no other specific plans at the time. I was damn glad to see him leave. He had been a black cloud around the office for quite a while. On the other hand, over the past three years he had developed into quite a capable agent, and was well liked by most of the artists we represented and by the talent buyers as well. Furthermore, he handled the majority of the fair business for the company. It would be very difficult to replace him or to explain his departure from the agency satisfactorily.

In light of these developments, I could not help but wonder what damage he had done to the company while he was representing us at the Fair Buyers' Convention in Las Vegas during the first week of December. He had surely known at that time that he intended to leave the company. Lane was up to something, but I did not yet know what it was. He had resigned but he did not want to leave just yet. He wanted to hang around until the end of January. Normally I would have given any employee two weeks' pay and sent him packing on the day he resigned. I generally do not like to keep someone around, paying him to run up the phone bill while he is busy setting up his new deal. In this case I wanted to see what Lane was up to, and this would be easier if he was there physically. Furthermore, I felt that I needed some time to think things over. Perhaps I should come to some kind of agreement with him and get him to stay. I really did not know what to do.

The week before Christmas, Gilley was in town and called

me. I told him to come on over. He showed up a little while later
with Eli Nelson, a steel-guitar player who had been promoted to
road manager after Cliff Wildeboer had resigned. Gilley announced that he was leaving In Concert. Nothing could have
been a greater shock. I could not believe it. What made matters
worse was that Eli Nelson sat there like some type of philoso-
pher interjecting his ill-informed observations about Sherwood
Cryer, as if he was anything other than Mickey Gilley's yes-man
and parrot. The meeting lasted about half an hour. I answered
Gilley's ravings about Sherwood Cryer by more or less agreeing
with him but suggesting that matters between them should and
could be worked out.

My greatest fear was that Gilley had already made a deal with
some other agency. He told me that he had not spoken with
anyone else and did not know what he was going to do. I asked
him to delay any formal announcement until I had time to
inform my agents as to his decision. I also wanted some time to
finish up the things we were working on. He agreed.

There are many instances of this nature in the life of an
agent. At times like these, one must act decisively and correctly.
You can only guess what has already happened. It becomes
necessary to plot an immediate defensive strategy to keep the
client, knowing full well that it may already be too late. I felt in
this case that it was already too late, and yet there was still hope,
even though Gilley had been quite clear about his intentions. I
felt that in light of Sherwood and Mickey's long history together, and in consideration of the complexity of their various
financial arrangements and holdings, some reconciliation could
be worked out.

I called Sherwood and told him what had happened. he
seemed a bit more concerned this time. He had reason to be. He
was about to lose everything he had worked for all of his life.
Next, I called the agents into the office and gave them the news.
As usual, I told them to get on the phone and set every date
possible, regardless of how far in the future it might be. I was
not happy about this situation at all, but there was nothing
much I could do about it then.

Needless to say, I had a bad Christmas. It was indeed a far cry from my Christmas three years before when I had just taken Gilley on as a client and the world seemed so bright. To make matters worse, we were nearing the end of 1986 and things were looking bad financially. The money that we had made in the prime summer months did not seem sufficient to carry us through the hard winter into spring. We had $90,000 in the bank going into December and our expenses were running around $50,000 a month. I did not know how we would survive, but I knew that somehow we would.

I kept calling Gilley with dates, but he wouldn't accept them. I had heard no word of any other agency pitching dates for him, so I was encouraged. Usually that is the first thing that happens. Finally, sometime toward the middle of January, Gilley started taking dates from us again, and it looked as if the crisis had passed. I quickly rebounded and regained Lou Rawls, and then picked up Ronnie Milsap. In Concert was stronger than ever. Things happen that quickly on the front lines in the music business in Nashville. You can be saved or destroyed by a couple of phone calls.

Lane Cross left and went to work for Jimmy Jay about two weeks later. My suspicions had been correct. I think that Jimmy Jay and Lane had tried to get Gilley to come over to them while they were with him down in Florida in November. I really believe that Lane expected to end up working for Jimmy Jay at Jayson Promotions and thought that Gilley would be there also. It must have been a shock to Lane and to Jimmy Jay when this did not happen, especially after Gilley had told us he was leaving.

We rolled along until the first week of May 1987, at which time I again received a call from Mickey Gilley, wanting me to join him for dinner at Ruth's Chris Steak House. We ate there frequently so I expected nothing out of the ordinary. When I arrived, I found Gilley, his stooge Mike Taylor, and Eli Nelson. Gilley told me that he was leaving the agency. I jokingly said "Again?" But this time it was no joke.

He told me that this time it was for good. Again he explained that his decision had nothing to do with me, that it was all about Sherwood Cryer. Gilley claimed that he had been "screwed,

blued, and tattooed" for the last time by Sherwood Cryer.
"Screwed, blued, and tattooed" was probably Gilley's favorite
expression. He used it frequently.

He said that he knew for a fact that Sherwood Cryer owned
the agency, regardless of whose name or names were on the
papers. He was through with Sherwood Cryer and he hoped
that they could part on good terms, meaning that he wanted
Sherwood to give him everything but the kitchen sink. He
didn't know if this would happen, but was prepared to fight in
court if necessary. A split was certain; all that remained was the
property settlement. In any case, Mickey did not want to pay
commissions to Sherwood Cryer by way of In Concert. He did
say that he would honor all contracts and pay us all commissions
that he might owe at that time or in the future as a result of our
efforts on his behalf.

Lying begets credulity, as they say, and I believe that in his
own mind Gilley intended to pay us the commissions that he
owed. On the other hand, looking back, I realize that he had not
paid us for what he owed us for the month of April. I do not
believe that he ever intended to pay us. Instead, I think that
Gilley came back to us after Christmas with the intention of
letting us set all of those dates for him free of charge.

Even at that point I still thought that things could be worked
out between Gilley and Sherwood. But it was too late. I asked
him to let me moderate a meeting between them, but Gilley
refused.

At this point, Eli Nelson said, "I gotta tell you that when we
were in Reno the people from the William Morris Agency came
over to see us, and we have been talking to the Brokaws. Their
old man [Norman Brokaw] is a big wheel over at William Morris
and they promised us TV and movies, which Gilley needs, so we
are going with the Morris office."

I said that I thought that the Brokaws, Gilley's publicists, were
already being paid to do that, to which Eli replied, "They are,
but it will be better this way."

The William Morris Agency had once again used its TV-and-
movie rap and Gilley fell for it. I knew then that it was already
too late. Gilley suggested that he join William Morris for a year
and during that time we could both get free of Sherwood Cryer.

Then if William Morris wasn't doing the job, I should call him and we could pick up things again as we had left them. At this point, a year seemed like an eternity, and I knew that the William Morris Agency was not going to let Gilley go after one year. I felt sick.

Gilley, however, was in a jubilant mood. He had just wasted $95,000 on a piece of land on Seventeenth Avenue South, in the Music Row area, upon which he intended to build a recording studio. I could not help but think how stupid it was to build a recording studio in Nashville. It was like selling salt water beside the sea. There were already too many studios in Nashville. Furthermore, the cost of setting up and operating a studio is incredible. The expensive equipment must be updated constantly. Gilley and his yes-man, Mike Taylor, thought that all that was necessary was to build a studio and hang a sign on the door saying GILLEY'S RECORDING STUDIO, and everyone would come running. Almost six years later the land is still vacant and marked with a FOR SALE sign.

I was also subjected to more tales of Sherwood Cryer's alleged misdealings. Mike Taylor told me how Sherwood roughed him up over a $60 bad check. The sage Eli Nelson put in his two cents' worth. It was a circus performance with the two parrots squawking and prating their yesses to everything ringmaster Mickey Gilley said. I listened to their incessant ramblings, but in the back of my mind I was trying to figure out what to do. I knew there was going to be a war and that I would be seriously affected by the outcome. However, it was not my fight and I should have stayed out of it and let the chips fall wherever they might. Of all the artists I had ever represented, I was closest to Mickey Gilley. I liked him personally and I know that he liked me. We ended the meeting with Gilley offering to come over to the office on Monday morning and explain to my staff what was happening. I told him that I would appreciate that gesture.

On Thursday, May 14, Gilley called me and said that he would be in town to close the deal for the land he had bought, and wanted me to meet him at Ruth's where he would buy me a steak. By this time, I had regained my equilibrium, and again thought that I might yet be able to save the situation, not between Sherwood and Gilley, but between Gilley and myself. I did not know whether Gilley had actually signed a deal with William Morris, but I felt that his invitation to dinner was a good sign.

When I arrived at the restaurant I found Gilley and Connie Moore waiting to be seated, as well as Mike Taylor and some wench. I was surprised to see Fluff since Gilley had told me that they had broken up, but there she was. Gilley sent Mike and the girls ahead and we talked. What he wanted was $500,000 to put into his studio project. We had both dined with my friend Dr. Doug Parker in Fort Smith a year or so before and Gilley wondered if we might want to get involved in the project. I said that it was unlikely unless we could also have agency representation, to which he replied that he did not want to mix the two together. Fluff came up and said to him that it was time they were going. She then walked back to the table and joined the other two. As she left Gilley said that Connie was a real pain in the ass and that he would not fool with her at all if she "weren't such a good lay."

We started walking in the direction of the table where the other three were seated. He said, "I'll call you tomorrow," meaning that he no longer expected me to join them for dinner. This suited me since I knew that from that moment forward our relationship was going to be all downhill.

On Saturday afternoon I checked my answering machine. Gilley had called to say he was flying back to Houston that morning and to call him at home after four o'clock. There was nothing more to say. The time for action had come.

I had been in touch with Sherwood Cryer throughout this period. When I had told him that Gilley was leaving he asked me what I was going to do. I replied that I was going to try to work things out. I was somewhat annoyed with him since I felt that this escalated situation was more or less his fault. I called him the first thing Monday morning and told him that I was not going to be able to resolve matters. He again asked me what I was going to do. I told him that I did not know. "You have him under contract, don't you?" he said, meaning that he wanted me to backdate a contract like we had done with Johnny Lee. From the tone in his voice I determined that it was not a negotiable issue.

I summoned Linda Edwards, told her what we were going to do, and asked her to type up a contract between Mickey Gilley and In Concert just like we did with Johnny Lee. I told her to backdate it to December 28, 1983, and Federal Express it to Sherwood Cryer for his signature. As I have said, Linda is very sharp, and managed to find a sheet of our stationery from that period. She typed up the contract on one of our IBM typewriters. After she had done this I destroyed the typewriter ball.

On Monday morning, May 18, 1987, I sent a telegram to the William Morris Agency in Beverly Hills informing them that In Concert International had an exclusive booking agreement with Mickey Gilley and that we were prepared to defend our interests. I had consulted with my lawyer, Peter Curry, prior to sending the telegram and he had told me to keep it simple and to the point without being threatening. Almost as soon as I had sent the telegram, I regretted what I had done. I figured that I would receive a call from Mickey Gilley as soon as William Morris received the telegram. It was not long in coming. At around four my secretary informed me that Mickey Gilley was on the phone.

I answered and he seemed in a good mood, so I suspected that he hadn't heard about the telegram yet. I was wrong. He asked me if I had sent a letter to William Morris and I replied that I had sent a telegram, not a letter. He then asked who had authorized me to do that. I replied, "Sherwood Cryer."

At that point Gilley went berserk and started shouting, "Sherwood Cryer and Mickey Gilley are through. Scott Faragher and Mickey Gilley are through, and In Concert and Mickey Gilley are through. Finished. If you and Sherwood ever pull another stunt like that, I will get on a plane and come up there and whip some ass. I am not paying In Concert another cent. If you want it, sue me."

There was a moment of silence after which I replied, "Do what you have to do." He slammed down the phone and that was it.

I did not know whether William Morris would heed my telegram. I imagined that they would stop claiming to represent Mickey Gilley, at least until they found out whether a contract existed. Why should they risk a heavy lawsuit over an artist who was almost totally booked for the year? I did not wish to sue William Morris or Mickey Gilley, but once I had started down that road it seemed too late to turn back.

I had been told by Sherwood that he had a management contract with Mickey Gilley and that it was still in force. Sherwood further told me that he had signed Gilley to the William Morris Agency in the first place and that by virtue of his management contract with Gilley, he had the authority to sign Gilley to In Concert. When he put it in those terms, what I had done did not seem so bad. I was just following up on what should have been done to begin with.

My intention in suing the William Morris Agency was to stop it from booking Mickey Gilley. When Gilley defaulted on commissions he owed us, I sued him as well. I wanted to sue him in Nashville but he filed a countersuit, bringing in Sherwood Cryer as a third party. He succeeded in having the jurisdiction established in Houston.

Gilley claimed that a management contract had existed between him and Sherwood, but that it had expired on March 31, 1983, prior to the date of our contract. He sought damages from Sherwood Cryer and In Concert. He then went on to say that if a booking agreement had existed between In Concert and Mickey Gilley, In Concert and Sherwood Cryer had both failed in their fiduciary responsibilities to notify Mickey Gilley of the existence of such an agreement.

We sought a partial motion for summary judgment but it was denied, and we were put on the back burner until the suit between Sherwood and Gilley was settled. This is not what I wanted at all. If we had been able to go to court before that trial and had sought only the commissions we were owed, we would most likely have won.

As it turned out, the management contract between Sherwood Cryer and Mickey Gilley was not admitted as evidence because Sherwood would not or could not produce the original. Instead, he submitted some photostat that the court determined had been altered. Since our suit was based upon Sherwood's right to enter into an agreement with us on Mickey Gilley's behalf based upon the validity of his management contract, this left us out in the cold.

Not only was Sherwood Cryer's contract ruled to be invalid,

but the court declared all management fees paid to Sherwood after its expiration date (beginning April 1, 1983) to be held by Sherwood Management in constructive trust for Mickey Gilley. In other words, Sherwood now owed Gilley all the money that he had received from him for the past five years.

On June 30, 1988, the jury awarded Mickey Gilley $7,999,000 from Sherwood Cryer and his accountant, Gerard Willrich, jointly and severally. It also awarded Mickey Gilley an additional $8,000,000 from Cryer and an additional $1,027,500 from Willrich.

The court further appointed a receiver to take possession and control of the assets of all of Sherwood Cryer's other companies. The receiver was directed to pay the debts of these companies including the judgment to Mickey Gilley. Gilley was also awarded attorney's fees in the amount of $375,000 plus 10 percent interest, as well as an additional $50,000 from each person who might appeal the decision if there was an appeal and Gilley won. Last but not least, Gilley won the exclusive use of the trademark "Gilley's," which meant that Sherwood had to remove the name from the club.

There was no chance now that I would win my case against Mickey Gilley in Houston. I finally withdrew, nearly $30,000 poorer for legal fees. I would see Gilley from time to time, and we even had dinner occasionally. He never denied that he owed In Concert $150,000, and always said that he would pay us as soon as everything was settled with Sherwood Cryer, but he never did. Gilley did not hold me responsible for what had happened, but felt that Sherwood Cryer had corrupted me and that I had acted under duress. He said that Sherwood had corrupted him, the Brokaws, and everyone else he had come in contact with. I wish that I could say that it had happened that way, but what I did was my own fault.

Was Gilley really an honorable man, and would he have paid In Concert the money he owed? I will never know because I never gave him the chance. When I sued him he reacted in the only way he could have. I lost $150,000, and in the crash that followed I lost In Concert and everything I had worked so hard to build. I hold no resentment toward Mickey Gilley, and what happened to me was directly the result of my own actions.

I really thought that Sherwood would win in court. The

picture that Gilley painted of him was completely contrary to
my own direct experience. Sherwood had always been a friend
to me personally and had gone way beyond the bounds of
friendship in helping me on many occasions. I was a loser no
matter whose side I took. Sherwood Cryer and Mickey Gilley
had both been my friends. As far as the trial between Sherwood
and Gilley was concerned, all I can say is Gilley must have had a
hell of a lot of damning evidence against Sherwood. A judgment of $17 million sounds like something involving a major
defense contractor. The sad thing is that it was all so unnecessary. There was enough in the pie for all of us to have
everything we ever could have wanted. What is sadder still is
that Sherwood Cryer and Mickey Gilley had once been close
friends.

There was much speculation around town that Gilley's wife
was behind it all, egging Gilley on, knowing that Sherwood
Cryer was the only person alive who could and would bring
Gilley's many marital infidelities before the public eye. It was
thought that after the trial between them was over, she would
present herself as the long-suffering wife who had stood by
Mickey Gilley through the hard times, only to find out in court
that she had been betrayed, at which point she would take Gilley
for everything he owned. Under those circumstances she would
come out on top, regardless of who prevailed in the *Gilley vs.
Cryer* suit. I halfway expected this myself and am somewhat
surprised that it did not happen.

There is no doubt that Sherwood intended to bring all of this
to light. He had Connie Moore's deposition taken, and it was
certainly incriminating. He sent me a copy of the deposition
and she denied nothing, saying that she had been in love with
Mickey Gilley. For some reason this was not admitted in court,
but it should have been since Sherwood sought to prove that
Gilley had used the company plane on numerous occasions to
fetch Fluff to places where Gilley was playing.

Gilley's closed in March 1989 as a result of the lawsuit. On
July 5, 1990, the building was destroyed by fire at the hands of a
sixteen-year-old arsonist angered over personal problems. It was
indeed a sad ending for the club and a loss for the city of
Pasadena, Texas, which otherwise has little to offer. More

unfortunate still, Gilley's was a larger-than-life place, and its loss truly represents the end of an era.

Sherwood appealed Gilley's judgment and Gilley sued him again for attempting to avoid paying the judgment by conveying assets to friends and relatives. Finally both actions were dropped by mutual agreement. Gilley took everything Sherwood Cryer owned except his modest house, and what was left of Gilley's was bulldozed.

Personally, I feel that what happened to Sherwood Cryer was a complete and total miscarriage of justice. Without Sherwood Cryer Gilley most likely would never have made it. Sherwood did, however, possess several major character flaws, and they were his undoing. He sought to control everything himself, kept poor records, and was unable to trust people who could have helped him. I have not spoken with Sherwood Cryer since 1988. I miss his friendship and have tried to reach him several times but he continues to refuse my calls. I did the best for him that I knew how with In Concert. All of us lost as a result of what happened. Sherwood lost everything he had worked for, especially Gilley's. I lost two close friends and In Concert International. It may sound strange in light of Gilley's incredible financial victory, but I feel that Gilley was the biggest loser of all, for by destroying Sherwood Cryer, he lost his own integrity.

In looking back at the situation I think that several factors contributed to bring things to this point. Life was fine for Mickey Gilley until his fiftieth birthday. He was making more money than his arch-rival, cousin Jerry Lee Lewis; he had a $2 million home, an airplane, property, money in the bank, a girlfriend whom he loved, and a successful career. When he reached fifty, however, things turned around for him quickly. He lost his girlfriend Fluff, the love of his life. I never knew why it ended, but my guess is that she got tired of waiting for Gilley to dump his wife.

Careerwise, Gilley's records were no longer selling and he had been dropped by CBS after ten years. Like most hillbillies on the skids, he needed a scapegoat, and Sherwood Cryer fit the bill nicely. It was not Sherwood, however, who picked or recorded songs that did not sell, nor was it Sherwood who cost him his one true love. For somebody looking for an excuse, any will do, and it is my opinion that Sherwood got the blame for everything wrong in Mickey Gilley's life. Sherwood did nothing to help the situation, and I still believe that if he had addressed the problems decisively back at Christmas in 1986, all of the carnage that followed could have been avoided.

When I had backdated that contract on Johnny Lee I had known that it was dishonest, but I had gotten by with it and everything had turned out all right. My conscience had bothered me a little at first, but I got over it. The ends justified the means. By the time I elected to do the same thing with Mickey Gilley, I had almost no choice, for I had lost all sense of right and wrong.

There is no doubt in my mind that there is a certain economy in the universe, and that as a result of my actions with Johnny Lee and with Mickey Gilley I brought about my own ruin as far as In Concert was concerned. I like to think that if I had it to do over again, I would be incapable of backdating those contracts. The ancients said that man learns through suffering. If this is the case, then I have learned my lessons well. I was on a self-destructive path, and what happened gave me plenty of time to think about who I was and what I wanted to do with my life. I apologized for my actions, both to Johnny Lee and to Mickey Gilley. As far as their careers were concerned, they both reached their zenith while at In Concert.

Chapter Nineteen

Billy Ray Cyrus: Elvis on Steroids

At In Concert I generally maintained an open-door policy and accepted unsolicited material from new writers and artists. Most people in my position were too cool or uninterested to see anybody without some references. I was busy as hell, but knew that there were great artists walking the streets just looking for an opportunity.

While my intentions were good, I usually did not have the time to listen to tapes that came in the mail and often passed them along to other people in the office with instructions to let me know if they heard anything worthwhile. Ringing phones and frequent interruptions distracted me at the office, and by the time I finally got home at night I was too tired to hear anything that required concentration or attention.

Aspiring artists called me often and sometimes dropped in unannounced. I did not appreciate anyone coming by without an appointment, but always admired courage and audacity. If someone dropped in and I was free, I would generally see him or her.

It takes a lot of guts to come in cold off the street and sell oneself to someone else. The environment is usually hostile and intimidating. The artist understands that he is a nobody and that everybody else realizes it too. Everyone also knows his actual chances of success are almost absolute zero. He is very self-conscious, and feels that all eyes are upon him as he slinks down the hall toward the office of some big wheel. Hopefully he will make a good impression. He is under incredible pressure to say and do the right thing, knowing that he only has a few minutes and that his presentation can be cut off at any moment without notice.

With nothing but a dream and a few bad tapes, the artist seeks to make a future for himself in the music business. Most of the people I saw did not have what it took. They did not look right, could not sing, or had poor material. Others had some talent, but lacked the burning desire to succeed. They were willing to become rich and famous as country singers, but only if they could do so without too much trouble. They did not wish to move to Nashville or to be away from their girlfriends or boyfriends.

To the others I offered encouragement, steering them to publishers and producers if I thought they had potential.

This business of music concerns a great deal more than singing. It is a metaphysical thing in many ways, like the search for the Holy Grail. This might sound strange and farfetched, but it's not. It is a calling that only the person who gets it hears or understands. When someone embarks on any career outside the norm, he immediately becomes a target. It is as if he suddenly steps away from the safety of the crowd, waves a red flag at fate, and says, "Here I am. See if you can get me."

Others, after having considered various career options, decide to be country singers. The above considerations do not apply to this group, since theirs is a conscious choice and not a calling.

In the summer of 1987 I received a call from Billy Ray Cyrus, another act off the street. Unlike many, he had enough manners to call first. He asked for ten minutes of my time and wanted an appointment. I told him to come the next day. That morning he called again to make sure that I would be in. I told him to come on over.

When I first saw him I thought that he was an attractive fellow. He was about twenty-five years old, a little over six feet tall, well-proportioned and muscular, with a nicely chiseled face. I also liked his attitude. He was humble and appreciative, a far cry from most of the artists I was dealing with at the time. It was obvious from his manners that he had been properly raised and was, as we say in the South, from "a good family." Everything was "yes, sir" and "no, sir." In that sense he reminded me of Jerry Lee Lewis and Elvis Presley at the beginning of their careers. If you look at any of their early interviews it is interesting to note how courteous and grateful they were. They appreciated the fact that people liked their music. They seemed glad to be alive.

Billy Ray was from Flatwoods, Kentucky, a small town on the border of Ohio, in Greenup County. The population of the entire county is less than forty thousand. His mother was a bluegrass musician and his father a gospel singer who ended up in the Kentucky State Legislature. His parents divorced when he was five, a very painful experience for young Cyrus.

He originally intended to become a professional baseball player, but changed his mind when he discovered the guitar. Billy Ray dropped out of college and formed his first band, Sly Dog, in the early 1980s, playing regularly at a joint called the Sand Bar in Ironton, Ohio.

Billy Ray wanted help and career guidance. He had just spent $2,875 putting out his own record on an independent label called Stargem. In addition to the money he paid he gave up publishing rights to the song, "All Night Love." He wanted me to listen to the record right then, but I told him to leave it and call me in a couple of days and I would tell him what I thought. I did not like to listen to someone's music for the first time with him standing there, and still don't, unless I know the artist well. This is especially true if the artist is an unknown act. If the music is terrible I might need some time to think of something honest to say that won't destroy the singer.

Our meeting did not last more than ten or fifteen minutes. Billy Ray left and I went back to work.

Later that afternoon when there was a break in the action, I gave his record a spin. There is something really neat about placing a 45-r.p.m. record on the turntable and watching it go around. This is the way it was done at the beginning of rock and roll. It's too bad that they don't make 45s anymore. The A side, "All Night Love" was a self-written moderate-tempo tune with rather juvenile but saucy lyrics: "I want your all night love, I want your all night love, I want your all night love, that's what I want from you." I liked the song. It was kind of country but not really.

The producer and the musicians had done a great job. The artist was listed on the record label as "Billy Ray and the Breeze." The other side of the record contained a song entitled "Remember." This number was about three minutes long, but seemed longer. It was definitely not country and would never get country airplay. The guitar introduction sounded like an elevator crash.

Despite the shortcomings in these two songs, I felt that Billy Ray showed promise as an artist and possibly someday as a songwriter. I thought no more about the matter one way or the other. He called back and asked my opinion. I told him that he needed to get some stronger material and go into the studio and cut a good demo and then shop it to the labels. I told him that he would be better off not shopping the record he had left me.

We kept in touch over the phone for the next few weeks as Billy Ray decided what he should do. In the meantime, I was interested in moving more into artist management. I was co-managing a group from Arkansas called Razorback, as well as a Texas girl named Margaret Lester.

In the meantime, I formed a management company called In Concert Group with surgeon Doug Parker and producer Peter Sullivan. Doug was the money-man and Peter Sullivan had been a staff producer for Decca in England and had produced most of the hits recorded by Tom Jones and Englebert Humperdinck. I signed Billy Ray Cyrus to this company on March 3, 1988, with myself as his personal manager. The management fee was 20 percent.

I felt that Billy Ray had what it takes, but I knew that unless some good music could be transferred to records, he was not going to make it as an artist. I sent Peter Sullivan to him to see if they could find some material to record. Peter went to Ohio to see him perform, and a regular correspondence developed between them, with Billy Ray sending Peter tapes of new songs he had written. Billy Ray possessed a charm and innocence that proved refreshing. One of his notes on the lyric sheets he sent said:

"Peter, Thanks for taking time out of your life to help me. I appreciate it. Once again, you came along at a time when I was and still am very hungry for guidance. I will repay you. The sooner, the better!"

Most of the songs he gave Peter were pretty bad. "Never Ever Thought I Would Fall in Love With You," "Appalachian Lady," and "Snooz You Looze" were all terrible, but there was something in his style that made these otherwise less than average songs interesting. Producer Peter Sullivan was always very conservative in terms of who he thought was likely to make it as an artist. He bragged that no act he had passed on ever subsequently reached stardom. His feeling that Billy Ray "had potential," as uninspiring as that might sound, was for Peter Sullivan a major endorsement.

With the management contract signed, I got to work. In January 1988 I put Billy Ray with producer Greg Humphrey. Greg is a rather interesting character. A large fellow, about six feet tall, with long hair and a beard, he had come to Nashville from California and had set up a little twelve-track studio over on Villa Place in the Music Row area. I remember singer Jennifer Warnes coming into my office one day in the fall of 1985 with "The Hump" as we called him. She talked about what a great producer he was. A couple of days later the three of us attended the Country Music Association Awards show together. I had heard some of the material he had produced for artists like Michael Smotherman and was impressed. I had also used him to do some songs for Margaret Lester, and was pleased with the results. Consequently, I selected him as a producer for Billy Ray Cyrus.

We chose "All Night Love," "Fire," "If Tomorrow Never Comes," and "Someday, Somewhere, Somehow" as the songs we would record, two fast songs and two slow songs.

Billy Ray would play Tuesday through Saturday at some

nightclub in Huntington, West Virginia. He would then drive six hours, work in the studio Monday and early Tuesday, and drive back to Huntington to work at the club. This went on during most of February 1988.

Using Greg Humphrey as the producer on these sessions proved to have been a big mistake, but by the time we realized this, we were too far into the project to back out. Greg was just plain not interested. I remember climbing the stairs to his studio to find him crawling around on his knees with his big fat ass up in the air. He had a flashlight in one hand and tweezers in the other as he moved around the floor, inch by inch, trying to find enough marijuana in the rug to roll a joint.

Billy Ray was extremely serious and couldn't understand the Hump's actions. The end came one night at about 10:15 P.M. The Hump told Billy Ray that he had to run down to the store and would be gone about fifteen minutes. He left the studio. He did not phone. He just did not come back, leaving a perplexed Billy Ray in the middle of the session with nobody at the console. Billy Ray and a couple of musicians finished the songs themselves, securing the aid of a neighborhood black girl to do the background vocals on "All Night Love."

I was ready to kill Hump for putting me in this position. I went to see him, stole the master tape from the session, and personally delivered it to Billy Ray. The Hump did not care for my actions, but I didn't give a shit. I had put my reputation on the line using him in the first place. As far as I was concerned, he forfeited any and all rights he might have had by his irresponsible behavior.

The songs turned out surprisingly well considering the circumstances under which they were recorded. "Fire" is a great up-tempo song, and "Someday, Somewhere, Somehow" was later rerecorded for his multi-platinum first Mercury album, *Some Gave All*.

All of us at In Concert Group had been dealing with a legal firm, Zumwalt, Almon, and Hayes, and were seeking its expertise in helping us secure recording contracts for some of our artists. Jim Zumwalt liked Billy Ray and suggested that I put him on the South by Southwest festival in Austin, Texas, in March 1988. This annual festival was a several-day affair that consisted of various music-related seminars during the day, followed by live performances at night. The festival was spread out all over town, with different types of acts playing one right after the other at almost every nightspot in Austin. The function was supposed to serve as a giant showcase for a large number of bands in a short period of time. Most of the major record labels had representatives there looking at new acts possibly to sign for record deals.

I called Louis Meyers, the man in charge of scheduling the events. I had never met Louis, but had known him from my days of pushing Jamaican music. In addition to running South by Southwest, he operated a nightspot called the Liberty Lunch.

He scheduled Billy Ray to play at an Italian joint called Birraporetti's on March 10, 1988. It was a free show, so the band did not make any money. I then called Sherwood Cryer and sold him Billy Ray Cyrus for $2,000 at Gilley's.

So far, I had not seen Billy Ray perform, so I was looking forward to joining him and his band, the Players, in Austin. It was cold when I left Nashville but nice and warm in Austin. When show time came the band in front of Billy Ray bitched and complained about the sound system, the monitors, the microphones, and everything else. The lead singer was really nervous and on edge. When they played I felt uptight due to all of the tension they generated. I think the audience felt it too. It was all unnecessary and very unprofessional.

When Billy Ray and his band hit the stage after a brief set change it was all different. There were not very many customers in the place, but Jim Zumwalt had succeeded in getting some people from the various record companies to attend. The sound system, as I mentioned, was not that great. What was great, however, was the way Billy Ray performed. He handled the situation with ease.

I have always found that one of the hallmarks of a successful act is that he is able to make the best of a bad situation on stage. There are so many acts who refuse to play unless things are exactly right. Sometimes at a show there may be an equipment breakdown or other technical problems of some sort. The few really great acts accept the situation and do the show even though things are not perfect. The others bitch and moan and finally do the show, complaining to everybody, including the audience, the entire time. It was all in a day's work to Billy Ray Cyrus. He was a trooper.

Billy Ray's show consisted of the songs he had recorded for me, as well as other songs that he had written. I instructed him to do original material. Very few new acts get signed by doing cover material. The show itself was bizarre and unexpected. Billy Ray shook, ground, and gyrated through the thirty-minute set to the amusement of some and the astonishment of others. I looked at the audience, and it was obvious that the majority of them had no idea what was happening. They sat there in bewilderment. I laughed my ass off, both at Billy Ray's exaggerated gestures and at the blank expressions on the faces of the audience. I was not laughing at Billy Ray, I was laughing at the entire situation. Pearls before swine.

There were a few people whose musical tastes were broad enough to understand the show. It was obvious that they were enjoying what they saw. The club manager was laughing also, and said that Billy Ray looked like "Elvis on steroids." He also mentioned that he would be glad to take him back if he was ever in the area again.

In terms of a career move, the appearance in Austin had not been productive, since none of the record company personnel in attendance that night rushed out to sign him.

Back in Nashville, I took Billy Ray to Mercury Records boss Steve Popovich. He did not hear anything interesting. I brought Billy Ray to Shedd House, a publishing company owned by Alabama's former producer, Harold Shedd. Perhaps I could get him a publishing deal so that he could concentrate on his writing. The company did not hear anything noteworthy in any of his songs, and was not interested in signing him. Attorney Jim Zumwalt kept telling me that Billy Ray was the "real deal," but I don't think that Zumwalt ever set any meetings for us at any of the record companies. I called producer Mark Wright at RCA and he promised to go see Billy Ray perform one weekend. When he canceled at the last moment, Billy Ray was devastated.

Billy Ray worked on his songwriting and came up with "Whiskey, Wine and Beer," "Suddenly," "It Ain't Over 'Til It's

Over," and others. These were all pretty good songs, but still not suitable for radio airplay at that time. They lacked polish, and Billy Ray's vocal style was still undefined.

On September 12, 1988, I sent a proposal to Rob Sanders at Gary Reynolds and Associates, the advertising agency responsible for the Miller Genuine Draft sponsorship. The bands selected for this program were given money, band equipment, promotional help, and the prestige of being associated with this national campaign. I had already signed Razorback, an Arkansas band, to Miller Genuine Draft and the group turned out to be a success.

I received a letter from Rob Sanders passing on Billy Ray. CBS Records also passed. Things were not going very well. I was disappointed but not overly discouraged, since Nashville is notoriously slow-moving in most matters pertaining to the music business. I knew that if we kept punching we would hit something sooner or later. I had no intention of giving up.

By this time, I knew Billy Ray fairly well. We had spent a considerable amount of time together, and I enjoyed his company. We talked about our objectives and goals. He was very determined and focused. We both believed in the power of visualization and positive thinking and frequently talked about these things, as well as the concepts of destiny and synchronicity. We both felt that our paths had crossed not by chance, but for a specific purpose. This turned out to have been an accurate observation, although more from his end than from mine.

He wanted to do a showcase in Nashville. At a showcase, the act plays and you try to get some record companies to hear the performance with the hope that one of them will be impressed and sign the act. I put him at some short-lived joint called the Cuckoo's Nest during the week preceding the Fourth of July, but nobody came. In fact, he was fired after one night because the manager did not like his music or his style. Billy Ray was depressed over this turn of events, as might be imagined. We seemed to be striking out everywhere.

The Miller Brewing Company had its 1988 national convention at the Opryland Hotel October 31 through November 4. Our group Razorback, as I have mentioned, was part of the

Miller Genuine Draft network, and Rob Sanders thought that it would be good to have them perform for the brewery bigwigs. By this time, Razorback had also been signed to Mercury Records as the result of a deal with Steve Popovich.

I remember Steve Popovich because of his conduct at the Mercury/Polygram Records convention dinner held in Nashville back in the summer. All of the big wheels were in town from all over the world. I had been invited to a banquet at the Opryland Hotel at the conclusion of the week-long gathering. Steve Popovich was from somewhere up north and had been moved down here to run the Nashville branch of Mercury Records. His forte had always been rock and roll, and he was credited with having discovered and signed acts like Meatloaf and John Cougar Mellencamp. That he was here at all was most unusual, especially in light of the fact that country music at that time was heavily under the influence of traditionalists like Randy Travis.

Steve was truly a stranger in a strange land. He was notoriously loud, foulmouthed, rude, and short-tempered. I liked him, to the extent that I knew him, and considered him colorful. Others around town, however, considered him boorish, lacking in gentility, and actually an embarrassment to Mercury Records and to the music community in general.

As I said, he had passed on Billy Ray Cyrus for Mercury, but I was invited to the dinner, probably because I represented Johnny Paycheck and Razorback, both of whom were on the label at that time. The dinner was a formal affair with designated seating. There were the standard speeches, with company president Dick Asher reaffirming the label's commitment to the Nashville office. David Lynn Jones performed, as well as some other acts. There was some incredibly long-winded and boring emcee who droned interminably. The guests listened respectfully for a reasonable period of time, but finally, bored beyond endurance, they began talking among themselves.

Steve Popovich, who was sitting at the table in front of mine, went crazy at this point and stood up, shouting and pointing. "Hey, you. Shut the fuck up! Don't you have any fucking manners? Can't you see that the son of a bitch up there is trying to fucking talk? Shut the fuck up!"

Popovich stood there in the middle of the room pointing and yelling at specific people in this fashion until things understandably quieted down. I enjoyed this performance, but others in the audience were visibly shocked by his actions. It was not long after this dinner that he left Mercury.

Steve Popovich had left Mercury at a rather inopportune time as far as our management company was concerned. Razorback had been signed by him and, as I recollect, had not done that well as a recording act. The immediate concern from my partner Doug Parker was to get them into the good graces of new label boss Harold Shedd. Harold owned the Music Mill recording studio as well as Shedd House. He had also produced most of vocal group Alabama's hits. If Razorback could become a priority for Harold Shedd, then they might survive the change in administration at Mercury. Otherwise, it was likely that the group would be dropped from the label.

Attorney Jim Zumwalt also represented Harold Shedd. It was up to him to persuade Harold Shedd on our behalf to see the group perform. By this time, money-man Doug Parker and I were pretty much on the outs. He had invested almost a million dollars in a band that was destined never to make it. His position at this point was that he had spent so much money already that he could not afford to quit, but he could not afford to keep going either.

The first thing that had to happen was for Harold Shedd to hear the band. I arranged for Razorback to perform at the Stage Door Lounge at the Opryland Hotel on November 2, 1988, for the Miller Beer people. Jim Zumwalt got Harold Shedd to attend.

At this point, I did not particularly care what happened with Razorback. I figured that they were not going to make it anyway. I was, however, concerned with Billy Ray Cyrus and put him on the show in front of Razorback. Mark Wright from RCA had promised to come. With Harold Shedd there from Mercury as well as the people from Miller Genuine Draft, I thought that maybe I could get Billy Ray some kind of deal. I once again instructed him to do all of his Elvis moves. This was one of his strong points. Country music had become so boring that it was time to liven things up. People want to be entertained, and entertainment means giving the people a show. Billy Ray understood and has used this kind of showmanship to his advantage. If people want simply to hear music, they can buy a tape and stay home and listen to it in peace and quiet. I told Billy Ray to entertain the audience, and he did.

He shook all over as if he had the DTs, waved his arms in the air, gyrated his hips, and did everything else he could think of. He was entertaining, but most of the people there did not notice. They were too busy drinking beer and talking. Mark Wright left without comment before Billy Ray's set was over. He had promised me he would come, and he had, but it was obvious that he felt I had wasted his time. I never heard what Harold Shedd had to say about Billy Ray, although he is the one who ended up signing him later to Mercury Records, the label that had passed on him for a second time.

By the end of 1987, I was sick of country music, disgusted with what I had become personally, and nauseated by everything having to do with all of those bastards. I had had a good time as an agent, more or less, for the past fourteen years, but it had been an insane roller coaster ride, and I wanted off. The whining, complaining, and lack of gratitude by the artists had become unbearable. The competition had been fierce, and I had enjoyed the fight, but it was time to slow down. I intended to stop being an agent for a large number of singers, and concentrate my efforts henceforward on the management of a few clients. I knew that there would still be problems, but not as many. Billy Ray Cyrus was one of my three management clients.

His first album for Mercury, *Some Gave All*, has already sold in excess of four million, an incredible though not unprecedented amount. Driven by the success of the first single release, "Achy Breaky Heart", Billy Ray became the fastest-rising debut in the history of *Billboard* magazine's top-album charts.

Billy Ray has caused quite a stir nationally. Many of the more established artists complain that he isn't country and that he has no musical ability at all. In June 1992, during Nashville's Fan Fair, hillbilly singer Travis Tritt made a fool of himself by condemning Billy Ray publicly. He complained that Billy Ray was being marketed as a sex symbol and that his career would ultimately suffer as a result. I doubt that Travis Tritt is overly concerned with Billy Ray's career. Travis Tritt won the Country Music Association's 1991 Horizon Award as well as the 1992 Music City New Star of Tomorrow Award, but apparently his career is not moving fast enough.

Tritt said, "It's as if he [Billy Ray] were drawing fifteen thousand people into a concert hall. He's stepping out of a limousine and being mobbed as he goes into a concert. This is a guy that's not even been recognized yet; this is his first single."

Obviously Billy Ray has already been recognized by more people than recognize Travis Tritt. Almost all of these hillbillies are jealous of any other artist who is doing better than they are.

As far as the controversy about whether Billy Ray Cyrus was a Chippendale dancer, he told me that he was. He confessed with lowered eyes that he had been forced to do some things that he was now ashamed of in order to survive out in California, and being a Chippendale dancer was one of them. I think that this is an issue now because he is being marketed as a sex object and his musical ability is being questioned.

Since Billy Ray Cyrus has become the next Music City phenomenon, everybody is taking credit for discovering him. The fact of the matter is that I discovered him. Everybody I took him to passed on him, including Mercury Records, the label that ultimately signed him.

Timing is everything. Billy Ray was in a hurry, but some things can't be rushed. His career was one of them. Mercury Records, despite its power internationally, has often been re- garded by Nashville insiders as a second-rate record company. There was an old saying around town that the only artists Mercury ever had were the Statler Brothers and Johnny Rodriguez. This is obviously no longer the case. They deserve credit for the success they are having with Billy Ray Cyrus since they were probably the only label in town that had the courage to sign him. Billy Ray also owes a great debt to the Kentucky Headhunters, another Mercury Records act. Had they not done so well and broken new ground, it is doubtful that Billy Ray Cyrus would have gotten a record deal anywhere in Nashville.

It goes without saying that I feel somewhat left out by the fact that Billy Ray Cyrus is doing so well and I am no longer representing him, especially in light of the fact that I worked so hard in his behalf. The sting is even worse considering that he ended up at Mercury Records, a label that passed on him twice while I represented him. On the other hand, Billy Ray Cyrus is truly one of the nicest and most genuine people I have ever met. He has paid his dues and is deserving of the renown he is rapidly acquiring.

In less than six months, his price has gone from $2,500 to $100,000 a night. This is all based upon one song off one album. A strong foundation? I doubt it. His agency is not to be blamed for getting the money now, while it is there, because nobody may want him in another six months. But where does Billy Ray, who is thirty now, go from here? How long can he sustain his career at this level? And does it matter? If he can make $5 or $6 million in the next two years, what difference does it make if he has no career beyond that?

In the past, a country singer looked forward to a lifelong career. Not all of them made it, but a great many did. Those who succeeded may not make as much money now as they did twenty or thirty years ago, but they have made a living in their chosen field. Twenty years from now, most of these singers who are out there now will not even be remembered. So how long does a hillbilly last? Nobody really knows.

And is Billy Ray Cyrus the next Elvis? Only time will tell.

Chapter Twenty

The Kentucky Headhunters

Greed, ego, and stupidity are the most destructive and unfortunately common character traits possessed by the average country music artist. While this is probably true with all artists, it is particularly so with hillbillies. Their need for recognition and approval is insatiable. They thrive on the applause and adoration of the public. This desperate search for respect, acceptance, and admiration extends into all aspects of their lives, both public and private. As long as they receive the adoration they require, they feel loved and problems generally can be contained.

When there is a drop in an artist's fame, there will inevitably be more trouble afflicting everyone in his immediate circle. This is an accepted fact of life here in Music City. Sometimes, however, it is at the zenith of his or her career that an artist says and does the stupidest things.

The Kentucky Headhunters are a case in point. The group consisted until recently of two brothers, Doug and Ricky Lee Phelps, who were the bass guitarist and lead singer. The remaining members of the Kentucky Headhunters are guitarist Greg Martin and his cousins, brothers Richard and Fred Young, guitarist and drummer respectively.

The Kentucky Headhunters were originally a rock-and-roll band named Itchy Brother who sought a record deal with Led Zeppelin's Swan Song label. As a result of their aspirations they met Mitchell Fox, an employee of that company, who subsequently became their manager. According to group leader Richard Young, the fat one with the long hair, they made a cold call that accidentally got past the receptionist to be answered by Fox. This was in 1978. Fox received a tape, came to see the band, and became their manager. Nothing really happened and they parted company in 1981.

By 1985, the band had undergone numerous personnel changes and had reached its full strength. Now a focused unit and less rock-oriented, the Kentucky Headhunters again sought Mitchell Fox as a manager. They recorded their first album, *Pickin' on Nashville,* on their own independent label, and as a result were signed to Mercury Records. The Kentucky Headhunters seemed to be an extreme long shot for the record company when the album was released in late 1989.

In the first place, they were wild-looking. This itself was no big deal, except that country music was at the zenith of its traditional phase again with acts like Randy Travis, George Strait, Ricky Van Shelton, Clint Black, and others topping the charts. All of them were well-dressed, closely cropped, and noncontroversial, if not actually boring. The Headhunters all had long hair, except for drummer Fred, who was bald as a cue ball. He wore a coonskin cap, and onstage removed his shirt. A man of few words, with his muttonchop whiskers and serious demeanor he resembled an 1840s preacher. In addition, the bass drum he played was his old high school marching drum. It was tremendous. The drummer's brother, Richard Young, resembled a fat Jerry Lee Lewis with hair like French monarch Louis XIV. They all looked like rockers and bikers. Many said they were not country at all and thought that Mercury Records had gone way overboard in signing them.

And then there was the music itself. *Pickin' on Nashville* contained ten songs. Instead of "Side One," the A side was labeled "Over Here" and the B side was called "Over Yonder." Their first release, "Walk Softly on This Heart of Mine," an old

Bill Monroe tune, became an immediate hit, despite some resistance from the old guard. Part of the resistance was due to their appearance and part of it was the result of Greg Martin's rock-flavored guitar solo in the middle of the song. Some radio-station copies of the record were subsequently sent to stations with the guitar portion of the song deleted. Some stations would not play the Headhunters at all, saying that they were not country. But there was no doubt that Bill Monroe was country, and the song "Walk Softly" was a country song. The Headhunters had merely reinterpreted it in their own way.

In fact, the Headhunters were and are country. They may look rough, and they may have long hair, but the fact is that they represent a large segment of the population. Coming from rural parts of Kentucky, the Young brothers practiced with guitarist cousin Greg Martin in an old Metcalf County farmhouse given to them by their grandmother. Their band, Itchy Brother, was too country to be rock and too rock to be country. It disbanded, and the musicians went their separate ways. Fred Young became a drummer for country singer Sylvia, while brother Richard tried his hand as a songwriter for Acuff-Rose, a music publisher in Nashville. Greg Martin joined singer Ronnie McDowell's band in 1981. It was here that he met bass player Doug Phelps.

Richard, Fred, Greg, and Doug began playing together locally as a group in 1986. A few months later, Doug Phelps brought brother Ricky to a practice session and the Kentucky Headhunters came into being. As a band, and as individuals, they are like many others in the thirty-to-forty-year-old bracket in that they were influenced by everything from Elvis, the Beatles, black gospel, and heavy metal to hillbilly music. That they finally decided to express themselves musically as country artists is not surprising. That their music was influenced heavily by other forms of music was inevitable. The result of this diversity of musical influences was indeed legitimate country music, despite the criticism of hard-liners. On any given night in hundreds of clubs in cities throughout the nation, one can find patrons who resemble the Headhunters in dress and demeanor, and who also listen to and play the same type of music. Where the group Alabama tapped into the country market in the 1980s, the Headhunters easily slipped into the groove of the 1990s.

Their next release, "Dumas Walker," was written by the Headhunters and also went to number one. This song is about having a good time, eating "Slawburgers," drinking soft drinks, and playing marbles out in the country. The tune was not the fabrication of some Madison Avenue public relations firm, but is a legitimate expression and outgrowth of the rural lifestyle.

Behind the scenes, the Kentucky Headhunters had been signed by the Jim Halsey Agency, where I was working at the time. Nobody at the agency except agent Terry Cline, who brought them there, was very excited about representing them since at the time their first single had not yet been released.

They played a showcase at the Ace of Clubs, a Nashville joint, so that the agents and the record company could become familiar with them. We immediately started selling dates, seeking to place them in major markets. This is where a good agency kicks in with the career of a new artist. Most of the *Billboard* reporting stations are in large cities. It is therefore crucial to get radio airplay in these markets. The best way to do this with a new act is to schedule a show in a major market. The place of performance should be a popular spot. The show should be tied in with the most important radio station in the area, and the ticket price should be lower than normal in order to fill the place. The idea is to get as many press people and radio personalities as possible to attend the show, with the intention of having the act's record played in that city. When the record receives enough airplay in enough places, it hits the charts nationally, and the act becomes more valuable in the marketplace and can charge a higher fee.

At this point it might be appropriate to look at how a record enters the charts and actually becomes a hit. In the past there were several important publications that printed weekly charts. When I started in the music business in the early 1970s, the big three were *Billboard, Record World,* and *Cashbox* magazines. Each more or less had its own methods and procedures for determining what songs eventually made its charts. To make matters worse, these publications often decided to change their methods of setting up the charts. It was alleged, and often with good reason, that there were gross inequities in the methods employed to determine which acts made the charts. As usual, the artists who complained the most were those who did not achieve good chart action. There were, however, legitimate complaints. A record might, for example, be listed as one of the top ten in one publication and among the bottom forty in another.

Record World eventually folded, and *Cashbox* became less significant in the overall picture. *Billboard* remains the leader in the field of record charting, although some people prefer *Radio and Records* or even the *Gavin Report*. It all depends on which publication happens to be giving your artist the highest position at any given moment.

Beginning in 1990, *Billboard* sought to bring some coherence to the procedure for determining the record chart position for singles. It did away with the former method of using regular reporting stations in specific areas and switched over to a new system called the Broadcast Data System (BDS). At present, 110 country radio stations are electronically monitored in eighty markets, twenty-four hours a day, seven days a week. Every time a record is played, a computer picks up an encoded audio signal on the record. It notes when the song was played and how often. This information is fed every day into a larger computer that sorts everything out and determines chart positions based upon airplay and the projected number of listeners to which a particular song has been exposed during the previous week. The reporting period each week runs from Monday to Sunday, and on Monday morning the new charts are ready.

The album charts are determined in a different but even more accurate fashion. Since the public does not generally buy single records anymore, the singles charts are determined by projected listenership. The album charts, on the other hand, are determined by actual sales figures. In the past, many country albums that may have sold well did not necessarily get properly reported, for one reason or another.

Starting in 1991, *Billboard* instituted its new album system. This system, known as Soundscan, reads the actual bar code on the product at the register as it is being sold at over nine thousand retail outlets throughout the nation. While the system obviously does not record every sale, it does provide an accurate indication of what is going on nationally. The two procedures outlined above have understandably placed *Billboard* ahead of its competition. The Headhunters' first album went gold (500,000), and then platinum (1 million). This was an incredible showing for a group that had been perceived as an unlikely long shot by most of Nashville.

We booked the Headhunters in Pittsburgh, Atlanta, Greensboro, and other important cities. They were fairly easy to sell because they were new, interesting, different, controversial, and, at that time, cheap.

We were, as I mentioned, more concerned with getting them airplay and breaking them nationally as an act than we were with getting them maximum money on each date. Since they were unknown then, with their first song just released, we played the group wherever we could for whatever we could get, as long as we also picked up radio airplay. They were getting as little as $700 a night in some instances in October 1989, when we first put them on the road.

In several cities like Baltimore, for instance, they played rock clubs. In this case they were the first country act ever to play Hammerjack's, a well-known and respected rock venue. The date was a great success. I had them scheduled to play a listening room in Philadelphia, but they did not make it because they were snowbound. In Pittsburgh they played another rock club.

I scheduled the Headhunters into the Lonestar Roadhouse in New York City on October 28 and 29, 1989. This was their debut in the Big Apple. Mercury Records threw a party preceding their show at the club. Members of the press were invited as well as the Nashville staff of the record company. Everybody had a good time and the Headhunters conquered the city. On the night before the show at the Lonestar, the group gave another performance at the invitation of the Country Music Association in another part of town. This show was not well attended, but it did help establish a relationship between the Country Music Association and the Kentucky Headhunters. The group eventually won three CMA awards and a Grammy. Their second Mercury Records album, *Electric Barnyard,* was released in April 1991 and sold 500,000 copies. This was a very good showing in terms of sales, but it did not equal the figures generated by their first album.

During the annual Nashville Fan Fair festival in June 1992 Ricky Lee Phelps and Doug Phelps announced on television that they were leaving the Kentucky Headhunters, then and there. According to the Phelps brothers, they wanted to pursue different musical directions. This is the standard excuse usually given when somebody starts thinking he is more important than the other members of the group that brought them fame. This announcement came as a complete shock to the other members of the band as well as to the public at large. The move must have been one the Phelps brothers had been planning for quite a while because by the time they made their announcement, they already had a booth at Fan Fair, and T-shirts printed. Those arrangements were not made overnight.

The Kentucky Headhunters are an extremely popular act, one that is truly known and loved by the public. The three remaining members of the band will keep the name Kentucky Headhunters and remain together as a group. In fact, they have already replaced Doug and Ricky Lee Phelps with two other players, first cousin Anthony Kenny on bass, and Mark Orr as lead vocalist. Both of the new members were originally part of their first band, "Itchy Brother," so the new arrangement is really a homecoming.

In the world of country music, there are often personal and musical differences, which sometimes result in one or more members of a group deciding to leave and start another band. The Statler Brothers lost Lou De Witt in the early 1980s, replaced him with Jimmy Fortune, and remain very successful in spite of that change. The group Exile suffered some serious shake ups a few years ago but has survived and prospered. During their run, the Oaks have had more members than the Democratic Party and are still going strong. The Kentucky Headhunters are finishing up their third album. Having heard some of the material, I can say that it is every bit as strong as anything to date. They are still, and no doubt will remain, the premier band in country music for many years to come.

As a career move for Doug and Ricky Lee Phelps, I think that this will prove to have been a big mistake. There are few singers, especially in the country music field, whose music is so significant that the world can't live without them. It was an extremely stupid move, one that in all probability was precipitated by ego and greed. They had everything going their way. Before the advent of the Headhunters Doug Phelps was merely a sideman in singer Ronnie McDowell's band and Ricky Phelps had no recognition at all. Most likely they will sink back into obscurity.

I saw Doug and Ricky Lee at their booth at Fan Fair a few days after they had announced their departure from the group. There was some goofy-looking stooge in a top hat shouting at passersby that they were there. "Here they are, folks, Doug and Ricky Lee Phelps, formerly with the Kentucky Headhunters." They were running a contest trying to get suggestions for the name of their new act. The fans were asked to complete a card by filing in the blank, "The ____ Brothers." I watched them from the CBS booth and felt sorry for them. If the name Headhunters had not been mentioned, hardly anyone would have recognized them. I felt like filling out a card myself, "The Foolish Brothers."

I went over and said hello. Doug said that they would now have the artistic freedom they wanted. As I listened to him, I could not help but wonder how they could possibly want any more artistic freedom than they already had with the group. The Kentucky Headhunters are without doubt the most musically liberated band in all of country music.

Chapter Twenty-one

First and Foremost

The Artist and the Manager

In these three chapters I shall briefly try to describe the players in this sideshow that we call the music business. While I readily admit that some of my observations may seem biased in favor of the agent and the agency, they are the outgrowth of much experience.

Most of the interactions between these various players are fueled by an ego-driven lust for power, with greed and the desire for wealth being an important, but secondary, consideration. All of these characters feed off each other in a symbiotic way, as in the relationship between a parasite and its host. The manager, artist, publicist, agent, radio station, promoter, songwriter, producer, publisher, road manager, spouse, lover, attorney, and record company are all part of a game in which the dynamics are in a state of constant flux, where the rules often change from day to day, and usually without notice. It is almost always a cutthroat affair with various parts of the artist's so-called "team" attempting to gain power for themselves at the expense of the other players. Very seldom are all of the horses pulling in the same direction, and the artist almost always suffers from these head games that frequently take place without his or her permission or awareness.

Before we proceed, some attention should be directed toward the term "conflict of interest." I used to say jokingly that the only conflict of interest that I recognized was one that conflicted with my own interests. Almost all of the players conduct themselves as if this were their unspoken motto. Although each of the players "wishees to do what's best for the artist" and to act in the "artist's best interests," reality is something else altogether. If any of the players truly act in the artist's best interests, it is only when their own interests are being served as well. It is true that there may be some exceptions, but in my experience, they are extremely rare.

Another term I mention only because it exists in relation to its opposite. The word is "loyalty." Enough said. Anybody in the music business is capable of anything at any time, often without reason and almost always without notice. While certain players are more prone to acts of disloyalty than others, the most blatantly disloyal acts are usually executed by the artists. As a group, there is nothing they will not do to further their own interests. In these instances, as in most others, the artist is only interested in himself or herself. Nobody else matters. The victim, whether spouse, agent, manager, or whoever, will sometimes have the last laugh, for what goes up must eventually come down, and very few artists hit the bottom gracefully. Well, folks, here they are—select your favorites.

THE ARTIST

The country music singer is frequently a tortured soul, for while it is true that the music business revolves around the artist, it does so only to the degree that an artist succeeds. Here, as elsewhere, nobody is interested in failure. Above all else, the artist must achieve and maintain success. This is extremely difficult for most singers since the public is notoriously fickle. The artist is in constant career danger, subject to the ever-present threat of being supplanted in his fans' shifting affections. His fears are certainly justified, and may become reality in a number of ways. If the artist is identified with a certain kind of music, say progressive country, or traditional country, or outlaw, or bluegrass, or whatever may be popular on a given day, he is likely to suffer when that kind of music becomes unfashionable. The artist is also likely to be eclipsed within his own style of music by another artist, perhaps a younger one. He lives in fear of ceasing to be a priority with his manager, his agency, his record company, and others he depends on for his success.

In the first half of this century, most country music singers were really "country." They sang country music because that is what they did. The singers frequently sought success, and sometimes achieved it, but their music was generally an outgrowth of their lifestyle and a genuine reflection of their culture and background. The competition to "make it" was not as great as it is today. If they failed, they could always return to the farm or get a job at the co-op, and life went on pretty much as if nothing had happened.

Today very few so-called country singers are really "country." They are no longer rural, ignorant, or illiterate, and many of them have never ridden a horse, milked a cow, hitched a ride on a train, or performed any hard physical labor. Most of them have been to college and have made a conscious career decision to seek fame and fortune in the music business. They are seldom "discovered" in the classical Hollywood sense, but have instead decided to become country music singers. Many have made this choice after having failed in the rock and roll field, or after not making it as movie stars and actors. Most of them have very little to offer as singers, entertainers, or "stars," other than rehashing a particular style or type of music that might have fallen by the wayside, waiting to be brought back again to the next generation of country listeners.

This is not to say that some significant artists have not emerged recently. How many will pass the test of time of course remains to be seen. Today there are few country artists in the traditional sense, and this means that those who have chosen careers as country singers have to work much harder than they did in the past, with the price of failure much higher than ever before. Someone who devotes ten or twenty years to a career as a country singer has few options in an already flooded job market if things don't work out in the music business.

While it is true that there are more people listening to what passes for country music, this increase in listeners and record buyers does not offset the fact that the pie has been sliced so many times that there is less available for anyone trying to make it as a country entertainer. The June 1992 issue of the *Journal of Country Music* featured an article under the "Briefings" section entitled "We Are Young Country, Can You Tell Us Apart?" In this story there are photos of and brief information about each of thirty-six new male country acts. The real question is, "Who the hell are they?"

Of the thirty-six acts mentioned, I have worked with five of them: David Lynn Jones, Rich Grissom, Billy Ray Cyrus, Mark Collie, and Larry Boone. Of that five, only one, Billy Ray Cyrus, can accurately be said to be a star, but so far that is solely on the basis of one record, "Achy Breaky Heart." Where will he be a year from now? As for the remaining thirty-one, some of their names are familiar to the public, but most are not. Of the names that are familiar, many are not even associated with faces or even songs. The bottom line is that there are too many new acts out there in the marketplace. There is not enough radio airtime for them, not enough rack space for their music at the stores, and not enough places for them to perform. In answer to the question posed by the article: No, the public can't tell them apart and, furthermore, doesn't care one way or the other.

Ultimately, the country music singer is at a great disadvantage in the scheme of things. The music business is oriented toward many acts, not just one. It seeks continually to create more and more stars and to sell more and more records. The record companies will run through many artists, as will the agents and managers, but the individual artist has only one career, his own. Small wonder that an artist resents other singers and is jealous of relationships that his team maintains with other artists.

How Long Does a Hillbilly Singer Last?

The question is similar to that posed in an advertisement used by Mack Trucks a few years ago. "How long does a Mack

Truck last?" The answer is, "We don't know yet," meaning that many of the early versions are still around. This is true also with country singers. While many of the original, well-known country singers like Jimmy Rodgers, Lefty Frizzell, Patsy Cline, and Hank Williams have disappeared, others are still on the scene and doing well. Ray Price is again on Columbia Records, forty years after he signed with them. George Jones had his first hit in 1955 and is still going strong. Willie Nelson, Merle Haggard, Conway Twitty, Loretta Lynn, Mel Tillis, and others are still working and successful.

Record deals and radio airplay are another matter for most of the older artists. I would prefer to use the term "established" rather than older, but older is the way most of them are viewed today by radio and the record companies. It is extremely difficult for these artists to get airplay or record deals.

While it is convenient for the older artists to blame everybody in power, after a certain period of time, an artist—any artist—may have really said all that he has to say as a singer or a songwriter. I think that this is ultimately the truth. Music changes along with everything else, and what was relevant a few years ago may not seem as important today. An artist is successful in my estimation if he or she has made a unique and lasting contribution to the art form. If years from now somebody can say, yeah, so and so's music remains as original and important today as it was when it was first recorded, then the artist in question is successful.

Success from a historical perspective is not as important to most of the older artists as financial success. A country artist who at the height of his career in the 1960s made $2,500 a night is understandably resentful when some kid these days make $50,000 a night.

It is tougher for the newer artists. Much of what has come to be known as country music has already been done. Out of the multitude of contenders for stardom, few offer anything original or lasting. Most of these performers will be dropped by the record companies and abandoned by the public fairly early in the game.

So how long does a hillbilly singer last? There is no set

answer. In these days, a successful career of twenty years is very good. In the future, I imagine that a successful one of five or ten years will be considered lengthy.

MALE VS. FEMALE ARTISTS

It has been my experience in country music that men are as a rule more likely to succeed than women. By success in this instance, I mean making the most money. While there are notable exceptions such as Dolly Parton, Barbara Mandrell, and possibly Reba McEntire and Wynonna Judd, these are in the minority. Dolly and Barbara are in fact the only female country singers who come to mind who have consistently made over $50,000 a night for any extended period of time.

With male singers it has been different. The Statler Brothers, the Oak Ridge Boys, Dwight Yokam, Clint Black, Randy Travis, Garth Brooks, George Strait, and Hank, Jr., have all made $50,000 and more at their zenith.

At the same time there has been only one truly well-known black country music artist, Charley Pride from Sledge, Mississippi. At his first major concert in Detroit in 1966, few of the ten thousand fans who waited to hear Charley sing—he had already become a star on the radio and on records—knew what he looked like. When he appeared on stage under the spotlight the applause suddenly stopped. He launched into a rendition of *Just Between You and Me*. When he finished singing, the applause was deafening.

Talent buyers expect to pay more for a male superstar than for a female. It has always been this way. At the time when the most money a country singer earned for a night's performance came to $10,000, those fees were paid to Ray Price, Willie Nelson, or the Statlers. When the ceiling reached $20,000 a night, males still were the recipients, and that practice continues to this day. In brief, male singers make the most money in country music.

According to promoters, male artists on average sell a disproportionately higher number of tickets at shows and concerts. While there are many theories for this state of affairs, they do not alter the facts.

At the level of record sales, most country records buyers are women, and they buy records by male singers far more often than they buy records by females. The result is that female country singers generally do not sell as many records as men. It is therefore harder for women to get a record deal than it is for men.

THE ORIGINS OF COUNTRY MUSIC

While country music has certainly changed and evolved recently, what has come to be country music as we know it today is the result of a rich and varied history covering several hundred years. Although many people simply assume that country music is American in origin, it is in fact a derivative of Scottish, Irish, and English folk ballads that were brought here by the early settlers.

In the development of white rural America, particularly in the South, country music played a large part. It was easy enough to play, and always dealt with themes of importance to working-class people. As time passed, the first professional singers made their appearance, playing at local dances, picnics, and other functions. In the era before television, when radio was all there was, many stations added country music to their programming. This usually occurred in the form of weekly programs known as "Barn Dances," which were live broadcasts from the radio station.

With shifts in population from decade to decade, the music spread to other parts of America. Soldiers from rural areas serving in the two World Wars also introduced their music to people from other parts of the nation. Like country's sister, the blues, it was carried north by rural workers seeking jobs in the factories. Country music continues in the working-class tradition; at least to the extent that it has not been diluted in an effort to make it more palatable to a broader audience.

During its evolution and development, country music has been divided into many categories, such as bluegrass, traditional, progressive, regressive, hat music, outlaw, hillbilly, rockabilly, countrypolitan, and so on. For a long while, country music was combined with cowboy music and known as "country and western." The "western" was eventually dropped by the mid-1970s.

Like gospel, blues, and to a large degree, rock and roll, country music is predominantly a Southern phenomenon, an evolution of white Southern culture. While this is true enough, country music is no longer limited in any sense strictly to the South, but has become extremely popular throughout the nation, and indeed, the world.

THE MANAGER

The manager's function is to guide, counsel, and allegedly further the artist's career. I use the word "allegedly" since it seems appropriate in terms of my own experience with so-called managers. Sarcasm aside, the manager is supposed to act as a general liaison between the artist and everybody else. He deals with the record label, agency, publicist, attorney, and all others on the artist's behalf, thus freeing the artist from day-to-day business problems and permitting him the leisure to work on his music. The manager is in fact the captain of the team and in charge of getting the various players to work together in the artist's behalf.

In the rare case where a real manager is encountered, it will most likely be found that he has secured a record deal for his artist. The average manager in country music usually comes into the picture after the artist already has a record deal. It is much easier for the manager this way, since it is usually more difficult to get an unknown singer a recording contract than it is to take on a client who has already overcome that major obstacle.

As in almost every other phase of the music business, the selection of a manager for an artist who already has a record deal is a case of whom you know. Often a manager receives a call from a friend at the record company who tells him that they have just signed a deal with a new singer and are looking for a manager. This call might just as easily come from a producer or a publisher, or anybody else on the inside track. Obviously it is important to maintain good relationships within Nashville's music community.

While it is true in theory that a singer has the freedom to choose his own manager and booking agency, it is not uncommon for the record company to recommend strongly a particular manager and agency for its new artists, especially in cases where no manager is already on the scene. In this way the record company makes certain that the manager is someone who it knows is not going to cause it too much trouble, someone it can control. Since the record company placed the manager, he will owe some loyalty to the record company from the very beginning. While this might seem like a conflict of interest for the manager, such an arrangement is not necessarily the worst possible scenario for the artist. If everybody is on good terms, things might actually move more easily for the artist than they would if the record company did not approve of or actually disliked the manager.

At the record company the manager must negotiate many things on the artist's behalf. He must be certain that the timing is right for the release of a client's record. He must seek the record company's assistance with expenses associated with the release of a new product. This could mean getting money from the record company for independent record promoters. It might mean talking the record label into providing money for tour support, or to pay a band, or to buy or lease a bus. While it is true that all advances to the artist by the record company are charged against the artist's account, it is still difficult to get the record company to open that billfold, especially if the artist has already been to the financial well a few times.

The manager must do everything in his ability to see that his artist becomes and remains a high priority at the record label, though he must walk a thin line while doing so. If he is not strong enough personally, or is afraid to rock the boat when necessary, he will be of little help to his client. He likely will be humored or ignored and actually becomes a liability for his client as far as the record company is concerned.

The relationship between the manager, the artist, and the record company fluctuates constantly according to several factors. Everything is moving at once and the dynamics of the situation change constantly. The manager who has been avoided by the record company can suddenly become very popular if his client unexpectedly starts having hit records and high sales, or if the artist's contract is up for renewal and another record company wants to steal him.

On the other hand, when an artist's career dips to the point that the record company is about to drop him, a manager who was once merely tolerated becomes totally unnecessary and finds that his repeated phone calls for the most part go unanswered.

While the manager may sometimes actually serve some purpose at the record label, he is almost always a liability to the artist he represents at the talent agency. A new manager will almost always move his client to another agency just as soon as he feels that he can get away with it. This is good for the manager since he can start out fresh with the new agency and retain control of the overall situation.

This move is seldom good for the artist, but the manager tells him that the agency is not getting him enough dates or enough money. The manager knows that the agency is the prime source of the artist's income, and consequently represents the greatest threat to him personally. The threat is real enough, since most agents believes managers to be an unnecessary nuisance, despite the respect and courtesy they may be forced to show them in order to keep a client.

The manager is justifiably threatened by a preexisting relationship between the agency and the artist he represents. The artist can easily look at his booking page and see if the agency is getting him enough work at the right price. It is harder to tell whether the manager is doing anything or not, since the agency is producing most of the artist's income.

If the manager can get in the middle of the agency's business and persuade the unwary artist that he should approve all dates submitted by the agency, he can make it look as if he is actually doing something. The manager is paid a percentage based upon the artist's income, most of which is generated by the booking agency. If the manager were paid only on the actual income he produced himself, and not on the money generated by the agency, he would in many cases starve to death. By making the agency call him with offers, it gives him something to talk to the artist about.

He can discuss the dates with the artist and act as if he knows what he is doing.

For the manager, the best defense is a good offense as far as the agency is concerned. By badgering, threatening, and browbeating the agency he can keep it on the defensive. While the artist should probably approve all dates himself directly with the agency, there are other things that a busy and successful artist has to do besides worry about whether he is going to be working enough to pay his bills. The effective manager can sometimes help the situation by refusing dates he knows would not be acceptable to the artist.

The cry of the manager has always been, "My artist is not getting enough money, and it's everybody's fault but mine." There are some managers who actually know almost as much as some agents about booking dates, but they are rare, and their knowledge is the result of thousands of miles on the road with their artists. Among those few in Nashville are Irby Mandrell, Barbara's manager, and George Richey, Tammy Wynette's manager. While it is true that they have both been a pain in the ass to agents for years, they have earned respect as a result of their experience on the road.

At the Halsey Agency, George Richey came by the office frequently, knew all of the agents personally, and talked to them often, politely suggesting that they call particular buyers and then following up a few days later to make sure that it had been done. When an offer was brought to Richey for Tammy Wynette, he always told the agent to go back and get more money, no matter the amount offered. Although this drove the agents crazy, almost invariably the agent obtained more, even if the amount came to only $500.

The long-term result of this approach is that, over the years, a small amount here and there has amounted to quite a large sum of money. In some cases George has forced the agent to get several thousand dollars extra on some individual dates. I have the utmost respect for him as a manager and as a person.

Many of the managers in the music business today are in their twenties and thirties, younger than ever before. They have degrees from various colleges and new and fresh ideas. The downside is that they frequently lack experience and seek to cover their asses by harassing the agency.

The manager, like the agent, is frequently terminated without reason and consequently lives in fear to some degree. Like the agent, he is subject to being cast off when the artist starts making money, or when the artist isn't making enough money, or at any other time, with or without reason. Ricky Skaggs got rid of manager Chip Peay, Lori Morgan dumped Jack McFadden, Ronnie Milsap disposed of Jack Johnson. Clint Black is suing manager Bill Ham. It's the same old story in Nashville every day.

For example, Gene Ferguson discovered, managed, and guided singers Charly McClain, John Anderson, and Larry Boone, only to get the ax at the zenith of their careers. Originally from Washington, D.C., Gene started with Columbia Records as a regional promotion man in 1956. By 1959 he was living in Nashville and had been promoted to national head of promotion for country product. Having been with CBS (Columbia) Records twenty-three years, he was eighteen months away from retirement when he received a call from Nashville company head Rick Blackburn saying that CBS was going to "dissolve his position." Although he received a substantial settlement fee, it was not near the amount he would have been awarded on full retirement. I might add that twenty-three years is a long time anywhere these days, and I sincerely doubt that many record companies have any employees who have been around anywhere near that long. There is no job security in the music business in Nashville, Tennessee.

Charly McClain was at that time a singer for CBS-owned Epic Records. She called Gene and asked him to be her manager. Due to the potential conflict of interest, with Gene still at CBS/Columbia then, Gene entered into an agreement with attorney John Lentz, where John would serve as the front man but Gene would handle her musical career. They both split a management fee of 10 percent. Charly, due to her increasing popularity, quickly developed the standard artist's syndrome: The more successful artists get, the less appreciative they become and the more problems they create. The transition in attitude is usually from "Anything you can do to help me, please" to "I'll tell you exactly how it goes, get out of my way, I don't need you anymore."

In 1986 Gene received a letter from an attorney in Memphis informing him that after eight years, he was no longer Charly McClain's manager. The letter understandably came as a complete shock to Gene Ferguson. This is not an uncommon turn of events here in Hillbilly Heaven. Artists quite frequently end long-term relationships with a letter from a third party, usually an attorney. In this case, Gene feels that his relationship with Charly was undermined by her husband, Wayne Massey. A settlement figure was agreed upon and Charly paid monthly until the figure was reached.

At the time Gene Ferguson began managing John Anderson, John was sacking groceries for a living at a convenience store in Nashville. John Anderson, originally from Apopka, Florida, had come to Nashville in the late 1970s, seeking fame and fortune as a country singer. He is almost six feet tall, with long blond hair and a scruffy-looking beard. I represented him at In Concert during 1985 and 1986. While he eventually had many successful records, he is perhaps best known for his offbeat hit "Swingin'." Vocally, John Anderson is one of the finest country singers of all time. Unlike much of the generic garbage that is being machine-gunned into the marketplace, John Anderson's style remains unique and original. His voice is immediately recognizable on the radio. It is obvious that Anderson, like many other singers, was heavily influenced by George Jones. But John has gone beyond that to establish firmly his own place in country music.

It is difficult for me to describe John's unusual vocal style, but a line from his hit song "Black Sheep" may help. "Look at me, I'm the black sheep of the family" is actually sung by John Anderson as: "Look at me, I'm duh black shape ub day fam-uh-lay."

John Anderson had already been through two managers, neither of whom had done much for his career. Gene first heard John Anderson by accident. He was at Warner Brothers Records talking with Norro Wilson, head of the label, in his office. Gene asked Norro whom they were listening to, and Norro told him that it was John Anderson. John had been recording for Warner

Brothers for about a year, but had not achieved much success. Norro put Gene and John together and it was decided that Gene would become John's manager.

Until that point, John had had several single releases, but none of them had done anything. "Girl at the End of the Bar" went to the forties in the charts and was his only noteworthy song. The first record that really did anything at all was "Lyin' Blue Eyes," which went to thirteen. At this point John was willing to listen to Gene's advice. Gene, who had years of experience at CBS, began selecting songs for John to record. Among them were "1959," "She Just Started Liking Cheatin' Songs," and "I'm Just an Old Chunk of Coal," each of which turned into big hits. John Anderson had initially refused to sing all of them. According to Gene, John Anderson upon hearing this last song said, "I don't know where you find this shit," and walked out of the building.

Fortunately for Gene Ferguson, he had a seven-year contract with John Anderson. When John eventually broke it, they went to court on January 8, 1989. The judge ruled in Gene's favor.

John had called Gene one day and said, "I'm not going to need you as a manager anymore." This announcement came as a complete surprise to Gene. Anderson then said that he would manage himself, to which Gene responded that he had another four years on his contract. John then said, "I don't give a shit what you got, I'm not paying you anymore." Gene replied that perhaps the court might see it differently. The reader should bear in mind that at the time of this call, John Anderson had already made over $5 million as a result of his three-year association with Gene Ferguson.

Next, Gene received a call from John's new manager, an accountant whom Gene had brought into the music business to handle John's books. On behalf of John, the accountant offered a settlement figure of $80,000. Never mind the original contract. This first figure was unacceptable to Gene, and a second figure of $168,000 was agreed upon. John Anderson began payments, but stopped when these reached the original but unacceptable figure of $80,000. Since Gene had accepted the settlement, when they went to court the matter was decided upon the basis of the settlement instead of the original contract.

Gene won, but not what he would have received under their original agreement. He attributes the decline of their relationship to John Anderson's ego combined with heavy use of alcohol and marijuana.

Gene Ferguson became very excited by a new act he had discovered. The singer was Larry Boone. Larry actually looks like Robert Redford, and is a talented songwriter as well. Gene had discovered Larry playing guitar for tips at the Wax Museum in the tourist section of Nashville's Music Row. This type of discovery does not happen often, and the musicians playing at such places usually return home at the end of the summer, having had their fill of Nashville. Gene played me some of Larry's songs one afternoon but I didn't really hear anything that knocked me out. He was excited, though, and succeeded in getting Larry signed to Mercury Records in May 1986.

"Stranger Things Have Happened" was the first release and went to sixty-four in *Billboard*. The second record, "She's the Trip That I've Been On," went to fifty-two. Larry eventually had three albums on Mercury, but none of them were big sellers. Gene and Larry became dissatisfied with Mercury and received a release from the record label in late 1989.

In January 1991 Gene Ferguson signed Larry Boone to CBS/Sony and the first release appeared a little more than a month later. His last Mercury release had appeared on December 20, 1989, and he did not have another single until he signed with CBS. This much time without a record usually hurts an artist, and Larry was no exception. His first CBS album, *One Way to Go,* came out in early 1991 and went only one way, down. Larry had written seven of the ten songs on that album. None of the single releases did anything, so the first CBS album was abandoned and a new one scheduled for release in 1992. Gene Ferguson also signed Larry Boone as a writer for Tree Publishing, a lucrative arrangement that nets Larry Boone $5,400 a month. But when things are not going well with an artist's career he usually lashes out at those closest to him. In this case, it was Gene Ferguson.

As a gesture of his sincere appreciation for the major-label record and publishing deals that Gene got him, Larry is suing Gene at this writing for $100,000, alleging that Gene ruined his career. When Larry told Gene that he no longer required his services, Gene asked him if they would be having this problem if Larry had a hit record on the charts. Larry replied, "No." Larry wrote seven of the ten songs on the album and yet blames his manager because he did not have a hit. Another example of hillbilly logic.

Due to the extreme disloyalty and unpredictability of artists in general, the manager should always protect himself with at least a three-year ironclad contract, one that Perry Mason himself couldn't break.

I might add that it is almost always easier to get the artist to sign a paper at the start of the arrangement. As times passes, doing so becomes more difficult, especially if the artist becomes successful. The existence of a contract may serve as a deterrent to some degree, but a successful artist will not be stopped from doing anything he wants to do by the mere presence of a written agreement. The contract becomes useful only later in court when the artist is ultimately forced to pay the manager the amount they had agreed on at the outset.

For example, I should have signed David Lynn Jones to a management contract, but didn't. I was mistakenly more concerned with what I could do for him than I was with protecting my own interests.

David Lynn Jones is one of the greatest acts to come out of Nashville. He is from Bexar, a small town in northern Arkansas, where he still lives. I first met him in 1988, when he and his producer came to my office to talk about representation. He was at that time being managed by the late Bill Graham but was not satisfied with that arrangement.

David is tall, solid, and attractive with a definite charm and a dry but active sense of humor. He was at that time with the Halsey Agency and had a deal with Mercury Records back when Mercury was run by Steve Popovich. He had a multi-album contract with Mercury and was expected by everyone to be a great success. Musically, he was hard to define, and while that might have been one of his greatest assets, it turned out to be one of his greatest problems as well. For lack of a better comparison, he is somewhere between Bob Dylan and Bruce Springsteen.

David had a big hit right out of the starting gate with a self-written song entitled "Bonnie Jean" ("Little Sister"), a song about a woman who dumps her no-good husband and becomes a successful truck driver. His first album on Mercury was called *Hard Times on Easy Street* and received incredible acclaim from all of the critics. There were several singles off that album, but none of them, except for the first, really did that well. His song "Living in the Promiseland" was a big hit for Willie Nelson. David also had a successful duet, "High Ridin' Heroes," with Waylon Jennings.

For some reason, success on the radio eluded him. He is an incredibly talented and intelligent artist, and I think his intelligence has hurt him to some degree. Much of his music is "message music" and most country listeners are more interested in getting drunk and getting laid than they are in social issues. When I met him initially, I felt that he had the big head a bit too early in the game for his own good and that perhaps he needed to take a few knocks before it would be possible to deal with him. Nothing happened for him at Mercury Records, in spite of the effort that had been made.

In late 1989, during the final days of the Halsey Agency, I saw his new video for the song "Lonely Town" from his forthcoming second album on Mercury Records. He was fantastic and I thought that this single would surely be a hit, but again, it was not. David floated around for a while with nothing happening, even though he had a new album out. He was signed to a production agreement with a company called Bald Eagle Productions, which had placed him on Mercury Records. Richie Albright, who had produced both albums, had acted as his manager, even though he had no idea what he should be doing.

I had known Richie for a while, since he had been the drummer for Waylon Jennings for years. When I told him that I wanted to manage David Lynn Jones, he thought it was a good idea. What he really wanted and needed were some dates on the books so that they could keep the band together. Since Richie had been with David Lynn from the beginning, had produced both albums, had played in the band, and had served as road manager, I knew that without his help and approval, I would not successfully be able to act as manager.

With his approval, I told David what I wanted to do. He agreed. So I went to work, both with the record company and setting dates. There we faced a big problem. A large number of buyers had never even heard of him.

Mercury intended to release a couple of more singles from the second album. The record company finally decided on a song called "I Feel a Change Comin' On." It was not the record company's intention to put out a video on this single but I successfully lobbied for one. The single was released, but did nothing, perhaps because of some controversial lyrics: "I know it takes salvation to make it through eternity, but I never knew that Jesus lived in Nashville, Tennessee."

I did not find this line controversial. However, radio station program directors would not play the record because they thought that their listeners might be offended. I argued with them, but to no avail. What the offending lyrics actually meant was that many of the people in the music business in Nashville act as if they are God. It was the wrong choice for a single release, but after it was out, it was too late.

One problem for many artists, especially if their debut is highly acclaimed, is that they have a tough time following their initial performance. In addition, if several records are released and none of them do particularly well, a backlash occurs and DJs become reluctant to play the artist's records at all, no matter how good they might be. I think this happened to David Lynn Jones at Mercury. Furthermore, David Lynn Jones was perceived to have an attitude problem, both at the record label and elsewhere.

This was true to some degree, but was mainly the result of poor communications. David was tired of repeating the same things over and over. He wanted to be released from Mercury Records and try again with another company. He felt that Mercury was killing his career. The label, however, planned to schedule another single, "One Song," a tune about world peace. This would have been a great choice, but the trouble with Iraq ended before the record was released. They planned to release the record anyway.

The record company also had every intention of recording another album, and possibly several more. Attorney Craig

Hayes had been trying unsuccessfully to get David out of his contract. All of this was taking a psychological toll on the artist, and no doubt affecting his creativity. One day I phoned him to tell him I thought I could get him released by the label if he would give me his permission to do it my way. He said to go ahead if I thought I could do something.

I called Paul Lucks, the head of the Nashville Mercury operation, and asked for a meeting. After a few pleasantries we got down to business. I told him that Mercury had done a great job for David Lynn Jones, but that nothing had happened despite its efforts, and that David wanted to be released from the label. He explained that they were planning to issue "One Song." I countered by saying that it was too late for that record to be relevant in the marketplace, since the Gulf War with Iraq was over. He disagreed but was willing to consider what I had said.

I knew that Mercury wanted to do another album, so I told him, "Your company has invested over $750,000 in David Lynn Jones, and it has not worked. He does not want to record another album for you. You can force him contractually, but it will not be the best he can do because his heart won't be in it. I think that you will be just throwing good money after bad. You have the two best albums he will most likely record anyway. Why don't you let somebody else start over? If by some quirk of fate they can do something else with him, then your first two albums may start selling. Let another company pick up the tab henceforward."

There was one problem, Mercury had advanced David Lynn $25,000 to start preproduction on a third album, and he had already spent that money. I addressed this matter and said that if he let David off the label, we would find a way to repay that money. Paul told me he would think it over and call me at the end of the week with his answer. On Monday, March 11, 1991, Paul told me Mercury had decided to release him from the label, with a few provisions pertaining to the repayment of the advance he had received.

Before I had asked for this release from Mercury, I had called Jimmy Bowen at Capitol. David and I met with him. He said that he could not discuss anything with us as long as David was on another label, but that he was interested in pursuing matters if Mercury released him.

David put together his ten favorite songs from the two albums he had recorded for Mercury, along with comments about them—what he liked and what he did not like. I delivered this material to Jimmy's office and it was sent to him in Hawaii. When Jimmy returned to Nashville, the three of us had a second meeting at Jimmy's house on Franklin Road. I was very enthusiastic about the meeting and felt that we were going to be offered a deal that very day with Capitol.

David disagreed. "It would be bad business to offer me a deal," he said. "He hasn't even heard any of my new stuff."

His negative attitude irritated me. Jesus, I was there to make a deal. I hate negativity. Not only did Jimmy offer David a deal, but he said that David could use whatever musicians he wanted, that he could record at his own studio in Bexar, Arkansas, and that the record company would bring in additional equipment if needed. He was actually giving David Lynn Jones a carte blanche to record his own music however he wanted to do it. Needless to say, David left the meeting in much better spirits than when he had entered.

My strategy was to get David accepted by radio disc jockeys, which would create a demand for paying road dates. When Richie Albright heard about the record deal, instead of congratualting me for a job well done, he started to hassle me about the fact that there were almost no dates on the books.

During the last few years, nothing had been happening for David Lynn Jones at all. I had quickly started turning that situation around. Now that things were about to get rolling again, Richie wanted to get rid of me. He told me that the deal with Capitol had to go through Bald Eagle Productions because that was the company to which David Lynn was signed. In other words, even though I had done the impossible, getting him off Mercury, followed by a carte blanche with the hottest label in town, Richie did not think I deserved anything for my efforts. The fact of the matter is that Richie Albright had only produced one hit out of twenty songs. The talk around town was that David Lynn Jones needed another producer.

I knew that I would never be able to overcome the talk behind my back, so I said "Fuck 'em!" I never even received as much as a thank-you from Richie or David Lynn Jones. I was told by an insider at one point that I could kill the deal for David Lynn Jones with a phone call if they were planning to get rid of me. I do not doubt that this could have been done, but I like David and Richie Albright in spite of the way things turned out. The new product is out on Capitol now and I hope it does well. I did a phenomenal job with David Lynn Jones in a very short period of time, and would have really kicked ass if I had been able to pursue my intentions without interference.

So what should the function of the manager be on a day-to-day basis? The manager should try to obtain commercials, television shows, and corporate sponsorships for his artist. He should work with the publicist, the record company, and the managers of other artists in maximizing the artist's career in every way. A good manager is a great asset to any artist, but a bad manager can kill his career.

Chapter Twenty-Two

Every Artist Has One

The Publicist, the Record Producer, the Lawyer, the Fan Club, the Record Company, and the Agent

THE PUBLICIST

Many country acts hire public relations firms that represent them with the media. The fee for these services is generally paid monthly by the artist, and in some case by the record company. At certain times, a publicist can be very beneficial to an artist's career by seeing to it that the artist stays in the public eye as much as possible. This means going after and securing television features, newspaper stories, interviews, magazine covers, and other press-related items for the artist. These duties include phoning music writers and local television personalities in cities where concerts are scheduled and lining up special stories about the artist, both before and after the dates are played. A good public relations firm can increase ticket sales at concerts and record sales in the area where the show is scheduled.

The publicist often works hand-in-hand with the record company, the agent, and the manager, coordinating and scheduling radio interviews, autograph sessions at record stores, and other such functions. Unlike some of the other players on the artist's team, the publicist is generally able to operate freely without much interference from anyone since his job does not represent any direct threat to the record company, the agency, or the manager. There are, of course, exceptions, and every once in a while a publicist may try to become the artist's manager. This arrangement usually does not last long, but can throw a wrench into the artist's career for a few months.

The main problem public relations firms face is that they are often hired to make a silk purse out of a sow's ear. Even the best publicist can do only so much with an artist who is uncooperative or whose career is stagnant. When a favorable buzz about an artist already exists, the public relations company can amplify the excitement and further the artist's career. On the other hand, if there is really nothing to brag about, then the publicist has to fabricate something that sounds newsworthy. For example, the publicist might create a story by visiting the neighborhood where the artist grew up and interviewing former classmates and teachers. In this way a feature about an artist's roots can keep the singer in front of the public during a dry point in his career. If an artist is new and unknown, the publicist can help put his career in motion.

In Nashville, perception and image are all-important, and it is understandably difficult, with so much competition, for an artist to develop his own unique style. Within the realm of country music, many images have been employed. Originally, there was not much concern about image. The hillbilly singers were more or less themselves. As time progressed and the music business developed, things became competitive. Artists wanted to make a name for themselves. They sought public recognition and fame. Nobody knows for certain just when the first image consultant was called in, but consultants are now a reality. They seek to take someone average and endow him with a unique and recognizable, though perhaps artificial, persona. Among the trends we have witnessed were the brightly colored and flamboyant Western suits. This particular style was eclipsed by the coming of the "Outlaws" as personified by Willie Nelson, Waylon Jennings, Billy Joe Shaver, and others. Their particular image was counterculture. They often wore raggedy-looking jeans, had long hair, openly smoked marijuana, and sometimes intentionally looked like bums.

One group similar to the outlaws were the former jailbirds. They were considered tough and authentic spokesmen of the working class. Among them were Johnny Cash, Merle Haggard, Freddy Fender, David Allan Coe, and others. Their prison stripes were their badge of honor. Among the most interesting and certainly the most enigmatic of this bunch is David Allan Coe, the self-proclaimed "Mysterious Rhinestone Cowboy."

Coe was released from the Ohio slammer in 1967, where he was doing time for a series of uninteresting minor offenses. He came to Nashville and got his first recording contract with producer Shelby Singleton.

I started handling him in early 1974. By then he had his first album on Columbia, entitled *The Mysterious Rhinestone Cowboy*. It was an incredible offering musically. David considered himself to be one of the outlaws, and had earned the title.

David Allan Coe was mysterious indeed. He is a bit taller than six feet, and at the time looked like a biker. This visual impression was offset by his very large cowboy hat and rhinestone suits.

Conversationally he was a moron, but he was an incredible writer. Columbia, his record label, had wanted me to have him play at the Exit/In, a Nashville listening room that at the time was dubbed "Nashville's Music Forum." David, however, had already earned a reputation as an asshole, and Owsley Manier, who was in charge of booking the club at the time, wanted to see him play somewhere else before he put him in the club. With this in mind, I booked David at the Caribou Lounge, a club in

Bowling Green, Kentucky, not too far from Nashville, where Owsley went to hear him play.

The club owner, Kirk Richardson, later told me that David Allan Coe spent a great deal of time bragging and said that he never left Nashville for less than $10,000 a night. The club owner found this to be extremely amusing since he was only paying Coe $200.

Before David signed to Columbia he had a couple of albums released on Shelby Singleton's Plantation label. These albums were anything but country. In fact, one of them sounded to me like a shameless rip-off of blues singer Screaming Jay Hawkins. I asked David if he had ever heard of Screaming Jay. He replied angrily that he had been in a jail cell with Screaming Jay Hawkins and that he, David, had "taught him everything he knew." He may have been in a jail cell with Jay, but I sincerely doubt it.

Most artists attempt to establish some sort of persona for themselves. David's was the "Badass." He wanted everyone to know just how tough he was. To prove his toughness he sometimes sucker-punched some innocent member of the audience. This happened at the Dean Scott Club in Houston in the mid 1970s, as well as in other places. As I heard the story, someone had heckled David, so he jumped down from the stage and sucker-punched the wrong guy, a customer who was just sitting there minding his own business.

In addition, he obviously spent a great deal of time in the Freudian anal stage, since he frequently mooned the audience at the end of his shows. He once released an album entitled *Texas Moon*, which featured himself and his band mooning the camera on the cover.

I have not seen David in years, but he still has a great many fans and has made a very significant and lasting contribution to country music as an art form. As a writer, he has penned numerous hits, both for himself and other artists, such as "Would You Lay With Me" for Tanya Tucker and "Take This Job and Shove It" for Johnny Paycheck. Artistically, he has provided many interesting diversions, both musically and personally, as a result of the different stages through which he has passed. As an outlaw, pirate, biker, Confederate officer, and sea captain, he has expanded the boundaries of country music.

As a result of his pioneering efforts, he helped clear the path for many of the unconventional artists who have followed him. He proved that it was possible to do his own thing and he succeeded in spite of himself. I cannot help but wonder how much more money he could have made if he had been more sociable and easier to work with. I have heard that he has mellowed out a bit over the years, but other artists have come along and it doesn't matter much anymore.

From the artist's standpoint, the publicist is somewhat like the manager in the sense that it is often hard to determine exactly what contribution is being made to the artist's career. If an artist is really up and coming, he gets a lot of press anyway without the help of a PR firm.

In Nashville, PR companies are similar to agencies in some respects. They may do a very good job representing a few artists, at first, but as their reputation for getting the job done grows, they tend to take on more and more artists until they reach the point where they have spread themselves too thin and lose their effectiveness for the majority of their clients. In this case, and it happens often, an artist ends up spending a great deal of money for nothing.

THE RECORD PRODUCER

The record producer generally selects the music that the artist will record. He confers with the artist, the record company, songwriters, and publishers in choosing songs for the artist. He schedules recording time according to the artist's availability, books the studio, and lines up the musicians for the session. More important, the producer serves as the captain in the recording studio, seeking to bring out the best musically from both the artist and the session musicians.

Ideally, the producer is able to help the artist develop and create his own unique style of singing. He is paid by the record company a flat rate per side, a percentage of the total product sales, or both. He is usually selected jointly by the artist and the record company. If the artist is very successful, and if it is a part of his contract with the record company, he may use whomever he wants as a producer or may decide to produce his own music. If the artist is new or lacks clout, the record company may tell him who will be his producer.

Some producers work directly for the record company, while others are considered to be independent or work for a "production company" consisting of several producers who have formed their own company and produce a number of acts for different record labels.

In Nashville, producers are often a slippery bunch, and sometimes force the artist to record songs from their own publishing companies. They often make songwriters share writing royalties or publishing rights with artists in return for recording one of the writer's songs. For this reason, several writers' names frequently appear on many country songs. In this manner, a producer who works with famous artists can frequently force the singer to record a majority of songs from his own publishing company.

Not only does the record producer make money as a producer in this way, but he also earns money through his own publishing company. If the songs his artist has recorded become hits, the publishing company becomes more valuable since its catalog is loaded with hit songs. This is a very important point if the owner should wish to sell the publishing company later. I am not suggesting that the average successful record producer will intentionally cut bad songs on an artist just because the songs are in his own publishing company, although this does happen. What I am saying is that the more songs on an album from the producer's publishing company, the better it is for the producer.

In the past, almost every major record label had its own recording studio, and that is where the artist recorded. It was that simple and, for the most part, was nonnegotiable. As time passed, and after much fighting within the music business, independent, non-label-owned studios made their appearance. As more and more artists achieved and began to wield power, they demanded the right to record wherever they wanted to. Ultimately the record companies had to accept their wishes and independent studios became the norm. As a result, some producers either bought their own studios or made deals with friends who owned studios to record there in exchange for kickbacks or other favors.

Consequently, it is not an unknown or uncommon practice for the producer to record an artist in a studio that he owns, either partly or completely. In this way he can take his time, run up the studio bill, and then tag the record company for a larger than necessary amount. This is not in the best interests of the record company, but someone at the label may be getting some type of kickback, so such things happen from time to time. This does not help the artist either, since recording costs constitute an advance against his record royalties.

As far as the selection of a producer is concerned, the artist should choose someone he likes personally, who is familiar with the artist's work, and who will most likely be able to put the artist's best and most representative music on tape. As much as I hate to say this, it does not hurt the artist to have a producer who is well connected politically within the music business community, or, to be more specific, someone who is liked by the artist's record company and the major publishing companies.

Producers, like the rest of the players, have their day at the top and then fall by the wayside. Like artists, some of them last longer than others, but with their potential for feathering their own nests, it is unlikely that many of the really successful ones will ever miss a meal.

THE LAWYER

Lawyers are, unfortunately, a necessary evil. Like managers, they have a pronounced tendency to get in the middle of a smoothly running situation and create problems that otherwise would not exist. They then pretend to solve the problems that they have created in an effort to justify their fees and to make it appear that they are actually doing something worthwhile, which in most cases they are not. They frequently use form letters for commonplace circumstances and then bill the artist for several hours' worth of work when in fact what they actually did required no more than fifteen minutes.

I am certain that there must be an honest lawyer somewhere who also possesses a high degree of competency, I have just not met one personally. Most of them will try to talk their own clients into settling so that they will not have to go to court. It would be awful if they actually had to work. Have you ever noticed that lawyers always seem to be "practicing"? Practice makes perfect. Perhaps one day they will get it right.

They remind me of import-car mechanics. You know in advance that they are going to be expensive but you never know for sure if they have done what you have paid them for. Most lawyers...well, never mind. I wish the artist luck in selecting an attorney who won't sell him out.

THE FAN CLUB

The artist should at some point establish a fan club. Not only does this organization provide a profitable outlet for some of the entertainer's merchandise, but the fan club potentially provides clout.

For example, if an artist's record does not receive enough radio airplay, a call to the fan club president can mobilize dozens, hundreds, or even thousands of fans who will phone radio stations all over the country requesting the artist's song. If an artist is having trouble getting booked into a particular city or venue, the fans with the sheer volume of their phone calls can influence a talent buyer in their artist's favor.

Fan club members also support shows in their geographical areas and sometimes work with the promoter to help increase the number of ticket sales. In view of the help a well-ordered fan club can provide an artist, it is extremely important to take the time to get this organization functioning smoothly. Where else can an artist get hundreds or even thousands of devoted, and unpaid, workers?

THE RECORD COMPANY

The record company is in business to sell records. It does not exist for the purpose of creating stars or building careers. Nor is it in business to humor country music singers, their managers, or anyone else. The record company exists for the sole purpose of selling records. That the record company does seek to build careers and to make artists famous and successful is only to move product, period.

The record company is certainly the most singularly important part of the artist's team. It all starts here. Without the record company, there are no records. Without records, there is no radio airplay. Without radio airplay, the artist has no exposure to the public at large. Without this exposure, there is no desire on the part of the public to pay to see the artist perform. Without paid performances, the artist makes no money.

The relationship between the artist and the record company is unusual in a number of ways. To the artist trying hard to get a record deal, the record company appears to be some mythical giant with the power to create or destroy careers. This is certainly true. To the artist who is selling millions of records, the record company does not seem so intimidating. To the artist whose records are not selling and whose career is on the skids, the record company is the evil cause of all of his problems.

As a result of the excesses displayed by some record companies in the past, many artists have come to expect the record company to be the provider of all their needs. Many artists feel that the record company should gladly give financial help for everything from transportation to wardrobe, and they become angry when the record company denies their slightest request. The artist also blames the record company when a record fails to progress up the charts, as if the record company did not want it to reach the top and could have stopped its decline with a phone call.

The record company is a corporate giant and can sometimes appear to act against the artist in that it has its own agenda and priorities. If an artist is a high priority at the record company, he does unquestionably have a better chance of making it. It is kind of a circular situation. The artist knows that if he does not have hit records then he has for the most part no career, and the record label will eventually cast him out. The artist contends that it is impossible to sell records if the public cannot hear them being played on the radio. He blames the record company for not adequately promoting his records, and becomes angry and resentful when another artist on the same label is doing well. There is some truth to this view from the artist's standpoint.

On the other hand, there is only so much a record company can achieve. If radio is not receptive to an artist's music after a reasonable or even excessive amount of promotional effort by the record company, there is not too much more it can do about it. The record company will try again with some more singles and another album, but if this does not work, then the artist is in a bad way.

One of the worst scenarios for the artist will occur when the executive who signed the artist leaves the record company and the artist is inherited by the new regime. This is especially bad if the executive who signed the artist was unpopular. The artist finds himself in the undesirable position of "a redheaded stepchild," as we say in the country. It is not necessarily in the best interests of the new regime for this holdover to succeed. It might make the departed label head look like he knew what he was doing after all. Furthermore, the new boss has his own priorities and special projects, and does not want to waste his budget on something that he did not initiate and will get little credit for if it succeeds.

Certain record labels are undoubtedly stronger than others in country music, and I have been told by some managers that they would rather not have a record deal at all than have their artist stuck on a particular label. Some labels succeed internationally but are weak in terms of their country operations, perhaps viewing their Nashville branches as provincial outposts in the wilderness. This is certainly the way many New York record company offices viewed the country market ten years ago. Fortunately, that has changed to a large degree, and recently the head of RCA Records in Nashville was promoted to president of that label, which is now called Bertelsmann Music Group and owned by the Germans.

Most of the older artists who formerly had substantial record sales have been for all purposes abandoned by the majority of record labels in Nashville, notwithstanding the fact that many

of them still have very large followings. In this respect, I feel
that the labels have failed substantially by ignoring an increasingly large segment of the population, specifically the over-
forty market. They are, it seems, leaving a large amount of
money on the table, but they say that the older artists do not sell.
Again the argument is circular in nature. The older artists do
not sell because they are not promoted by the record companies, and the record companies do not promote them because
they do not sell. It makes no difference to the older artists which
position one takes. They do not have record deals and are not
on the radio.

In the final analysis, the record company is the single most
important factor in getting the artist's career off the ground.
My advice to the aspiring artist in search of a record deal is to
play from his heart, develop his own style, and not try to copy
anyone else. The worst thing that can be said about any artist,
no matter how good he may be, is that he sounds like George
Jones or Merle Haggard or anyone else for that matter. Those
people already exist, and the record companies are not looking
for other ones.

Another thing to avoid is telling anyone anywhere that you
are not sure what direction you should take musically. Today
the record companies do not have the time, the interest, and in
many cases the intelligence and experience to figure out what
type of music an aspiring artist should play. The presentation
of an artist's material to the record company should leave
nothing to the imagination.

The worst possible thing for a would-be star is to be turned
down by a record company because he played what he thought
they wanted to hear. The artist should always be true to his own
music. If he is passed on by the record label, it should be
because the label rejected his music, not because of the style of
someone else he tried to imitate.

It is also very important when seeking a record deal not to
waste time auditioning for some twenty-year-old subaltern at
the record label. These people are paid to say no to prospective
artists. To present an artist's music to someone who has the
power to pass on an act, but not the authority to sign one, is self-
defeating and counterproductive. The prospective artist who

does get a chance to perform before someone in a position to sign him had better go in with his absolutely best material. He most likely will not get a second chance.

THE AGENT

The agent is arguably the most important single person in the artist's career. His efforts provide the artist's income and place him in front of the public. An agent is almost always there from the beginning, before the record deal, before the fame and renown. He is there through it all, and there after the fall. When the fame has come and gone for most of these artists, there is still some agent somewhere trying to get them work.

The agent's job is unquestionably the most difficult of all. He is under constant scrutiny from everyone and is most often criticized by people who have absolutely no concept of what is actually involved in being an agent.

It is one thing for the record company or the manager to receive an occasional call from someone wanting to use one of his artists for a date. It is another thing altogether to have to sell dates for an artist, and then more dates to tie those in. It is not enough to fill a Friday and Saturday night. The artist wants Sunday as well. If Sunday is booked, then the agent is instructed to see if he can find something for Wednesday and Thursday. This is not a onetime problem, but is repeated almost every week for every artist. So the more acts an agency has, the more agents it takes to get them all booked, the bigger the phone bill, the greater the expense, and the more problems.

It is indeed a thankless job for the most part, as I have mentioned elsewhere, and acts lose so much revenue by not taking care of the agents at their agency. It is a simple enough matter for an act to take an agent out to lunch from time to time, or to thank him for a particularly good date, but this is seldom done.

Often, a manager is involved in the neglect. He tells the act that he has things under control at the agency and discourages the artist from having any commerce with the agents at all. This is, of course, in his best interests, certainly not those of the artist he represents. If the act can be kept away from direct contact with the agency as much as possible, then the manager is in a much safer position personally. He gets to present the dates to the artist instead of having the agent present them. This method of doing things makes the manager seem important.

The intelligent artist will do well to sidestep his manager and make friends with the agents, at least on a business level. It is human nature to work harder for people you like. If the agent has no personal connection with an artist he will not do the best job for him. That's just the way it is.

Often, however, when an artist goes around his manager and contacts the agency directly, a dialogue between the two begins and the act may find out that the agent is doing the majority of the work. This is a decidedly unappealing prospect for the average manager. But most artists do not appreciate their agency and consider the agents to be a necessary evil, like lawyers. It always amazes me to see how important an agent suddenly becomes in the artist's eyes after he has been dropped by the record label and his career is on the skids.

As a result of all of this constant neglect and abuse, eventually even the best agent will develop a bad attitude, and although he may very well speak favorably of his clients on the phone, he will in many cases look forward to the day when he has some other, more profitable artists and can tell the artist who has been a prima donna and thief to hit the road.

I can understand this attitude as a result of my own experiences. While there are some acts with whom I have had serious differences of opinion in the past, I would consider working with them again, under certain circumstances. Mickey Gilley falls into this category, as does Ronnie Milsap, to a lesser degree. Other acts, Ricky Skaggs, for example, I just plain do not like and would not represent for any amount of money. There are some things more important than money, and one of them is not having to fool with inflated egos constantly. There are many artists whose company I genuinely enjoy and who are fun to be around. As far as getting any gratification from associating with the famous, that is a novelty that wears off very quickly.

In many cases there are some causes for alarm on the part of the manager and the artist as far as the agency is concerned.

The agency exists to sell dates, and as a result, agents will sometimes take dates that are not in the best interests of the artist, solely in order to make commissions. The likelihood of this happening increases as the individual agents are under pressure from their employer to sell more and more dates. Often an agent will take the path of least resistance in order to complete one transaction and move on to something else. This can be accomplished by selling the date for less money in order to get the deal done, rather than holding out for more money on behalf of the artist.

On the other hand, with so much ongoing competition, an agent who waits too long to wrap up a deal may lose it altogether. While the agent deliberates, a buyer will frequently book another artist so that he may conclude his own business and move on to something else as well.

The agent must always walk a thin line. He must obtain dates for his acts or he loses them, yet at the same time he must protect his buyers. If he overcharges a buyer for an act and the buyer loses money, then the buyer's trust in the agent diminishes and other acts on the roster may lose dates as a result.

The agent, like the manager, is in constant danger of being fired, and usually without notice or reason. One day an act listens to a presentation from another agency and decides to go with them for a while. He frequently leaves owing a big bill. It is really strange, but of all the people the artist must pay, the agency is usually the last to be paid. It is as if the artist actually resents having to pay the agency.

The best way for an agency to see that it is paid is to deduct its money from the deposit check before it is sent to the artist, after the date has been played. This is not always possible since on certain dates there are no deposits. It should be established clearly at the outset when taking on a new artist that this is the way things are handled by the accounting department. Believe it or not, some acts who have been permitted to run up a big bill sometimes feel so guilty about not paying the agency that they leave and go to another agency to avoid having to face the agents, knowing that they owe money to the agency. It is best for all concerned not to let the artist get behind on his commissions.

I enjoyed being an agent for most of my eighteen years in the business, but the lack of gratitude and the incessant complaining and disloyalty finally wore me out. I still handle Ray Price and occasionally work with Jerry Lee Lewis, and I enjoy those associations, but as far as handling and baby-sitting fifteen or twenty acts again, well, I think not. There are times, however, when I miss the action, and the ruthlessness and the exhilaration of slicing up one's adversaries, but luckily the feeling soon passes.

Any doubts that I may have had were put to rest at the Country Music Association's Twenty-Fifth Anniversary Awards this past October, when artist Travis Tritt received the Horizon Award. The Horizon Award was "created to honor an artist who for the first time in the field of country music demonstrated the most significant creative growth." His agents from the William Morris Agency were sitting a few rows down from me when the winner's name was announced. They all stood up and shouted and whistled, having worked very hard on his behalf. He took several minutes to thank everyone from God to the kitchen sink—everyone, that is, except the William Morris Agency. I saw the expressions on the agents' faces as a result of this obvious and inexcusable omission. That cinched it for me.

Chapter Twenty-three

"It All Begins With a Song":

From Songwriters and Publishers to the Country Music Association and Branson, Missouri

Around town there is a saying, "It all begins with a song." This is certainly true enough, for without a hit song the artist does not get enough airplay and record sales to keep his price or demand high enough to have much of a career. For this reason songwriters are extremely important.

The songwriter may write for a publishing company and receive a weekly or monthly advance, in which case the songs generally belong entirely to the publisher. If the publisher, however, fails to get the writer's songs recorded, then the songwriter will not make money over and above his weekly or monthly draw. Meanwhile, the publishing company still owns his songs. Many songwriters begin this way, writing for publishing companies, then stay with them until they have established their own reputations for hits. At this point, they frequently start their own publishing companies and keep all the money.

The biggest problem for the new songwriter is breaking into an already flooded market. While it is true that everybody in Nashville looks for a hit song, it is also true that thousands of terrible songs are written each year by hopeful writers. The publishers, artists, and producers are often overwhelmed by the sheer volume of songs, many of which arrive unsolicited and poorly recorded. Most of these writers never make it, and after starving for a while eventually return to their hometowns and to another, more profitable line of work.

The songwriter who does succeed foresees a life of relative ease. For a while, everybody praises the writer and wants to cut his material. There is, however, continual pressure to write more hit songs. Some writers are seemingly blessed with what seems to be an inexhaustible ability to keep turning them out. For others, a big hit song too early in their career can be the kiss of death, since everything they write from that point forward never equals their one really big hit song. Look at Kenny Rogers' hit record "Lucille," for example, written by Hal Bynam. It was the biggest song Bynam ever had, before or since.

The songwriter is also faced with other problems as well. He frequently has to share his proceeds with an artist or producer in order to have his song recorded by someone famous. In other words, I may have written a hit song, but in order to have it cut by a star, I might have to agree to give the artist credit as a cowriter, even though he actually had no part in writing the song. That is decidedly unfair, but it has always been that way in Nashville, and no doubt always will.

The songwriter is also subject to the same laws of success that control the artist, the producer, and the session musician. He might be on top one day, but then for some reason his songs are no longer in demand and the artists around town find a new writer whose songs become the rage. As with the other players, some songwriters defy the odds and have long and successful careers.

All in all, the successful songwriter has the best deal in the music business. He must be productive, and his songs must continue to be at the top of the charts, but he does not have to support a band, pay for a bus, and travel thousands of miles in order to make a living.

The publishing company hires songwriters in order to have a large catalog of hit songs. The more hit songs it owns, the more valuable the catalog. Hit songs are nearly always recorded by several artists, and often in different ways. A song may be recorded originally as a country tune, but then issued as a pop song, or the words may be slightly altered and recorded as a gospel song. "Handy Man," written in 1959, was a pop hit for Jimmy Jones. It was successfully revived over twenty years later by James Taylor. "What a Difference You've Made in My Life," a song written for Ronnie Milsap, has been rerecorded several times as "What a Difference God Made in My Life." "You've Really Got a Hold On Me," written by Smokey Robinson and recorded by the Miracles, was later a country hit for Mickey Gilley. The list goes on and on.

A hit song continues to be profitable for years. I read recently that Kris Kristofferson's "For the Good Times," a song made famous by Ray Price, and which sold 11 million records over twenty years ago, was just sold for almost $1 million to another publisher. The purchaser of that song obviously felt that it was worth what he paid for it in terms of its continued royalty-producing power. The article in the Nashville paper said that one would have to listen to that one song nonstop, twenty-four hours a day, for twenty-five years to equal the number of times it has been played on the radio. In Nashville and in country music, as in all other types of music, song publishing is big business. Sony Music recently bought Tree Publishing, a Nashville company, for a reported $50 million.

MASTERMINDS OF NOTHING

In the country music business an evil group of individuals often appear. Although they frequently know each other, they are not related in business terms. Some may be well known and perhaps even respected within the music community. Their chief function consists in throwing the proverbial wrench into the machinery. They may work in any capacity, as agent, manager, band member, attorney, or in any other branch of the music business. There are many of them and they are decidedly dangerous. The late, great talent agent Shorty Lavender referred to them as "masterminds of nothing." Like the legendary gremlins of folklore, they show up at the wrong moment and ruin things.

In the music business, these are the people who smile and speak pleasant words in your presence, but work behind your back to undermine your projects. They possess enough ability to cause problems for those whom they attack, but never enough skill to complete the projects they start. They sometimes have no conscious desire to cause trouble, but frequently intrude upon and destroy otherwise good relationships between artists, managers, agents, and record companies. More often than not, however, they intend to create turmoil, seeking to start a rift between parties so that they can have someone removed and then take his place. The perpetrator may be a family member, a friend of the artist, the bandleader, a producer, or anyone else seeking to further his own interests at the expense of someone else. These people abound, and cause a great deal of trouble for everyone with whom they come in contact.

THE BAND

The band is a mixed blessing for the country singer. An artist who uses the same musicians day to day over a period of months or years naturally has a tighter show onstage than the artist who employs a pickup band.

In the past, many smaller acts frequently traveled alone and would have another band back them up at the show. This is still done to some degree, particularly by older singers as well as artists who do not make that much money. Today, however, the newer artists all have their own bands. This is the ideal situation provided the artist is making enough money to be able to afford it. Most bands consist of four or five musicians in addition to the artist. Naturally, the larger the band, the more it costs the artist.

The artist's arrangements with the band may be handled in several ways. He may pay the band a weekly salary, in which case the band members are to work exclusively for him, though he may permit them to play sessions during their off-time. They are also expected to rehearse whenever required, and are paid the same whether they play five shows or none.

In other cases, the band members are given an agreed-upon amount, either per show or per day. In the latter case, they are paid for the actual number of days they are gone. The artist must let them know in advance when and where they will be playing.

An artist can also use one of several regional bands when necessary. In this way, the artist can be certain of having a band he is familiar with whenever he happens to be in a particular area.

Over time, the band becomes an entity with a personality of its own, and must be reckoned with by the artist. The relationship is often adversarial, with the band coming together as a unit and making demands of the artist, some of which may be unreasonable. The artist is not in the best possible position in such circumstances. Although he can ultimately fire the band, a band usually makes its power plays right before a big tour or at some other time when the artist does not have time to make other arrangements. Often the artist will dismiss the main troublemaker, an example that sometimes gets the band back under his control for a while, but the potential for conflict is always present.

THE ROAD MANAGER

The road manager is an extremely important part of the artist's performing troupe. He determines the times of departure and arrival, and makes certain that all of the band members are where they are supposed to be. He arranges lodging and transportation, schedules interviews on the road, acts as liaison between the band and the artist, oversees the setup and teardown of equipment, collects the money for the artist, and performs dozens of other functions. He is closer to the artist on a day-to-day basis than the manager, the agent, or anyone else. For this reason, and others, the road manager exercises some influence over the artist and must be dealt with carefully by the other players. Due to his constant presence in the artist's life, he has the capacity for helping or hurting the other members of the team.

THE UNION

The American Federation of Musicians, known as the musicians' union, performs a number of services for musicians. It forces companies to pay a uniform wage so that union musicians will not be undercut by competitors. For example, the Tennessee Network's popular show, "Nashville Now," pays the musicians $250 per show. This is a very desirable job for the musicians who work the show. There are plenty of musicians who would gladly work free just to have the exposure the show provides. The union protects the network's musicians from being dismissed unfairly. The union performs other protective services of a similar nature for its members.

THE COUNTRY MUSIC ASSOCIATION

The Country Music Association was founded in 1967. It exists for the purpose of promoting country music worldwide. The membership, in excess of seven thousand, is supposedly composed exclusively of people who make their livelihood from country music, but I imagine that a detailed investigation of its membership roster would reveal otherwise. Be that as it may, the CMA has done an outstanding job over the years, and all of my dealings with directors Jo Walker Meador and Helen Farmer have always been pleasant.

The CMA has not always been held in the esteem it now holds in Nashville. Twenty years ago, an organization known as the Association of Country Entertainers (ACE) came into existence. It was formed as an alternative to the Country Music Association by industry professionals and performers who felt that the CMA did not represent country music properly and was taking it away from its roots. Some important performers were members during its brief life, including Barbara Mandrell. Many factors contributed to the demise of ACE. The most significant were probably the success of the CMA's nationally televised awards show and the presence of the Country Music Hall of Fame.

There are many artists today who still feel that the CMA does not really represent country music, but then the CMA's objectives forced it to make a choice. The audience for country music had always comprised a very small segment of the listening public. While it can be argued that this was due to the fact that there were previously not very many country radio stations, it can also be said that country music did not appeal to the average American's tastes. For country music to increase its audience, it had to change, and that is exactly what has happened.

The music that passes for country today is indeed a far cry from the original plaints that characterized this art form. I am not referring to singers like Patsy Cline, Jim Reeves, or Eddie Arnold, although they have always been considered country. I am speaking of hillbilly music, most of which was not particularly soothing to the ears. A substantial amount of what is called country now would have been considered rock and roll twenty years ago. The choice for the CMA was whether to push traditional country music and maintain a continued small share of the radio audience, or to lay tradition aside and seek to gain a larger share of the market by promoting music that was more palatable to the American public at large. It seems that the CMA chose the latter course.

If the reader takes issue with what I have said, I suggest he or she listen to some of the guitar solos on records today that pass for country. Some of the artist's wardrobe selections are a far cry from what was considered country in the past. There was a time in the early eighties when country music stars dressed like clowns, and I am not referring to "Moe and Joe" (Moe Bandy and Joe Stampley, who dressed up like Boy George and Culture Club and did a novelty album on CBS Records in the early 1980s). This change was influenced by the West Coast and was a subtle attempt to further water down country music in order to appeal to a wider, more cosmopolitan audience.

Producer Jimmy Bowen once told me that most of the people at the Nashville record companies don't even like country music. This was a rather broad but accurate statement on the situation here. This attitude is much more pervasive than the public will ever know, and it applies to many artists as well.

Listen to the songs some of them have recorded. Barbara Mandrell, the princess of country music, had hit records with two remakes of black soul songs, "If Loving You Is Wrong, I Don't Wanna Be Right" and "Woman to Woman." Ronnie Milsap's "Lost in the Fifties Tonight" is an adaptation of "In the Still of the Night" by a black fifties quintet called the Five Satins. Milsap also did a remake of black singer Chuck Jackson's "Any Day Now." Mickey Gilley redid "You've Really Got a Hold on Me" and "Stand by Me," both originally recorded successfully by black singers.

It is not that these artists in particular do not like country music. It is that country music has changed, and as a result of that change has gained a larger audience, but has also lost some of its character.

This is unfortunate. That the CMA has chosen the course that it has taken is a source of irritation to many of the more traditional, or perhaps I should say older, artists. Many of them feel left out, and with good reason—they have been. They are paid lip service, but they know that they are constantly and intentionally overlooked. The Country Music Association is interested in what is new and hot.

The most blatant and obviously insensitive example of this occurs before millions of viewers every year on the CMA's awards show. The names of the nominees for the major awards are read to the public, along with background information on some of them, before the winner's name in each category is announced; and yet for the most important award of all, the Hall of Fame Award, the nominees' names are not even mentioned. What an insult. More attention is given to the Horizon Award for newcomers than to the Hall of Fame Award. So much for tradition.

The winners in the various categories are determined by votes from the active membership. What this means is that companies with something to gain from the voting sign up their secretaries, receptionists, and others as members of the CMA. The company pays the membership dues on behalf of the employees, and when the time comes, the company takes all of the ballots and votes them for their own horse at the big show.

I had all of my employees signed up as members of the CMA while I was president of In Concert. When the ballots came in, I had one of my secretaries drop them off at a particular record company. I did this frequently. I would like to say that the CMA has done everything possible to see that this type of thing does not happen, but it certainly occurs, every year.

There are so many artists in country music today that it would be impossible for all of them to be sufficiently honored by the Country Music Association. There are others, such as Jerry Wallace, Del Reeves, Stonewall Jackson, Billy Walker, Johnny Russell, Sonny James, and David Houston, who are consistently ignored by the CMA, presumably because they do not fit within the image the CMA wishes to promote. They are out there, though, perhaps considered too old, too dated, or simply too obscure now to warrant any mention, despite their contributions to their art.

And then there is the lunatic fringe of country music, acts like Lyle Lovett, k. d. lang, and others. These artists are out there also, selling records and playing shows, and are considered by the public to be country. This may perhaps be the supreme irony, for by expanding its horizons, country music has given birth to some bastard children the CMA would rather not mention. The wheel turns, and country music evolves and changes. As it does, it continues to be relevant to its audience today. The Country Music Association has done a good job in keeping country music alive and vital, but like society at large, it has for the most part left its elders to die, and it hopes quietly, having already squandered its inheritance.

THE ACADEMY OF COUNTRY MUSIC

The Academy of Country Music (ACM) is a California-based organization that exists for much the same reason as the Country Music Association. It was founded in 1964 and has an approximate membership of four thousand. Like the CMA, the ACM also has an annual televised awards show. The ACM awards show takes place in the spring and is an enjoyable event, although it is not quite as sophisticated and formal as the CMA show. It seems to be a more relaxed production, not in terms of quality, but rather in its overall atmosphere. It may be said to possess more of a West Coast flavor.

In Nashville the West Coast is a subject that almost everybody has some opinion about. Several years ago it was viewed as a big threat to Nashville, after the defection of several major artists to West Coast agencies and management companies. The alarm has died down to a substantial degree and things proceed here much as they did before the big scare. Nashville is, always has been, and always will be the home of country music.

Be that as it may, most people in the music business do not hold the ACM in the same esteem as they do the CMA. While ACM recognition is important, it is the CMA awards that count. Many in Nashville view the ACM as a regional fraternity that more or less tends to its own business.

The ACM is much more important than that, however, for several reasons. While it may be as political as the CMA, it acknowledges acts who are frequently overlooked or completely ignored altogether by the Country Music Association. It is not afraid, as an organization, to embrace the outside edge of country music as an art form, and thrives in a much less restricted atmosphere. While the ACM will most likely never achieve the status of its Nashville cousin, it will always provide a legitimate balance and offer artists ignored by the CMA significant and well-deserved recognition for their efforts.

RADIO

The radio stations determine which artists get airplay. This is, as might be imagined, extremely important, for if the public never hears an artist then they do not buy his or her records and do not pay to see his or her live shows. For this reason, the radio station is an essential factor in the artist's career.

Among the twenty-five hundred stations throughout the United States that play country music, some are more important than others. The most important are called reporting stations. These stations report the amount of airplay songs are receiving within their listening areas to national publications such as the *Gavin Report, Cashbox* and *Billboard* magazines, *Radio and Records,* and other publications that maintain record charts. The individual publications themselves determine which stations they will select as reporting stations.

For the purposes of establishing a national chart, most of these publications divide the country geographically into regions as follows: central, midwest, southwest, western, southeast, and northeast. The reporting radio stations then inform the publications which records are playing the most in their respective areas. Based upon this information, a record receives a national chart position. If a particular record is moving up the charts very quickly, it is given a "bullet," which indicates that it is still moving upward.

We jokingly refer to a record that has reached its highest point on the charts and started its downward movement as having "taken the anchor."

National chart position for a record is similar to winning a ribbon at a horse show. It not only shows that the horse is valuable, but the recognition conferred by the ribbon makes it even more valuable. This is true for the artist, the record company, and the talent agent in much the same way. The record company that can boast of having had *x* amount of number-one records during the course of the year is in a good position. The same may be said of the artist as well. This recognition is especially important to the artist in terms of the number of dates he works and the amount of money he receives per show, since his agent will use his popularity as a selling point, and number-one records are a great sales tool.

The chart system as practiced has its flaws and is a source of irritation to any artist who is not at the top. Those who reach the coveted number-one position do not complain much about it as long as they remain there, but when their record stops at number three, or fails to make the top ten, it is a different story.

Strange as it may seem, it is possible to have a hit record without reaching the top ten at all. There are hundreds of small, grass-roots stations that play records the reporting stations refuse to play. As a result, an artist may become very popular in a certain region even though none of the reporting stations will play his records.

Radio today is not what it used to be. It has lost its youthful spirit and has for the most part turned into a numbers game. One of the most pernicious of all possibilities for radio today has become a reality, the "consultant." The consulting company is hired by the radio station owners to determine the radio station's playlist. In other words, some moron in New York, Chicago, or somewhere else will, based upon his "study of the market," tell the radio station that has hired him what records the station should play. As absurd as this might seem to the average listener, it is an increasingly common practice. Regardless of the present state of radio, it remains an extremely important part of the country music artist's career.

THE RECORD PROMOTER

The record promoter is the individual who calls the various radio stations and seeks to persuade the program director to add a particular record to the station's playlist. Most record companies have their own in-house promoters who work only on promoting the records of the company that employs them. In addition, there are the independent promoters who are hired to promote specific records, but do not work for any one company.

The independent record promoter can be a very significant part of the artist's team. He may be hired by the artist personally, by the publishing company that owns the rights to the song, by the artist's manager, or by the record company as a temporary addition to its own staff. The independent record promoter is usually hired for "the life of the record," a time period that generally covers about eight weeks. The cost of his services in this instance is around $2,500. Like the attorney, he is a hired gun with no particular loyalty other than to himself. This should be taken into account when selecting an independent record promoter.

As with the publicist, it is hard to know for certain whether or not he is working for you and what, if anything, he may be doing in your behalf. That a record moves up the charts can be the result of several factors. An artist may be particularly hot for a while, and anything he releases is likely to be a hit, or the record may take off on its own. It is hard to tell.

The biggest problem with the independent record promoter is that most of them are pushing a dozen records at the same time, so an artist may or may not be getting the services the promoter is being paid for. Furthermore, a record promoter will often trade off one record to advance another. In other words, if the promoter feels that one of the records he is working has gone as far as it is going to go, he may ask the program director at the radio station to drop the dying record in exchange for adding a newer one to the playlist. This happens all the time. It is fine, as long as it isn't your record that is being traded.

THE OPENING ACT

The opening act, also known as the warm-up act, is the first act on the stage. The act has to be good enough to keep the crowd entertained and to work them into a state of excitement so that the main attraction will find an eager and expectant audience.

If the opening act is too good, the headliner may want to get rid of him and find another act who will not steal as much of his thunder. If the opening act is boring onstage, then the headliner might not wish to use him again. There is often a subtle, and sometimes not so subtle, competition between the opening act, who is jealous of the headliner's success, and the headliner, who is intimidated by the increasing popularity and arrogance of the opening act. When these factors come into play, the audience is usually assured of seeing a good show. Both acts have to be entertaining onstage as well as on record. It is not enough to be a good singer. The public wants someone who is an entertainer as well.

We used to joke about certain artists, as all agents do, and suggest a tour sponsored by the sleep aid Sominex. "And now, ladies and gentlemen, for your enjoyment, the Sominex Tour, featuring ____, guaranteed to put you to sleep in ten minutes or less!"

The opening act must also be a good draw at the box office.

He must be able to sell tickets and must be worth more to the promoter than he costs. The position of the opening act is usually reserved for the least famous, successful, and popular act on the bill, and as such it is not the most prestigious of all positions, but it beats playing clubs, and all successful artists must take this role at the beginning of their careers.

THE TALENT BUYER

The talent buyer is extremely important to the artist, for without him the act has no place to play and, for the most part, no income. Talent buyers exist in many forms, among them the military buyer, the club buyer, the concert promoter, the convention buyer, the fair producer, the college buyer, the telephone promoter, and so on. They are all important to the artist in varying degrees, depending on which category is most likely to want his services as a performer.

THE MILITARY BUYER

The military buyer is generally someone within some branch of the military who purchases entertainment. For country music artists, the military is not much help, since most purchases of country music are for the NCO clubs, which do not have enough money to pay the average country music star. In addition, the people who buy the entertainment have to have their purchases approved by their superiors. Frequently this takes weeks, only to find that the date you thought was there does not work out after all. Furthermore, the military buyer at a particular location is likely to have been transferred to another post the next time you try to get him on the phone.

For these reasons and others very few agents representing acts in the over-$2,500-a-night category have much luck with the military buyer. Nevertheless, I have always felt that if an agency could devote one agent exclusively to the military, for a long enough period, it might prove to be worthwhile. I never had the time to test this theory personally.

The Club Buyer

The club is the backbone of the industry as far as the income of the average country music artist is concerned. Clubs exist from the top of the scale to the bottom, with many clubs quite capable of paying an artist $20,000 a night. In addition, there are clubs that are open every night of the week in which an artist may secure a pickup date en route to or from a weekend concert. While almost all artists I have ever worked with do not like clubs, the fact is that were it not for clubs, many of them would not be able to pay their bills. Clubs are notorious for heavy smoke, and loud and obnoxious drunks, but there are nice clubs as well where the artist is appreciated and enjoys playing.

The club buyer is different from the majority of other buyers. He uses entertainment to get people to come and stay and drink at his establishment. If he can make money at the door over and above the cost of the entertainment, so much the better. If not, then he has the possibility of making it at the bar by selling alcohol.

Many club buyers know what is happening in their area. They keep accurate records and they know how much they made or lost on a particular singer the last time they had him. In addition, they all talk among themselves, so if an artist causes problems for one buyer, he will pass the information on to another club owner very quickly. I have always liked clubs and club owners, and enjoy the honky-tonk ambience in small doses, and on my terms. Artists as a whole should be more appreciative of the revenue they make from club engagements.

The Concert Promoter

The concert promoter rents an auditorium, hires an entertainer, and does a show. It sounds that simple, but the promoter must take into account many factors if he is to succeed. He must know the market in which he does shows. Not only must he know what artists the public wants to see, but he must select an appropriate date.

In some cities, where there may be several large manufacturing plants, he has to schedule concerts as soon after the first or fifteenth of the month as possible, if that is when most of the people are paid. He must also avoid certain times of the year, such as holiday weekends, high school or college graduations, and certain religious holidays.

He must also see that no other major entertainment of a competitive nature is scheduled too soon before or after his date. And he must pick the best venue for the type of show he plans to promote. For example, it would be foolish to attempt a country show in a predominantly black neighborhood, since blacks as a group do not generally like country music. It would also be dangerous to promote an outdoor show at a time when the weather is questionable.

The concert promoter has nothing to back him up at the box office. He is on his own. He cannot expect to make money at the bar or to be helped by the presence of rides and other amusements as at a theme park or fair. In addition, he has an incredible array of expenses that must be covered before he makes any money personally, such as those for entertainment, catering, security, sound and lights, advertising, transportation, auditorium rent, ticket printing, stagehands, equipment rental, spotlight operators, box office expenses, insurance, and in some cases transportation, hotel rooms, and additional musicians. Furthermore, there are always unexpected incidental expenses.

Many artists and their agents place a ceiling on the amount of money a promoter can actually make. Quite honestly, very many promoters come and go, having been at first intrigued with the glamour of show business, but later sorry that they wasted their money.

Promoting concerts is a great deal like gambling, in many instances. There is beginner's luck, which is a real factor. The successful first-time concert promoter, like the amateur gambler, should take his winnings and go home. Instead, he wants to roll the dice again. If he wins a second or third time, he may become overconfident and begin taking greater risks. Sooner or later he loses a great deal of money and ends up wondering what happened. There is always another sucker, however, and another agent willing to perform a walletectomy.

Although most promoters would be much better off putting their money into something else, they keep coming, and their money keeps the buses rolling.

THE CONVENTION BUYER

Convention dates are usually very desirable engagements for the entertainer. Frequently multiple dates, they almost always pay more than the artist is worth and are often on weeknights. Generally these dates reach the agent as call-ins. Almost always, the clients or organizations seeking entertainment have already more or less decided upon one or two artists they really want for their convention. There are, of course, some exceptions, but this is generally the way it works. Since they are looking for a specific artist the agent is in a good position to overcharge them, and frequently does.

The date itself is usually played in the ballroom of some large hotel, and proceeds according to a fairly predictable and standard format, or "floormat," as many country artists say. There is a cocktail party followed by a seated dinner, at which time there are many speeches and awards. After this the star does an hour show, followed by a local band for dancing until the wee hours. Convention dates are usually great fun and are almost always enjoyed by the artist and the crowd.

THE FAIR PRODUCER

The fair producer is very important to the country music artist. There are all types and sizes of fairs, from the small pumpkin roller to the large multiday state fair. All of them use entertainment, and most of them use country music. The fair producer represents many fairs and is consequently a volume buyer. The producer is able to provide entertainment at a lesser price than the fair board would be able to get if it negotiated directly with an agency. The artist who works with the fair producer on multiple dates gets less money per date, but is guaranteed a specific number of dates. The fair producer also provides sound and lights, staging, and other services for the fair in a complete turnkey package.

THE COLLEGE BUYER

College entertainment generally falls into two categories, the coffeehouse series and the major concert series. Within the coffeehouse class are the smaller acts, usually in the $2,000 range. These acts are most often booked by some member of the student activities committee.

For the agent wishing to sell entertainment to one of these institutions, several problems are encountered. The student buyer is hard to reach by phone, since he is in class much of the time. In most cases, he does not have the authority to purchase talent directly, but has to make a recommendation to the other members of the student activities board, many of whom are making suggestions themselves. After the board has agreed upon a particular act, their decision must be approved by a dean.

In addition, many of these student activities boards change personnel every semester or quarter, and it becomes more trouble than it is worth for most country music agents and artists.

In the past, many colleges would hire big-name entertainers and promote the shows themselves. The shows would be open to the general public, with a slightly lower-priced ticket available to students. This is still done, but to a lesser degree. It is easier for the college or university to rent its large auditorium to an outside promoter. In this way, the university is able to provide students with top-name entertainment at no financial risk to the institution at all. Instead, the college or university makes money from the outset, on auditorium rental, concessions, and in some instances, even parking.

There are other buyers, such as the telephone promoter, the private party, the charity benefit, and others, that I have neglected to mention, but the procedures involved are much the same, regardless of who is actually buying the entertainment. The talent buyer is one of the most significant factors in the success of every artist's career, and the degree to which an artist is liked and sought after by the talent buyer directly determines his income.

BRANSON, MISSOURI

Unlikely as it may seem, the pretty little town of Branson, Missouri, has become a major player in the high-stakes game of country music. Branson is nestled in the Ozark Mountains, about forty miles south of Springfield, Missouri, and just north of the Arkansas border. The entire population of the town is around 3,500 people, but swells to over 45,000 during the season, which runs May through October. The area is dotted with numerous scenic lakes and waterways, and is truly a fisherman's paradise. Rolling hills and lush foliage make it one of the most remarkable places on earth. How this small community came to be highly significant in terms of the country music business is as interesting as it is unlikely.

Branson had long been a destination for family vacationers. Visitors enjoyed fishing and other water sports during the daylight hours, but at night there was nothing much to do. Some musicians got together and began playing for their own entertainment. In time, however, a small theater was opened by the Presley family (no relation to Elvis), and things grew from there. Now there are over thirty theaters, most of which have been built in the last ten years. These operate full-time during the season and attract thousands of patrons daily.

There are also go-cart tracks, helicopter rides, water slides, souvenir shops, restaurants, motels, and other diversions, such as the Silver Dollar City theme park and the Shepherd of the Hills, an outdoor play dealing with the history of the area. Most of these attractions are located within walking distance of each other along a mile-and-a-half-long area of Highway 76 known as the Strip. There is virtually no crime. Everybody for the most part has a good time, and a carnival-like atmosphere prevails.

What should most likely have remained just another small, scenic Ozark town has developed into a major commercial operation. The stone that the builder refused in this case has been the acts that have been cast off by the music business machine in Nashville.

Unable in many cases to get enough work to survive on the road, these artists come to Branson to play. Here they have a built-in audience that appreciates their music and is turned off by the crap that many of the record companies are releasing these days.

Nashville has almost no country music stars playing on a regular basis, and outside of the Grand Ole Uproar, there is little opportunity for fans to see, hear, and meet country stars playing live music.

Branson has filled that void, both by offering the opportunity to hear a large number of acts in one location and by providing family entertainment. Artists like Mel Tillis, Boxcar Willie, Mickey Gilley, Roy Clark, Cristy Lane, Ray Price, Ray Stevens, Willie Nelson, Moe Bandy, Del Reeves, and even Andy Williams are playing Branson on a regular basis. They are doing shows, meeting their fans, signing autographs, and making large sums of money. They are also taking a big chunk out of Nashville's tourist industry.

While Music City dismissed Branson as an insignificant purgatory for its own cast-offs, the citizens of Branson were organizing, planning, and building. Today, Branson is kicking Nashville's assets and costing Music City millions of dollars a year in lost revenues. Branson is now too big to be ignored, and it's not going away. We have nobody to blame but ourselves.

We have briefly examined the players in the music business, and have looked at their roles and relationships, both with the artist and to each other. There are most likely some other members of the game who will feel left out, and I apologize for any unintentional omissions; for every player, no matter how seemingly insignificant or unimportant, has an effect on the outcome of events and careers within the music business.

The various players frequently fight among themselves over one thing or another, and tempers flare for a while. Then the wheel turns and two opponents will find themselves on the same side of the fence on another project. For this reason, it is unwise for anybody in the music business to hold a grudge. After all, it's just a game, it is supposed to be fun, and generally is. I personally hold no grudges of any kind, despite the way it might seem to the reader, and those who have beat me in deals have taught me very much indeed, not only about the music business, but about life as well.

In Conclusion

Nashville as I knew it is gone. Deaderick Street, the seedy and interesting haunt of my youth, consists of boring government office buildings. Crowds no longer line up at the door to the Ryman Auditorium, the real Opry House. Grammer Guitars, the Roy Acuff Exhibits, and Sho-Bud Guitars have all disappeared from lower Broadway. Hank Snow's music store and John G. Miller's store are also gone. The Ansley Modern Hotel is now a parking lot. The 100 Per Cent Fireproof Hotel on Fourth Avenue North burned down. The Greyhound bus station has moved and the old building was torn down. In fact, most of Nashville between Broadway and Commerce has been torn down in recent years in the name of progress, much the way the decaying mansions around the Tennessee State Capitol Building were demolished in the 1950s, the same way the older artists were forced out of the charts. Progress.

I could go on, but what I am really trying to say is that country music is dying. Like Nashville's, indeed America's, landmarks, the death has been gradual. Nobody noticed at first, one here, another there. The destruction started with the old buildings, then attached itself to our automobiles. Americans now drive cars that they would not have been caught dead in twenty years ago. They marvel at what was once commonplace, and the descent continues.

I have thought about it a great deal. Perhaps what is happening is not really the death of country music, but rather its evolution. I like to think so, but I am not so sure. If you are at the top or on the way up, then country music is evolving and growing. If you are on the way down and out, then country music is dying. It is largely a matter of perception. It has always been the same from generation to generation. The older artists always say that the newer ones are killing the music.

We as a nation have been very fortunate and have made much progress. We have always been the first to obtain and enjoy the new and different, also the first to disregard the tried and true. Music is no different. The Charleston came and went, along with the big band era, the doo wop groups, the Twist, folk music, acid rock, and so on. Things change.

The rural background and lifestyle that produced country music is rapidly vanishing, and along with it the fertile ground from which the music emerged. As this erosion continues, we all lose something essentially American, a part of our heritage, yes, but a part of ourselves as well. Every time an old building is demolished, or a large American automobile is crushed, or an old person is left for dead at a nursing home, we move ever more closely toward mediocrity and loss of identity. Will country music suffer the same fate? I hate to think so, but like everything else, we probably won't miss it until it's gone.

Index

Sun Records, 107
Swaggert, Jimmy, 29, 107

"Take This Job and Shove It," 130
Talent. *See* Artists
Talent agents. *See* Agents and agencies
Talent buyers
  and agents, 86, 301
  importance of, 316
  and Jerry Lee Lewis, 116
  and tickets sales, 27–28
Taylor, Mike, 237, 238
Television, and career enhancement, 31
Texas Dance Hall, 151
Thompson, Errol, 190
Thompson Brothers, 166
"Till I Met You," 82
Tillis, Mel, 271
Tiltor, Charlene, 53
Time, 83–84
Tomlinson, Dennis, 187
Tompall and the Glaser Brothers, 4
Top Billing Agency, 83
Tosh, Peter, 184
Travis, Randy, 25, 139–46
Triad Artists, 31, 196
Tribute editions, of trade publications, 199
Tritt, Travis, 256–57
"Turn the house," defined, 46
Twitty, Conway, 80, 225

Unions, 308
  and recording sessions, 101, 104–5
United Talent, 80, 225
Universal Amphitheater, 156–57
Universal Attractions, 163, 173
Urban Cowboy, 30
  impact of, 52–53

Vallon, Larry, 156
Vapors Club, 117, 119
Varnell Enterprises, 154

Wagoner, Porter, 131
Wailer, Bunny, 184

Wailers, 179
Waiting for the Sun to Shine, 149
Walker, Billy, 311
"Walk Softly on This Heart of Mine," 260–61
Wallace, Jerry, 311
Wardrobe, 309
Wariner, Steve, 11, 27, 68
Warner Brothers Records, 62, 139
Warnes, Jennifer, 249
Watson, Gene, 112, 142, 43, 144–45
Westwood One, 48
Whitcomb, Allen, 13, 18, 19, 24, 35–36, 80, 83, 156, 159, 160
  and In Concert, 137–39
  and Randy Travis, 140–46
White, Buck, 69
White, Cheryl, 69
White, Sharon, 69
Whites (group), 11, 69–70, 71, 150
Whites (race), and reggae, 180
Whitley, Keith, 148
Whitsen, Tex, 75
"Whole Lot of Shakin," 107
Wildeboer, Cliff, 227
William Morris Agency, 50, 51, 87, 221–22, 236–37, 238–39, 302
  and Mickey Gilley, 30–31, 32, 34, 53–54
  and Ronnie Milsap, 205–6
Williams, Don, 6, 74, 75–76
Williams, Franklin, 192, 193
Williams, Hank, Jr., 155
Williams, Jason D., 117, 119–20
Williams, Leona, 75
Wilson, Norro, 279–80
World Class Talent, 23, 129, 138, 140, 141
Wright, Mark, 252, 255, 256
Wynette, Tammy, 3, 74, 133, 136, 205

Young, Fred, 259, 260, 261
Young, Richard, 259, 260, 261

Zumwalt, Jim, 250, 252, 255